PRESCHOOL

The MAILBOX
IDEA MAGAZINE FOR TEACHERS®

2006–2007 YEARBOOK

The Education Center, Inc.
Greensboro, North Carolina

The Mailbox® 2006–2007 Preschool Yearbook

Managing Editor, *The Mailbox* Magazine: Kimberly Brugger-Murphy

Editorial Team: Becky S. Andrews, Kimberley Bruck, Diane Badden, Sharon Murphy, Karen A. Brudnak, Hope Rodgers, Dorothy C. McKinney

Production Team: Lori Z. Henry, Pam Crane, Rebecca Saunders, Chris Curry, Sarah Foreman, Theresa Lewis Goode, Greg D. Rieves, Eliseo De Jesus Santos III, Barry Slate, Donna K. Teal, Zane Williard, Kitty Campbell, Tazmen Carlisle, Kathy Coop, Marsha Heim, Lynette Dickerson, Mark Rainey, Margaret Freed (Cover Artist)

ISBN10 1-56234-816-7
ISBN13 978-156234-816-8
ISSN 1088-5536

Printed in the United States of America.

The Education Center, Inc.
P.O. Box 9753
Greensboro, NC 27429-0753

Contents

Departments

Features

Arts & Crafts for Little Hands

Arts & Crafts for Little Hands

Super Stoplights

When you display these printmaking projects, passersby are sure to stop and take a gander! Cut a green, red, and yellow apple in half; then notch the halves as shown to make easy-grip handles. Place the apple halves in shallow containers with thin layers of coordinating paint. Then simply press the red, yellow, and green apples on a black construction paper rectangle in the arrangement shown. If desired, mount the project on yellow construction paper. What a super stoplight!

Nancy Foss
Wee Care
Galion, OH

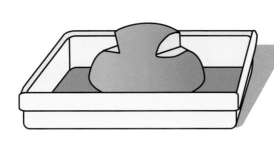

Puffy Prints

To prepare, copy a large clip art picture on tagboard; then use puffy paint to trace over the picture. Allow the paint to dry according to package directions. Secure the tagboard to a tabletop and lightly tape a large piece of paper over the painting. Then rub the side of an unwrapped crayon over the paper. Use crayons to add details to the rubbing as desired. Now that's a great way to integrate the current season or a classroom theme into craft time!

Kim Lopez
Kelso Christian Academy
Kelso, WA

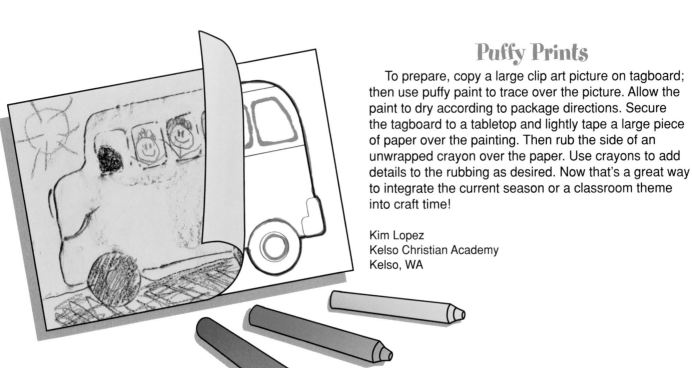

Splendid Suncatcher

Recycle deli container lids to make these nifty apple suncatchers! To make a suncatcher, brush a thick layer of glue on the inside of a lid; then press red tissue paper squares on the glue. Also brush glue on the inside of a second lid. Then press the lids together, sandwiching a yarn hanger and a green paper leaf between them. When the glue is dry, hang the resulting apple in your window!

Janet Boyce
King's Kids
Hutchinson, MN

Super Stampers

In advance, use a hot glue gun to make designs, shapes, and squiggles on each of several film canister lids. (The glue gun is for teacher use only.) When the glue has cooled, secure the lids to the canisters. To begin, use the canister as a handle and dip the lid in a shallow pan of paint. Then make prints on a sheet of colorful paper. Continue in the same way with other canisters and colors of paint.

Kimberly Barfuss
Riverside Preschool
Logan, UT

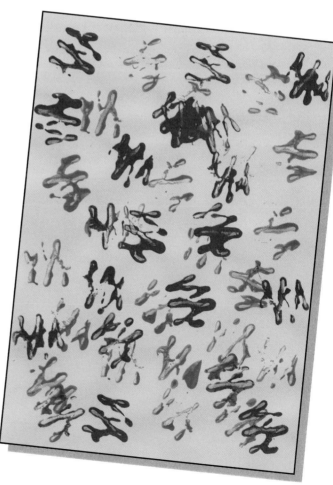

A Wonderful Web

These creepy spiderwebs are made with a unique painting technique! To make the project, dip a length of string into a shallow container of white paint. Then repeatedly drag the string across a sheet of construction paper. When the paint is dry, cut the paper into a simple web shape. Next, cut out a construction paper oval and two matching rectangles. Fringe-cut the rectangles to make eight legs. Then glue the oval to the legs to make a spider. Bend the legs to give the project a three-dimensional effect. Then draw eyes on the spider and glue it to the prepared web.

Nancy McComas
Lord of Life Preschool
Memphis, TN

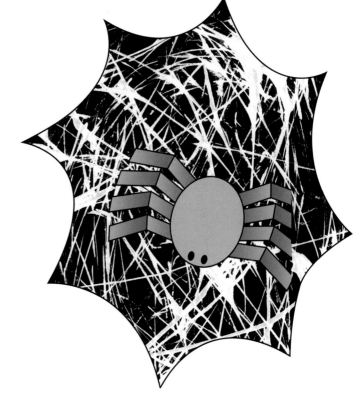

Look, No Hands!

Little hands are sure to remain paint-free with this nifty printmaking project! Fill several rubber gloves with rice and then secure the open end of each glove with a thick rubber band. Place a layer of paper towels in several shallow containers; then pour paint into each container, saturating the paper towels. Lay a glove in each container. To begin, choose a glove and press it on a sheet of paper to make a handprint. Continue in the same way with other gloves and colors of paint.

Sandy Barker
Children's World
St. Paul, MN

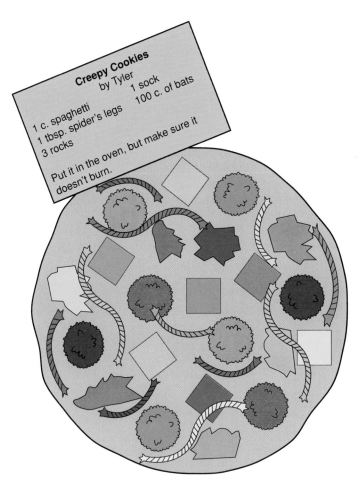

Creepy Cookies
by Tyler

1 c. spaghetti
1 tbsp. spider's legs
3 rocks
1 sock
100 c. of bats

Put it in the oven, but make sure it doesn't burn.

Creepy Cookies

Youngsters use oodles of creativity to make these creepy cookies! Place at a table a class supply of construction paper circles along with a variety of craft items, such as pom-poms, tissue paper squares, crayons, and construction paper scraps. Also place scissors and glue nearby. To make this project, decorate a circle cutout as desired to make a one-of-a-kind cookie. Then dictate the cookie's unique recipe while it is being written on a large index card. Display the cookies and cards on a bulletin board titled "Creepy Cookies."

Tracey Rebock
TBS Preschool
Cherry Hill, NJ

Pinecone Painting

This twist on marble painting is just perfect for fall. Obtain a lidded container. Then lightly tape a sheet of paper to the bottom of the container. Next, place two different colors of tempera paint in separate trays. Roll a different pinecone in each tray of paint. Then place the pinecones on the prepared paper and put the lid on the container. Gently move the container back and forth so that the pinecones roll over the paper; then remove the paper. When the paint is dry, trim the paper into a leaf shape. Lovely!

Mary Caldwell
First Baptist Preschool
Midlothian, TX

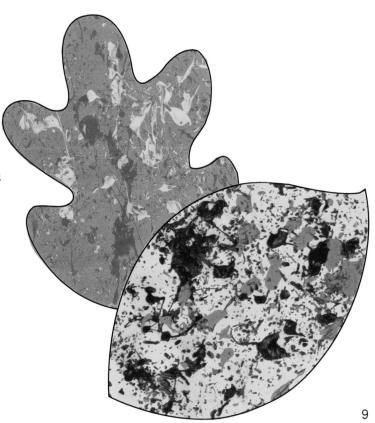

Arts & Crafts for Little Hands

Raffia Brushes

These fun little brushes look just like bundles of straw! Cut a bundle of natural raffia and use a rubber band to bind it together. Drip several colors of tempera paint on a colorful sheet of construction paper. Then use the prepared brush to spread the paint over the paper until a desired effect is achieved. If desired, mount the finished painting on a contrasting sheet of construction paper.

Jennifer Gebelein
Kids' Stuff Preschool
Land O' Lakes, FL

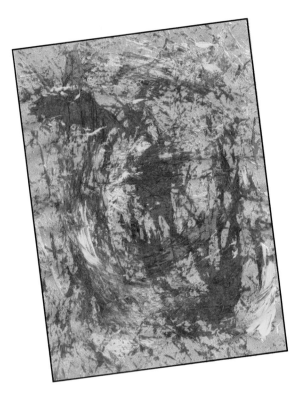

Turkey Time

Here's a cute little turkey with some seriously long legs! Drip tinted water on a large coffee filter. When the coffee filter is dry, fold it in half and glue it in place. Glue construction paper features to a small cardboard tube. Then glue to the inside edge of the tube a length of yellow crepe paper sliced lengthwise to resemble two legs. After gluing a foot cutout to each leg, glue the tube to the prepared coffee filter. That's one terrific turkey!

Sarah Weingartz
Small Wonders Preschool
Lakeville, MN

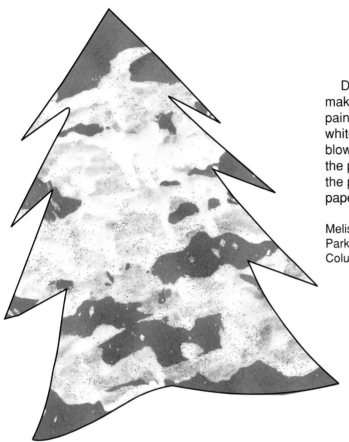

Frosty Evergreens

Display several of these evergreen trees together to make a frosty forest! In advance, dilute white tempera paint with water. Use a teaspoon to place small puddles of white paint on a green sheet of construction paper. Then blow through a straw to move the diluted paint around the paper. Sprinkle silver glitter over the wet paint. When the paint is dry, shake off any excess glitter and trim the paper to resemble an evergreen tree. Lovely!

Melissa Lee
Park Avenue Head Start
Columbia, MO

A Hidden Bear

Surprise! There's a polar bear hiding in this snow-storm! To prepare, cut a simple polar bear shape from newsprint. Then spritz the newsprint with water and smooth it onto a sheet of fingerpainting paper. Finger-paint a layer of light blue paint over the entire paper. When a desired effect is achieved, remove and discard the bear. Finally, dip a toothbrush in white paint and then run your finger over the bristles, spattering the picture with paint to resemble a snowstorm.

Shirley Bailey
Hallsville ISD
Hallsville, TX

Arts & Crafts for Little Hands

Hugs-and-Kisses Collage

This simple collage makes a lovely Valentine's Day gift! Print the letters *X* and *O* in several different fonts. Then cut the letters apart and put them in a container. Place the container at a table along with glue sticks and sheets of 9" x 12" red construction paper programmed as shown. Glue letter cutouts to a sheet of paper until a desired effect is achieved. If desired, mount the project on a larger piece of paper and add a decorative fabric ribbon. How lovely!

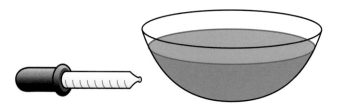

Paper Towel Splash

Add water to dilute several drops of food coloring in a bowl. Repeat the process for several different colors. Then use an eyedropper to drip the diluted food coloring onto a white heavy-duty paper towel. (Textured paper towels will result in a particularly attractive piece of artwork.) When a desired effect is achieved, set the paper towel aside to dry. Trim the dry paper towel into a desired shape and then mount it on a matching piece of construction paper as shown.

Danielle Owens
St. Paul Lutheran School
Cincinnati, OH

Handy Leprechaun Magnet

To make this leprechaun magnet, paint a youngster's fingers orange, the middle of her hand peach, and the remaining portion of her hand green. Have her press her hand onto a sheet of tagboard. Then use a paintbrush to fill in any gaps in the print. When the paint is dry, help each child add details to the print with a permanent marker. Then cut out the resulting leprechaun and laminate it for durability. Finally, attach a self-adhesive magnetic strip to the back of the leprechaun. This little guy looks adorable attached to a refrigerator door!

Colleen Zeoli
Look Who's Learning Preschool
Garden Grove, CA

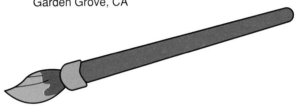

Mini Masterpiece

This simple project results in an appealing piece of artwork. Cut a 5" x 5" piece of Con-Tact paper and remove the backing. Sprinkle colored sand and glitter onto the sticky side of the Con-Tact paper. When a desired effect is achieved, shake off any excess sand and glitter over a trash can. Then mount the project to a square of brightly colored construction paper. If you should decide to display the artwork, keep it looking pristine by hanging it in an area where it won't be bumped into or brushed against.

Cari Christensen
Marywood Country Day School
Rancho Mirage, CA

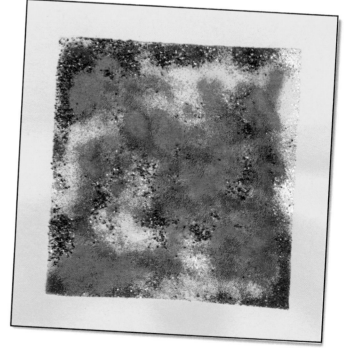

Pleasing Planets

Celebrate Earth Day with these supersimple projects! In advance, dilute liquid glue with water. Use a paintbrush to brush the diluted glue onto a paper plate. Place green tissue paper squares and blue cellophane squares over the glue in any desired arrangement. The green resembles the earth's land and the blue resembles the water. Cellophane gives the water a lovely, shiny appearance. Spread another layer of diluted glue over the plate if desired.

Amber Baker
Learn a Lot Christian Preschool
Mooresville, IN

Carrot Painting

The art that results from this process-oriented project looks good enough to eat! In advance, obtain two carrots, one with the greens still attached. Cut the end off of the carrot without greens. Prepare two shallow containers, one with a layer of orange paint and the other with a layer of green paint. Dip the cut end of the carrot in the orange paint and press it on a carrot cutout similar to the one shown to make prints. Then dip the greens of the other carrot in green paint and brush paint onto the stems and leaves of the cutout.

adapted from an idea by Angela L. Morlan
Holy Cross Lutheran Church Child Development Center
Colorado Springs, CO

Fluffy Chicks

These adorable chicks are all set to welcome spring to your classroom! To make a chick, dip a bath puff in a shallow container of yellow paint and press it several times onto a sheet of construction paper. Continue making chicks in this manner as desired. After the paint dries, embellish the chicks with yellow craft feather wings and paper beaks and eyes. These cute projects make a lovely spring hall display!

An Excellent Egg

To make an "eggs-traordinary" suncatcher, brush glue onto an egg-shaped piece of waxed paper. Press colorful Easter grass into the glue until a desired effect is achieved; then place another egg-shaped piece of waxed paper on top. Staple the two pieces of waxed paper together and attach the finished project to an oval construction paper frame. Hang the resulting Easter egg in your classroom window. Now that's "eggs-tra" special!

Amy Spencer
R. B. Stewart Elementary
Leoti, KS

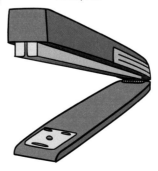

Arts & Crafts for Little Hands

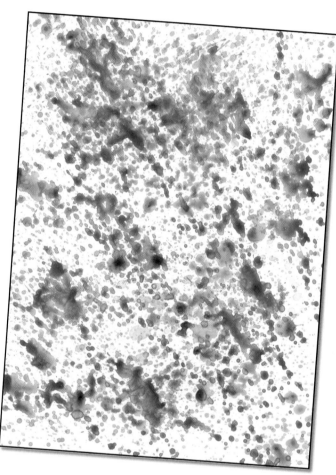

Spray Art

Obtain empty pump-style containers or spray bottles. Make sure the containers are cleaned thoroughly. Then fill them with diluted paint. Place them on a protected tabletop along with a supply of white construction paper. To make spray art, simply spray various colors of paint on a sheet of paper until a desired effect is achieved. What a fun way to make art and develop fine-motor skills at the same time!

Lisa Duffin
San Antonio, TX

A Splendid Sundae

This sundae looks good enough to eat! To begin, place a dollop of sugar-free chocolate pudding (or brown paint) on a white construction paper circle. Spread the pudding over the circle using your fingers. Then sprinkle colorful paper confetti on the wet pudding. When a desired effect is achieved, set the circle aside to dry. After it's dry, attach the circle to a sundae dish cutout. Finally, glue a red pom-pom to the sundae so it resembles a cherry.

Denise Dobbins
Elyria YMCA Preschool
Elyria, OH

BULLETIN BOARDS AND DISPLAYS

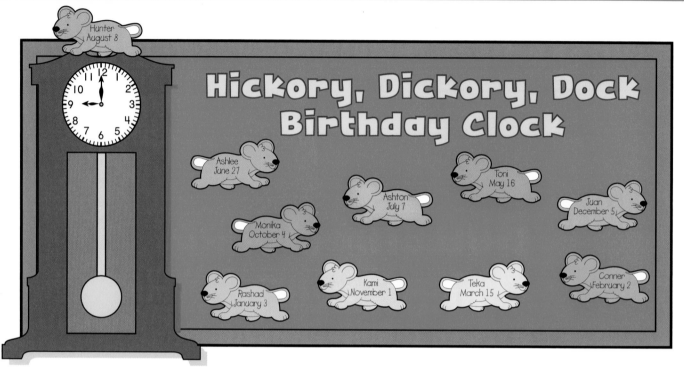

Make a grandfather clock cutout and attach it to the display as shown. Also make a class supply of mouse cutouts (pattern on page 29). Have each child color his mouse. Then label each one with the appropriate name and birthdate. Mount the mice to the display and add the title shown. During each child's birthday month, attach his mouse to the clock.

Bonnie Martin, Hopewell Country Day School, Pennington, NJ

Secure a tree branch in a pot to resemble a small tree. If desired, hot glue leaf cutouts to the tree; then place it near your classroom doorway. Mount the title shown nearby. Before preschool begins, mail a letter and a personalized apple ornament to each student, encouraging him to attach a photograph of himself to the apple. When he brings his apple to school, help him hang it on the tree display. Children love seeing their smiling faces among the branches!

Mary Hogan
Kidz Skool
Clifton Park, NY

Paint the palm of each child's hand to resemble his skin tone and the fingers to match the color of his hair. Then help each youngster make a handprint on a sheet of construction paper. When the paint is dry, add a smiley face to each hand and a speech bubble that says "I'm a helping hand!" Ask each student how he can use his hands to help either at preschool or at home; then write his words under his handprint. Attach the completed projects to a bulletin board titled as shown.

Tanya Tschombor, Childtime Learning Center, Brea, CA

Fold a T-shirt cutout in half for each child; then encourage each youngster to add a small amount of colorful paint to one half of the T-shirt. Help the student refold the shirt and then unfold it again to reveal a lovely design. When the shirts are dry, personalize them and use clothespins to secure them to a length of thin rope attached to a wall. Add the provided title above the resulting clothesline to finish this display!

Angela Stamper, Creation Station Preschool, Crawfordsville, IN

Have each child glue small gray construction paper strips to a longer strip as shown to make a rake. Encourage her to fold down the ends of the short strips and then glue leaves under the rake. Mount the rakes on your display with additional leaf cutouts and the title "Enjoy Fall Before It Leaves."

Tanya Alicea, Harleysville Learning Center, Harleysville, PA
Mary Caldwell, First Baptist Preschool, Midlothian, TX

To make a spider, help each child accordion-fold eight black construction paper strips. Have her glue the strips to a circle cutout to resemble a spider. After she adds hole-reinforcer eyes, mount the spiders on a display of artificial cobwebs. Then add the title "Our Preschool Web Site." If desired, add your actual preschool Web site address to the display!

Jeanette Frei and Debbie Schwarz
Enchanted Garden Nursery School
Hawthorne, New Jersey

No Turkeys Here!

Gather a class supply of inexpensive masks similar to those shown. Help each child make a simple turkey craft sized to fit the mask. Mount the turkeys on a wall and then attach a mask to each one. Label this rib-tickling display with the title "No Turkeys Here!"

Preschoolers Are Sweet!

In advance, drizzle light brown paint on bulletin board paper. When the paint is dry, mount the paper on a board or wall and add the title shown. Encourage each child to dip the top of an apple cutout into light brown tempera paint. Allow the paint to drip toward the bottom of the apple for a moment; then lay the cutout on a flat surface to dry. When the projects are dry, tape a craft stick to each apple. Then attach the projects to the display. If desired, enhance your display by adding a few caramel wrappers!

Lydia Hess, Chambersburg, PA

Clean an empty individual-size milk carton for each child; then tape the milk carton closed. Have each youngster paint his carton with a mixture of tempera paint and white glue. When the carton is dry, encourage each child to glue cutouts to the carton to resemble a door and windows. Have students glue cotton batting to the roofs of their houses to represent snow. Finally, display the houses on a bulletin board decorated with tree cutouts and more cotton batting snow. Title the display as shown.

Charlet Estes, Highland Wee Care, Hardy, AR

Make a three-dimensional snowman by stuffing a trash bag with paper; then use string to tie off the bag in three sections as shown. Mount the snowman on your display and add the title "Preschoolers Are 'Snow' Special!" Finally, have youngsters marble-paint snow-flake cutouts or make other snow-themed crafts. Then arrange the crafts around the snowman.

Kimberly Dessel
Pixie Preschool and Kindergarten, Spotswood, NJ

Amber Parsons
Kiddie Academy of Laurel Maryland, Laurel, MD

AND DISPLAYS

SHINING LIGHTS FOR EIGHT NIGHTS!

Trim one inch off each of eight cardboard tubes. Leave a ninth tube whole. Then have youngsters help paint the tubes blue. Encourage students to sprinkle silver glitter over the wet paint. When the paint is dry, glue tissue paper flames in each tube. Then display the tubes as shown to make a menorah. Finish the display with dreidel crafts and the title shown.

adapted from an idea by Frances Moskowitz, On Our Way Learning Center, Far Rockaway, NY

We Are All Different. We Are All Special!

To make this display, place tempera paint in a variety of skin tones into separate pans. (Mix dishwashing liquid with the paint for an easier cleanup). Help each student remove her shoes and press her feet in a pan. Then have her carefully walk across a length of bulletin board paper. When the paint is dry, attach the paper to a bulletin board. Then add photographs of your youngsters and the title shown.

Angela Fulk, First Baptist Church Garner MMO, Garner, NC

23

Special Delivery!

Leo · Michelle · Bobby · Mia · A.J. · Seth · Callie · Alex · Hannah · Susan · Darlene · Lynn · Jesse · Josh

Invite each child to decorate a heart cutout; then attach a photograph of each youngster to his cutout. Affix each heart to a personalized envelope so that it peeks out. Then mount the envelopes on a board decorated as shown. Title the board "Special Delivery!"

Pam Sartory, City of Palm Beach Gardens Recreation Department, Palm Beach Gardens, FL

Youngsters focus on healthy habits with this adorable board! Attach an inexpensive shower curtain to a wall. Make a copy of the bathtub pattern on page 30 for each youngster. Have her color the tub as desired and then glue it to a sheet of construction paper. Ask her what she does to stay clean and healthy; then use a permanent marker to write her words on the bathtub. Next, invite her to make prints above the tub with a bath puff to resemble bubbles. When the projects are dry, mount them on the shower curtain. Then title the display as shown.

adapted from an idea by Cindy Carswell
Central Methodist Preschool
Fitzgerald, GA

Bubbling Over With Healthy Habits!

Jill
I wash my hair.
I brush my teeth.

AND DISPLAYS

Lounging Leprechauns

Trim a sponge to make a small rectangle and a semicircle. Then have each youngster make sponge-prints on a sheet of construction paper to create a toadstool as shown. Invite her to add fingerprints to the cap to make spots. After the paint dries, have her color a copy of one of the leprechaun patterns on page 184, cut out the leprechaun, and then glue it above her toadstool. Display the projects with the title shown.

We're Leaving Winter Behind!

Your little ones are sure to look forward to the first day of spring with this adorable display! Invite youngsters to make simple bunny crafts similar to the ones shown. Attach the projects to a bulletin board decorated with grass, clouds, and student-made flowers. Then title the board "We're Leaving Winter Behind!"

Laurie Taivalmaa, The Ark Christian Childcare and Learning Center, Bessemer, MI

25

Showers for Flowers

You're sure to receive a shower of compliments on this lovely spring display! To make the display, attach an oversize watering can cutout to a wall as shown. Then tape lengths of blue cellophane to the spout so that they resemble water. Invite each youngster to decorate a flower cutout with crumpled tissue paper squares; then attach the cutouts below the watering can. Title this cute display as shown.

Karen Eiben
The Learning House Preschool
La Salle, IL

Have each child color a bunny pattern. Then have her paint an umbrella cutout with a mixture of corn syrup and food coloring. The result is a shiny, gorgeous umbrella! Mount the bunnies and umbrellas to a display titled as shown. Then embellish the display with aluminum foil puddles and raindrops.

Bonnie Martin, Hopewell Country Day School, Pennington, NJ

Here's an earth-friendly bulletin board that's bright and colorful! Have each child make a handprint on black construction paper with a desired color of paint. When the paint is dry, cut out each print. Have students help you paint a circle of bulletin board paper so that it loosely resembles the earth. Attach the earth and handprints to a board; then add the title shown.

Leslie Fowler, Tender Loving Care Child Development Center, Tracy, CA

These Special Ladies Help Us Grow!

To prepare for this display, have each youngster bring in a picture of his mother or another female caregiver. Attach the photos to a construction paper circle. Next, attach the circle to your display along with a class supply of petal cutouts to resemble a flower. Then, have each child describe something he enjoys doing with this individual. Write his words on a petal cutout. Then add a catchy title to the display.

Maryanne Restivo
Laurel Hall Early Childhood Center
North Hollywood, CA

My mom takes me to the zoo.

Lucas

BULLETIN BOARDS

Make a bucket and shovel cutout for each youngster. Have each child spread glue on the top of his bucket; then encourage him to sprinkle sand over the glue. Decorate a bulletin board or wall so it resembles a beach, and attach the pails and shovels.

Jennifer McDonald, Creative World Preschool, Wilmington, NC

This cute display will light up your classroom! Gather a class supply of compact discs. (Consider asking parents to donate the free compact discs they receive in the mail.) Have each child glue bug body and head cutouts to a disc. Then have her attach waxed paper wings as well as paper legs and antennae to the project. Mount these cute fireflies on a wall display decorated and titled as shown.

Jean Jaffe and Jennifer Prekup
Brandywine YMCA
Coatesville, PA

28

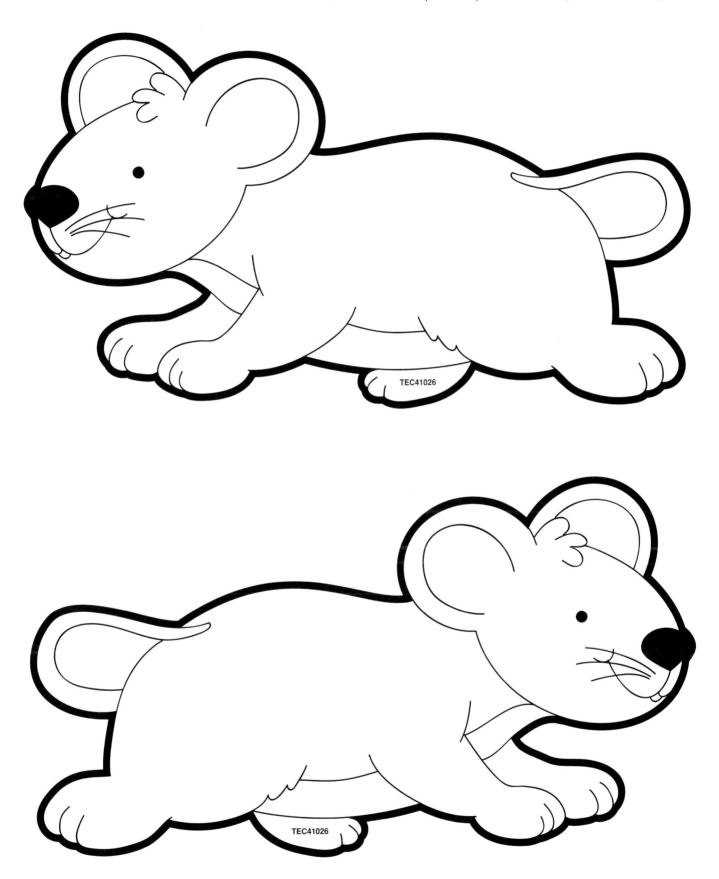

Mouse Pattern

Use with "Hickory, Dickory, Dock Birthday Clock" on page 18.

TEC41026

TEC41026

Bathtub Pattern

Use with "Bubbling Over With Healthy Habits!" on page 24.

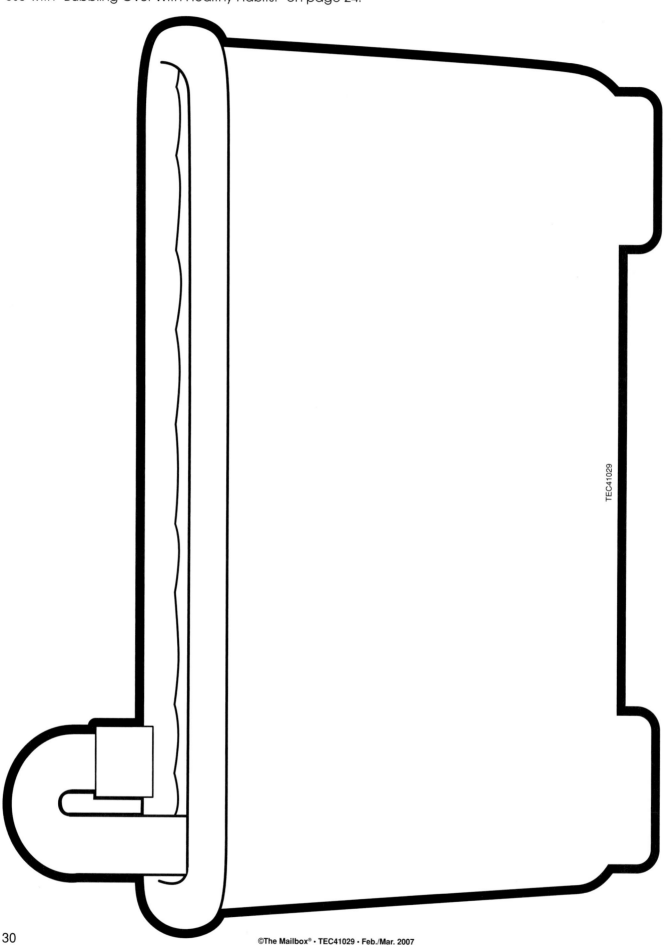

TEC41029

BUSY HANDS

BUSY HANDS

Creative Learning Experiences for Little Hands

BACK-TO-SCHOOL!

Invite little ones to explore items traditionally associated with back-to-school time! Crayons, backpacks, apples—the list is endless!

ideas contributed by Janet Boyce, King's Kids, Hutchinson, MN

ONE-OF-A-KIND WREATH

In advance, obtain a grapevine wreath and place it at a table along with a variety of cutouts with back-to-school themes. You may wish to add a supply of craft foam letter cutouts as well. Provide access to a container of white glue and a brush. Have youngsters brush glue on cutouts and then nestle them in the grapevine wreath. When the wreath is full of items and the glue is dry, top it with a bow and then display it in your classroom!

Michelle Lemaster-Johnson
St. Paul's School of Early Learning
Muskego, WI

PLACING PENCILS

Place a supply of unsharpened pencils at a table. (Hexagonal pencils work best.) Encourage students to visit the table and see how many shapes and designs they can make by arranging the pencils. Youngsters are sure to challenge both their fine-motor and spatial skills with this simple idea!

ROUND AND ROUND

After teaching little ones the traditional song "The Wheels on the Bus," record them singing the first verse of the song several times consecutively. Place the recording at a table covered with a sheet of bulletin board paper. Then provide access to crayons. Little ones play the song and then use crayons to draw on the paper, making their markings reflect the lyrics "round and round." No doubt the paper will soon be covered with lovely swirls of color!

REMOVING WRAPPERS

Label two empty containers as shown and place them at a table along with a supply of drawing paper and old worn down crayons. Encourage students to peel off the crayon wrappers and then scribble with the crayon on the paper. If they decide the color is attractive and the crayon is in good condition, have them place it in the happy container. If not, have them place the crayon in the sad container. Later in the year, use these crayons for rubbings or melt them down in muffin tins to make jumbo crayons!

PACK IT UP!

Collect a variety of school supplies, such as unsharpened pencils, crayons, glue, a ruler, folders, and notebooks. Then place the supplies near a backpack with a variety of different compartments. Youngsters give their fine-motor skills a workout by unzipping and opening all of the compartments and then organizing the items in the backpack.

BUSY HANDS

Creative Learning Experiences for Little Hands

SLIGHTLY SPOOKY EXPLORATIONS

Spiders! Candy corn! Pumpkins! With these fine-motor investigations, you're sure to hear screams of delight!

ideas contributed by Roxanne LaBell Dearman, Western NC Early Intervention Program for Children Who Are Deaf or Hard of Hearing, Charlotte, NC

APPLES AFLOAT!

It's easy to bob for apples with the addition of a few handy utensils! Make apple cutouts from craft foam, and place them in your water table along with a supply of small sieves and slotted spoons. Put a plastic container nearby. A youngster uses the utensils to scoop up apples and place them in the container. When he has collected all of the apples, he places them back in the water.

FUNNY FACES

Giggles abound when youngsters design these amusing jack-o'-lanterns! Cut a variety of facial features from old magazines; then place the features in a container near several pumpkin cutouts. A youngster places features on the pumpkins to make a variety of hilarious jack-o'-lanterns!

Paula Diekhoff
Head Start
Warsaw, IN

PEEPERS!

There are a bunch of creepy critters hiding out in this nighttime mural! Decorate a length of black bulletin board paper to resemble a night sky. Make a supply of yellow construction paper circles; then place them at a table along with dark-colored bingo daubers and glue. Students press the daubers on the circles to make eyes. Then they attach the eyes to the paper.

SNACKS FOR SPIDER

To prepare, tape a sheet of bulletin board paper to a tabletop. Then draw a supersize spider's web on the paper. Provide access to oversize plastic bugs and pans of shallow paint. A child presses a bug in the paint and then makes a print on the web. After many youngsters have had an opportunity to make multiple prints, allow the paint to dry. Then display the bug-filled web in your classroom along with a large construction paper spider.

CONCEALED CORN

Partially fill a transparent plastic bottle with dried corn; then drop one piece of candy corn into the bottle. Secure the lid and then reinforce it with heavy-duty tape. Shake the bottle to hide the candy. A youngster picks up the bottle and manipulates it to try to find the candy corn. There it is!

Busy Hands

Seasonal Explorations for Little Hands

Garland, presents, gift tags, and cards! Little ones are sure to enjoy exploring these popular holiday-themed items.

ideas contributed by Aimee Robertson, School for Little People
Sherman, TX

Totally Tags!

Label and hole-punch a supply of construction paper rectangles as shown; then place them at a table. Provide access to a shallow container of paint and mini cookie cutters in a variety of holiday shapes. A youngster chooses a cookie cutter and dips it in the paint; then she gently presses it on a gift tag to make a print. She continues in the same way to create oodles of colorful gift tags. If desired, help little ones tie bundles of tags together to give to parents as gifts!

A Big Fluffy Beard

Place a supersize tagboard Santa cutout on a tabletop as shown. Then provide access to a paintbrush, a container with a small amount of glue, and a supply of cotton balls. A child brushes glue over a small area on Santa's beard; then he places cotton balls on the glue. Other youngsters visit the center and add more cotton balls to the beard until it's completely white and fluffy!

SPLENDID SEWING

In advance, remove the front panels from used holiday cards; then hole-punch the edges. Attach a length of curling ribbon to a hole in each panel and place the panels in a container. A child chooses a panel and then laces the curling ribbon through the holes. When he is finished, he attaches it to a designated wall. Other children repeat the process as desired and add their lacing projects to the wall to make a holiday quilt display.

WHO'S BEEN HERE?

It looks as if reindeer have been prancing through this freshly fallen snow! In advance, tape a length of white bulletin board paper to a table. Cut a potato in half and then trim the halves to make reindeer hoof stamps as shown. (You may wish to cut notches in each potato half for easy gripping.) Place paper towels in a shallow container; then saturate the towels with brown paint. Put the container at the table along with the potato stamps. A youngster chooses a stamp and presses it over the paper to make reindeer prints in the snow. When the snow is filled with prints, replace it with a new length of paper.

GORGEOUS GARLAND

Have little ones use cereal to make this simple garland! Cut several lengths of colorful yarn. Then tie a piece of O-shaped cereal to one end of each length. Dip the remaining end in glue to prevent fraying. When the glue is dry, place the yarn at a center along with a container of O-shaped cereal. Invite children to string the cereal on the yarn. If desired, tie each finished length of garland and drape it over your classroom holiday tree.

37

Seasonal Explorations for Little Hands

Fresh green grass, green shamrocks, and new green leaves—green is certainly a popular color this season! Invite little ones to investigate the color green with these vibrant explorations!

ideas contributed by Rebecca Perruquet, Here We Grow Preschool
Danville, PA

SPARKLY SNAKES

Mix green glitter with green play dough. Place the play dough at a table; then encourage a youngster to visit the table and take a portion of the dough. Invite her to roll the dough carefully to make a snake. Then have her repeat the process to make snakes in a variety of different sizes. What a terrific and "ssssimple" fine-motor workout!

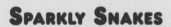

SHAMROCK MATCH

Make a supply of green heart cutouts. Trace a heart several times to make shamrock patterns on white bulletin board paper as shown. Place the hearts in a container and then put the container and paper in a center. A visiting youngster places a heart cutout over each leaf. Now those shamrocks are green!

LOVELY LEAVES

Got glue bottles? Then your youngsters can make these lovely green leaves! Draw a tree trunk and branches on a length of white bulletin board paper; then tape the paper to a tabletop. Place a layer of paper towels in a shallow pan. Pour green tempera paint over the paper towels until they're saturated. Then place the pan at the table along with glue bottles. A youngster visits the center, presses the bottom of a bottle into the paint, and then makes a print above the trunk to resemble a leaf. Youngsters repeat the process until the tree is filled with lovely spring leaves.

GORGEOUS GREEN

Write the word *green* on a large sheet of paper, using bubble letters as shown. Place the paper on a tabletop and provide scissors, glue sticks, and a variety of old magazines. Invite children to visit the center and flip through the magazines. When a child locates a picture of an item that is green, have him cut out the picture and glue it to any desired letter. Have students continue adding pictures to the word until it is filled with green items.

GRASS CLIPPINGS

Collect a variety of green craft items, such as construction paper, tissue paper, crepe paper, and cellophane. Place the items in a tub; then place the tub at a center and provide a supply of scissors. Encourage youngsters to cut the items into strips to resemble grass. Have youngsters use the resulting grass clippings to make beautiful spring collages.

Busy Hands

Seasonal Explorations for Little Hands

Flowers, frogs, rain, and seeds—here's a bouquet of seasonal explorations that are just perfect for spring!

*ideas contributed by Janet Boyce
Cokato, MN*

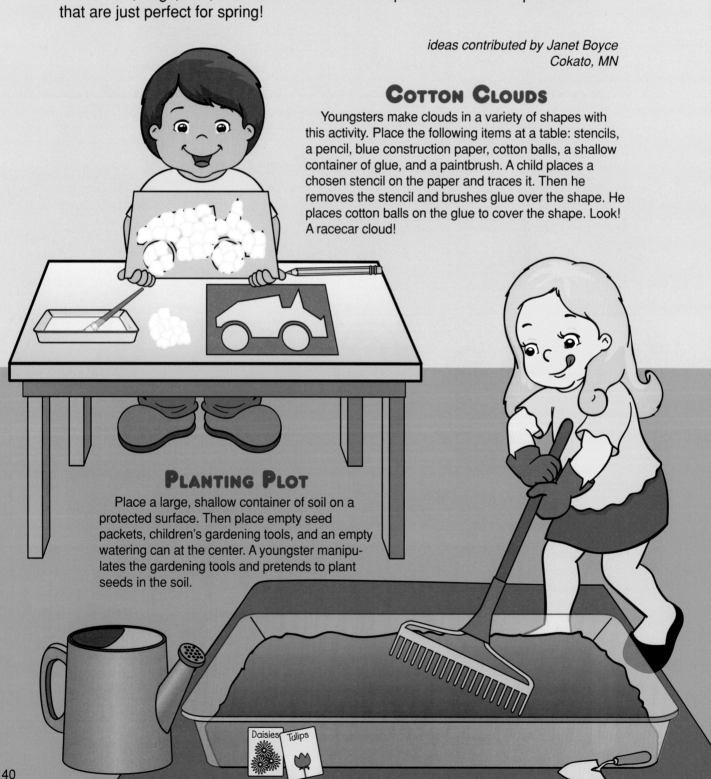

Cotton Clouds

Youngsters make clouds in a variety of shapes with this activity. Place the following items at a table: stencils, a pencil, blue construction paper, cotton balls, a shallow container of glue, and a paintbrush. A child places a chosen stencil on the paper and traces it. Then he removes the stencil and brushes glue over the shape. He places cotton balls on the glue to cover the shape. Look! A racecar cloud!

Planting Plot

Place a large, shallow container of soil on a protected surface. Then place empty seed packets, children's gardening tools, and an empty watering can at the center. A youngster manipulates the gardening tools and pretends to plant seeds in the soil.

Daisies   Tulips

FLIES FOR FROGGIE

Attach a frog cutout to a length of bulletin board paper. Then attach the paper to a table. Place at the table a black stamp pad and several foam packing pieces (the type shaped to resemble a figure eight). A youngster visits the center, presses a packing piece onto the ink pad, and then presses the inked piece onto the bulletin board paper to make a print that resembles a fly. Allow youngsters several opportunities to visit the center and make tasty flies for this hungry frog.

A RAINBOW GARDEN

Draw rows on a length of brown bulletin board paper so that it resembles a garden. Provide access to gardening and seed catalogs and glue sticks. Encourage youngsters to visit the area, cut out photos of plants and flowers, and then glue them to the garden. After students have had several opportunities to visit the center, display this abundant garden in your classroom. It's so colorful!

A UNIQUE UMBRELLA

Little ones give this umbrella pizzazz! Place a plain umbrella at a center along with paper, tape, crayons, scissors, and markers. Invite students to visit the center and create any desired artwork with the supplies. Then encourage each child to tape his artwork to the umbrella. After several youngsters have visited this center, the umbrella will be a three-dimensional masterpiece!

Busy Hands

Seasonal Explorations for Little Hands

Summer sun, ice cream, and fireworks! Celebrate the wonderful season of summer with these fine-motor explorations.

BANANA SPLIT

Place a supply of white and brown play dough at a table along with ice cream scoops. Then provide plastic bananas, empty ice cream–topping squeeze bottles, and plastic dishes. A youngster places scoops of white and brown play dough on a dish so that they resemble ice cream. She places a banana on the scoops and then adds any desired pretend toppings. Now that's some sweet fine-motor practice!

PATRIOTIC COLLAGE

Cut clear Con-Tact paper into squares. Place the squares at a table along with a variety of red, white, and blue craft materials and cutouts. Help a child peel the backing off of her square and then help her place the square on a flat surface, sticky side up. Next, invite her to choose items to press onto her square. When she is finished, encourage her to play I Spy with a partner using these patriotic projects. I spy with my little eye…a red dog!

Suzanne Moore
Tucson, AZ

IT'S CIRCLE TIME

It's Circle Time

Follow That Pattern!

With this daily activity, little ones consistently practice colors, shapes, numbers, and patterns. Make a supply of numbered shape cutouts that form an AB pattern. Each day, enlist youngsters' help in placing a cutout on your calendar to represent the date. When a pattern begins to emerge, encourage students to guess the color, shape, and number of each cutout before placing it on the calendar. Your super sleuths will be eager to crack the code to a new pattern each month!

Carole Bogar
Serendipity Preschool
Boardman, OH

Sunday	Monday	Tuesday	Wednesday	Thursday	Friday	Saturday
		1	2	3	4	5
6	7	8	9	10	11	12
13	14	15	16	17	18	19
20	21	22	23	24	25	26
27	28	29	30	31		

August

Sunday	Monday	Tuesday	Wednesday	Thursday	Friday	Saturday
					1	2
3	4	5	6	7	8	9
10	11	12	13	14	15	

September

Framed Friends

Decorate a picture frame with craft supplies. Then take a photograph of each child to fit the frame opening. To begin, use Sticky-Tac to affix one photo to the center of the frame. Display the frame as you lead the children in singing the song below. Then help students identify the name of the child and locate her in the circle. Play several rounds of this toe-tapping game, attaching a different photo to the frame each time.

(sung to the tune of "The Farmer in the Dell")
Who is this special friend?
Who is this special friend?
Look at the frame. Tell us [her/his] name.
Who is this special friend?

Kelly Ash
Waukesha Head Start
Waukesha, WI

Color Toss!

This simple beanbag toss is sure to be a hit. Gently toss a beanbag to a child, identifying the color of the beanbag and the child's name. For example, you might say, "I'm going to toss the [red] beanbag to my good friend [Bryan]." Then have him toss the beanbag back to you. Continue in this manner with other colors as you recognize each child in the group. What a fun way to acknowledge youngsters and help develop color recognition skills!

Lois Peterson
Mom's Day Out Christian Learning Center
Frederick, MD

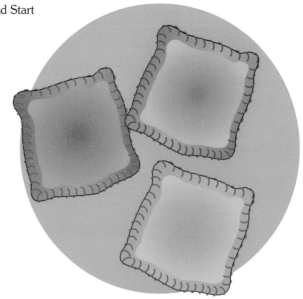

Marvelous Masks

Make several paper plate animal masks similar to those shown (or transform Hefty Zoo Pals plates into masks). Select a volunteer to choose an animal mask and hold it in front of his face. Then encourage him to travel around the room pretending to be the chosen animal as you lead youngsters in singing the song shown. When students reveal the name of the animal in the final line of the song, invite your young actor to remove his mask and take a bow. Continue in this manner with new volunteers and different masks.

(sung to the tune of "The Mulberry Bush")

A friend from the zoo is in our room,
In our room, in our room.
A friend from the zoo is in our room.
We see it is a(n) [tiger]!

Gail Madden
Great Escape
Littleton, CO

Musical Match

Youngsters match symbols with this engaging game! To prepare, write a different symbol on each of several cards to make a class supply. Make a second set of cards identical to the first. Then place one set of cards in a bag and give each student a card from the remaining set. Place a bell (or other musical instrument) in the middle of your circle-time area. To play, remove a card from the bag and show it to your youngsters. Encourage the child with the matching card to go to the center of the circle and ring the bell. Then help her identify the symbol displayed on the card. Continue in the same way until each child has had a turn.

Hilarie Hutt
Summit School
Summit, SD

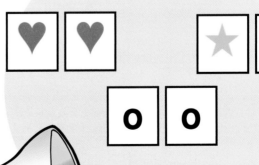

It's Circle Time

A Tidy Room

This nifty activity is a fun way to tidy up tiny toys! Cut a hole in one end of a shoebox as shown; then decorate the box. Have students place in the box small found items that need to be put away. When the box contains a variety of items, invite a volunteer to reach into the box and remove an item. As classmates slowly count to 15, have her return the item to its proper home. Continue in this manner until the box is empty.

Meg Thaler, Scarsdale Congregational Church Nursery School, Scarsdale, NY

Turkey Hideaway

Preschoolers identify shapes to find where this adorable turkey is hiding. Cut out a construction paper turkey and several haystacks. Program the front of each haystack with a different shape. Then have students cover their eyes as you hide the turkey under one of the stacks. Invite a youngster to point to a haystack and identify the shape. As children chant the verse shown, have the child lift the stack to see whether the turkey is there. Continue in this manner until the turkey is revealed.

Turkey, turkey in the hay,
Hiding on Thanksgiving Day!

A Super Scene!

Students solve simple riddles to make this fall scene! Display several fall-related cutouts near a posted sheet of paper. Then give students a clue describing one of the cutouts. When a youngster identifies the cutout, have him tape it to the paper. Continue in this manner until all of the cutouts have been added to the paper. It sure does look like fall!

Shelley Hoster
Jack and Jill Early Learning Center
Norcross, GA

I am thinking of something that can fly. It likes to sleep upside down!

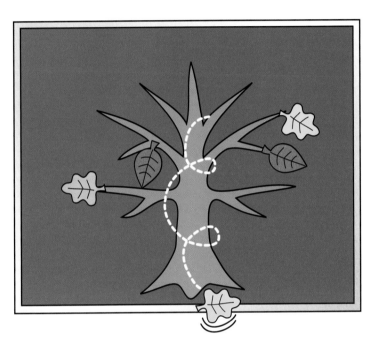

Five Little Leaves

This interactive rhyme is not only perfect for the season but it also introduces simple subtraction skills! Arrange a felt tree shape and five colorful felt leaves on your flannelboard. Then lead youngsters in reciting the poem below, pausing after the third line for a volunteer to remove a leaf from the tree and let it fall to the floor. Be sure to encourage all preschoolers to notice the silence of the falling leaf before whispering the last line. Continue in this manner until all of the leaves have fallen off the tree, altering the numbers as appropriate for each repetition.

[Five] little leaves are hanging on a tree.
Along came a breeze and blew one free.
The little leaf fell without a sound.
There are [four] on the tree and [one] on the ground.

Jenni Remeis, Graham Road Elementary, Reynoldsburg, OH

Letter Search

Write each student's name on a card and place the cards in a bag. Also write a desired letter on a sheet of chart paper. To begin, invite a volunteer to remove a card from the bag. Identify the name on the card and have the volunteer give it to its owner. Help the child decide whether the letter shown is found in her name. If it is, add her name to the page, writing the target letter in a different color. If her name does not have the letter, have her place the card in a discard pile and remove a new card from the bag. Continue in this manner for several rounds. Play this game many times throughout the school year, choosing a different letter each time!

Jennifer Schear
Clover Patch Preschool
Cedar Falls, IA

Rr
Barbara
Gerard
Richard

Sally

It's Circle Time

Snowy Classmates

To play this entertaining game, give each child a small piece of cotton batting to represent snow. Lead students in singing the provided song while they hold the batting on their heads as indicated in the first line. Sing repeated verses of the song, changing the name of the body part and encouraging youngsters to place their snow accordingly.

(sung to the tune of "The Farmer in the Dell")

The snow is on my [head].
It landed there, you see.
I went outdoors to play
And snowflakes fell on me!

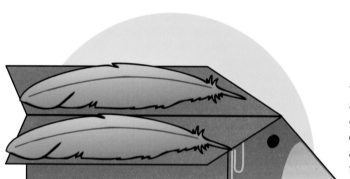

Flying South

Explain that many birds fly south to warmer places during the winter months. Help each youngster make a simple paper airplane similar to the one shown. Secure the underside of each airplane with a jumbo paper clip. Have each little one decorate his plane with crayons and craft feathers to resemble a bird. (Have youngsters use a minimal amount of glue.) When the projects are dry, lead youngsters outside, have them turn to face the south, and then encourage them to fly their birds!

Beth Baranowski, Roselle Park, NJ

Name That Color

Help little ones identify colors with some athletic gingerbread men! Make several colorful gingerbread men stick puppets similar to those shown. Read aloud the classic story *The Gingerbread Man*. Next, hold up one of the prepared puppets and encourage youngsters to run in place as you lead them in reciting the rhyme shown. At the conclusion of the rhyme, prompt little ones to name the gingerbread man's color and then stop running. Continue in the same way with each remaining gingerbread man.

Run, run, as fast as you can
Until you can name
The color I am!

Melinda Johnson, Hager Preschool, Owensboro, KY

Ho, Ho, Ho!

Little ones pretend to be Santa with this jolly activity! In advance, place a class treat in a box and wrap it like a present. To begin, ask a volunteer to sit in a chair and close her eyes. Then invite a second volunteer to play Santa. Santa picks up the present and quietly places it under the chair. When he sits back down, all of the children shout, "Ho, ho, ho!" The youngster in the chair opens her eyes and has three chances to guess Santa's identity. When Santa is revealed, choose two new youngsters for the next round. When each youngster has had a chance to play, share the present's contents with your little ones!

Anna Katrina Enverga
Alphabits Learning Center
Manchester, NH

Melting Away

Help each youngster make a snowman hat headband as shown. Gather five big red bows and make a large sun cutout. To begin, invite five youngsters to wear snowman hats and bows and stand in front of the group. Invite another volunteer to be the sun. Encourage the snowmen and sun characters to act out their roles while you lead youngsters in the chant below. When one little snowman is left standing, chant the final verse provided.

[Five] little snowmen, all in a row,
Each with a hat and a big red bow.
Out came the sun and it stayed all day,
And one little snowman melted away.

Final verse:
One little snowman, last in the row,
Wearing [his/her] hat and a big red bow.
Out came the sun and it stayed all day,
And the last little snowman melted away.

Sandy Barker
KLC—Children's World
St. Paul, MN

It's Circle Time

Golden Opportunities

Students match lettered coins to leprechauns' pots of gold with this activity! Label each of several margarine tubs with different letters. Then make a class supply of gold coin cutouts and write a different corresponding letter on each coin. Place the pots in the middle of your circle-time area and scatter the coins nearby. Tell students that the leprechauns have spilled their gold and need help picking it up. Have each student, in turn, pick up a coin and drop it in the matching pot.

Heather Miller, Creative Playschool, Auburn, IN

The dog is hungry. He ate up all the food. It was *yummy*. Then he played with his ball.

Ms. Rhine's class

Simple Story Starters

Use magazine pictures to jump-start student stories! Show youngsters a picture from a magazine; then ask students to describe what they see and predict what might happen next. Write their thoughts on a sheet of chart paper to make a simple story. Reread the story to youngsters, following the words with your finger. Then post the picture and story in your classroom.

Jennifer Rhine
Preschool Express
Millersville, PA

The Birthday Circle

Here's a fun game that helps each student remember the date of his birth! Have students stand in a circle. Give a child a birthday cake cutout and encourage the youngster to walk around the outside of the circle. As he walks, have him lightly tap each child's back as he recites the chant shown. The child who is tapped at the end of the chant gets to hold the cake cutout and recite his birthday (with help as needed). Then he repeats the process. Your little ones are sure to be eager to play several rounds of this game!

Apples, peaches, pears, and plums,
Tell me when your birthday comes.

Christine Wirt, Tiny Tot Station, Elk Grove, CA

Letters in the Mail

Program a class supply of decorative paper with different letters. Place each sheet of paper into a different envelope. Then personalize the envelopes and add a sticker or stamp to each one as shown. To begin, hold up an envelope and read the name. Lead students in singing the first verse of the song. Have the appropriate child remove the paper from the envelope and hold up the letter. Then lead youngsters in singing the second verse of the song, substituting the appropriate letter name. Repeat the process until each youngster has a chance to open a letter. For future rounds of this activity, place each letter in a different envelope.

(sung to the tune of "The Farmer in the Dell")

This letter is for you!
This letter is for you!
Hi-ho, now did you know?
This letter is for you!

The letter's name is *[M]*!
The letter's name is *[M]*!
Hi-ho, now did you know?
The letter's name is *[M]*!

Amber Baker,
Learn a Lot Christian Preschool
Moorseville, IN

It's Groundhog Day!

Write the poem shown on a sheet of chart paper. Then have each youngster make a paper bag groundhog puppet similar to the one shown. Instruct each child to place his puppet on either hand. As you lead children in reading the poem aloud, have them move their groundhog puppets accordingly.

Little groundhog in the ground,
Pop your head up; look around.
Is it cloudy? Is it bright?
Will your shadow give you a fright?
Come on out and have your say
Because today is Groundhog Day!

Jody Johnson, Little Lamb Preschool, Madison, SD

51

It's Circle Time

Highlighted Letters

Here's an easy activity that showcases featured letters in words! Write a chant or rhyme on chart paper and then display the paper. Cut a supply of brightly colored cellophane into squares. After reading the rhyme aloud several times, invite a student to locate a specific letter. Then, have the youngster tape a cellophane square over the letter. Continue in the same way with other students. Finally, reread the poem, pointing out the cool colored letters.

adapted from an idea by Paula Wright
A. A. Milne Elementary, Houston, TX

Humpty Dumpty sat on a wall.

Humpty Dumpty had a great fall.

All the king's horses and all the king's men

Couldn't put Humpty together again.

That's not a norse! It's a horse!

Trouble on the Farm

Youngsters develop phonological awareness with this adorable idea! Place several farm animal cards in a bag. Then don a straw hat and a bandana and introduce yourself as the farmer. Explain that you have had some trouble with the animals not answering your call. Next, remove a card from the bag and say the animal's name, replacing the initial consonant. No doubt youngsters will immediately correct your error. Continue in the same way with each animal card.

Gail Marsh, Pacific, MO

Be the Thunderstorm!

Youngsters can create a thunderstorm right in your classroom! Brainstorm with youngsters the many sounds they hear during a thunderstorm. Write student responses on a chart. Then help youngsters find common props in the classroom to re-create these noises. For example, rattling a tub of building blocks could resemble thunder, or tapping pencils on a table could resemble rain. When all the sounds have been decided, assign groups of youngsters to the different props. Then have students create a storm!

Jamie Matchett, A Child's Garden, Greenville, OH

rain—pitter-patter

puddles—splash, splash

wind— whoosh, whoosh

thunder— rumble, rumble

52

GET MOVING!

Get Moving!

Back-to-School Boogie

This action-packed dance has a back-to-school theme! Make a supply of two different cutouts, such as apples and school buses. Give each child a cutout; then sort the youngsters into two groups by cutout shape. Play a recording of fun, upbeat music. As the music plays, have the youngsters with apples jump up and down and those with school buses shake their hips. After several minutes, prompt each group to change to a new movement, such as spinning, leg wiggling, or stomping. This is a nifty activity to do any time of the year with cutouts that match the season or your current theme!

Sue Reppert
Widening World Pre-school
Mentor, OH

Sticky Hands

Get ready for giggles with this fun activity and song. Tell youngsters that your hands are very sticky. Then stand with your hands on your hips and pretend they are stuck in that position! Encourage students to pretend that their hands are sticky and to mimic your actions. With hands still attached to hips, lead youngsters in singing the song shown. Then guide students to remove their hands with exaggerated motions. While demonstrating relief, place your hands on your head! Then repeat the process, singing the song and removing the hands as before. You're sure to get many requests for the sticky-hands game!

(sung to the tune of "If You're Happy and You Know It")

Oh, my hands are sticky, sticky as can be.
Now my sticky, sticky hands are stuck on me!
Oh, whatever should I do
To get rid of all this goo?
So my hands will not be stuck—they will be free.

Jane Donaldson, Saint Susanna Preschool, Plainfield, IN

Movement Ideas for Preschoolers

The Name Game

Little ones learn each other's names with this twist on the action song "London Bridge." Have students stand in a line. Position yourself at the beginning of the line with one of your youngsters (or your classroom assistant) and hold up your arms to make a bridge. Then have youngsters walk under your arms as you sing the song shown, much like the traditional game. When the song is finished, bring your arms down around a child and encourage him to say his name. Repeat the game several times so many youngsters get an opportunity to say their names.

(sung to the tune of "London Bridge")

Learning names is so much fun,
So much fun, so much fun.
Learning names is so much fun.
What is your name?

Kelly Ash, Head Start, Waukesha, WI

Amanda!

Shape Hunt

Gather several plastic buckets, and use a wide-tip permanent marker to draw a different shape on each one. Place the buckets upside down in your outdoor play area, making sure they are located some distance from each other. To begin, call out the name of one of the shapes. Then blow a whistle and encourage youngsters to run and stand near the appropriate bucket. Repeat the process several times, encouraging students to scamper from bucket to bucket. Your little ones are sure to love this active game!

adapted from an idea by Melissa Ojasoo
The Child Development Center, Cape May, NJ

Get Moving!

The Copycat Game

With this activity, you'll actually *encourage* your little ones to be copycats! Lead youngsters in reciting the chant shown, inserting a child's name when indicated and altering the pronoun appropriately. Have the chosen child stand in front of the group and perform several movements, such as raising his arms above his head or hopping on one foot. Prompt students to watch carefully and copy each movement. When he is finished, repeat the process with other youngsters.

Let's play copycat just for fun.
Let's copy [Ryan], (s)he's the one!
Whatever (s)he does, we'll do the same,
'Cause that's how you play the copycat game.

Beth Iliff, Tri-County Head Start, Benton Harbor, MI

Autumn Actions

This movement idea invites youngsters to pile on the fun! To prepare, make a large tree cutout and post it in your group area. Then make a class supply of leaf cutouts and label each one with a different movement command, such as "Jump three times" or "Hop on one foot." Attach the programmed leaves to the tree, making sure they're within student reach. Invite a child to remove a leaf from the tree; then read aloud the command and ask all the youngsters to perform the action. After attaching the leaf to the bottom of the tree, play another round of this fun fall game.

Tammy Parks, Treehouse Daycare
Grandville Public Schools, Grandville, MI

Run in place.

56

Movement Ideas for Preschoolers

Hidden Honey

Place a piece of yellow play dough in a container to resemble honey. Choose a volunteer to be the bear, and ask her to pretend to be asleep near the honey. Invite the remaining children to "fly" around the bear, buzzing like bees. As they are flying, tap one of the bees on the shoulder and have her take the honey. This will be the signal for all of the bees to land, sitting in a circle around the bear. Have the child with the honey place it behind her back and encourage all the remaining bees to position their arms in the same way. Lead students in the chant shown to wake the bear. Then have the bear guess who has the honey. (Provide clues as needed.) Once the youngster with the honey is identified, she becomes the bear for the next round of play.

Isn't it funny how a bear likes honey?
Buzz, Buzz, Buzz. I wonder why he does!

Jacinda Roberts
Horace Mann Dual Language Magnet School, Wichita, KS

Indoor Obstacle Course

Try this idea to help youngsters develop their gross-motor skills and expend energy on a rainy day! In a traffic-free area of the room, arrange carpet squares, a table without chairs, large hoops, and two parallel tape lines. Each youngster, in turn, hops on each carpet square, crawls under the table, jumps in each hoop, and moves as desired through the tape lines. No doubt little ones will ask to complete this course again and again.

Kim Montanye
Glyndon United Methodist School, Glyndon, MD

Get Moving!

Frequent Fliers

There will be plenty of reindeer prancing in your classroom with this movement idea! To begin, take a photo of each child wearing an antler headband and a red sticky-dot nose. Then give your little reindeer a flying test! Have youngsters stomp to practice landing properly, follow the leader around the room to practice prancing, and practice picking up presents just in case Santa overturns his sleigh. You can also have them practice "flying" together as a team. Once each youngster has successfully passed his flying test, help him add his name to a signed construction paper copy of the flying license on page 64. Finally, attach his photo as shown.

Windy Ford
North Trenholm Baptist Church Weekday
  Kindergarten
Columbia, SC

Around and Around

Invite youngsters to practice a variety of movements as they celebrate the winter holidays with this festive song. Gather students around your class holiday tree (or a tree cutout). Then encourage children to skip around the tree as you lead them in singing the song shown. Continue in the same way, substituting different movements and holiday-related items such as those suggested.

(sung to the tune of "The Muffin Man")

[Skip] around the [Christmas tree],
The [Christmas tree], the [Christmas tree].
[Skip] around the [Christmas tree]!
We love the holidays!

Additional verses: *march, kinara; walk, menorah*

LeeAnn Collins, Sunshine House Preschool, Lansing, MI

Movement Ideas for Preschoolers

A Winter's Nap

Your little bear cubs will love this fun hibernation game! After a brief introduction to the concept of hibernation, gather youngsters in an open area. Play a recording of upbeat music and invite them to move to the beat. After a short time, stop the music and call out, "Hibernate!" Then prompt youngsters to lie down and pretend to fall asleep. To continue the activity, restart the music and call out, "Spring is here!" Play several rounds of this fun game!

Rita A. Clouse
Building Blocks Child Care Center
Cheyenne, WY

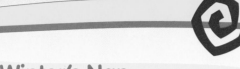

Spring is here!

On a Roll

Will youngsters have a ball with this idea? They sure will! Fill a large white trash bag with crumpled newspaper and tie it closed so that it resembles a giant snowball. Set up an obstacle course with a table, cones, and tape lines. Then invite each youngster to roll the giant snowball under the table, around the cones, and through the tape lines. What a flurry of activity!

Lois Otten
Kingdom Kids Preschool
Sheboygan, WI

Get Moving!

Running Rainbows

Reinforce colors with some fast-paced fun! Gather crepe paper streamers in rainbow colors and cut a length of streamer for each child, making sure that at least two youngsters represent each color. Give each child a streamer and take the class to an open area. Call out a featured color word, such as *yellow.* Invite each youngster holding a yellow streamer to run to a designated location and back, waving the streamer in the air. Continue to announce colors in this manner, periodically calling out the word *rainbow,* prompting all the students to run.

Cindy Hubbard
Bunche Early Childhood Development Center
Tulsa, OK

Gathering Gold

Little ones tiptoe through this gold coin search so they don't alert a slumbering leprechaun! In advance, make a supply of gold coin cutouts from yellow tagboard and scatter them throughout your classroom. Have youngsters move quickly about the room searching for gold coins, encouraging them to tiptoe so they don't wake the sleeping leprechaun. When a youngster finds a coin, have him place it in a designated location and then resume his search. Once all of the coins have been found, invite your little ones to join you in dancing a celebratory jig!

Sapna Datta
Endeavor Elementary, Orlando, FL

Movement Ideas for Preschoolers

Be a Butterfly!

At this center, youngsters transform themselves from a caterpillar into a beautiful butterfly! To prepare, place several leaf cutouts, a sleeping bag, and two colorful scarves at a center. Also attach several flower cutouts to the floor in an open area. A child pretends to be a caterpillar, crawling on the floor and munching on leaves. Then he crawls inside the sleeping bag (chrysalis) and pretends to sleep. After a short rest, he emerges from the sleeping bag with a colorful scarf in each hand (butterfly wings). Then he flies around gathering nectar from the flowers.

Angie Martin
Angie's Angels Childcare
Roxboro, NC

The W Walk

In advance, attach a path of *W* cutouts to the floor in an open area. Place along the path pictures of items whose names begin with *W*. Then invite a child to walk along the path of *W*s. Have her pick up and name each picture as she walks. If desired, invite her to pull a wagon behind her, placing the pictures in the wagon!

adapted from an idea by Leslie Boyett
Asbury Ark Academy, Bossier City, LA

Get Moving!

Rainy Day Romp

This obstacle course helps youngsters expend some energy on a rainy day! In a traffic-free area of the room, use Con-Tact covering to attach puddle cutouts to the floor. Tape a large rainbow cutout to a tabletop. Then suspend several cloud cutouts from your ceiling so that they are within students' reach. Each youngster, in turn, jumps on each puddle, crawls under the rainbow, and then jumps up to touch each cloud. As youngsters make their way through this rainy day obstacle course, consider playing a musical recording, such as "Raindrops Keep Falling on My Head" or "Singin' in the Rain."

Julie Witherell, Maywood Elementary, Monona, WI

The Bunny Pokey

Encourage little ones to get hopping as they pretend to be bunny rabbits in this version of "The Hokey-Pokey." Lead youngsters in singing the song shown, directing each student to place his hands on either side of his head so his hands resemble ears. Repeat the song in a similar way for each additional verse as suggested below, encouraging students to move appropriately.

(sung to the tune of "The Hokey-Pokey")

You put your [ears] in.
You put your [ears] out.
You put your [ears] in
And you wiggle [them] about.
You do the bunny pokey; that's the way that this song goes.
Wiggle your bunny nose!

Additional verses: *paws, tail, teeth, whole bunny*

Michele Harvey, Washington Early Childhood Center, East Alton, IL

Movement Ideas for Preschoolers

The Sideways Hop

Your youngsters will jump at this chance to practice their numbers! To prepare, label a set of tagboard rectangles with numbers from 1 to 10. Use Con-Tact paper to attach the rectangles to your classroom floor in a row. Have youngsters keep both feet together as they hop sideways from one rectangle to the next, saying each number as they go.

Karen Eiben
The Learning House Preschool
La Salle, IL

Letter Search

When the weather outside is frightful, try this indoor activity to get your children moving! In advance, prepare a supply of desired letter cards and hide them in the classroom. With a great deal of playfulness, lead students in stretches and simple exercises to "warm up" for the letter search. Then play lively music and have little ones groove to the beat as they look for letters. When a child finds a letter, have her identify it before handing it to you. Here's an *A!*

Kim Montanye
Glyndon United Methodist School
Glyndon, MD

Flying License

Official Seal of the North Pole

Place photo here.

Reindeer is officially licensed to fly.

Signed

64

KIDS IN THE KITCHEN

KIDS IN THE KITCHEN

Serve up pleasing pumpkins with this fun fall recipe! Then follow up the tasty snack with the project shown below. It's simply divine!

To prepare for the snack:
- Collect the necessary ingredients and utensils using the lists on the recipe card below.
- Photocopy the step-by-step recipe cards on page 67.
- Color the cards; then cut them out and display them in your snack area.
- Follow the teacher preparation guidelines for the snack.

Pumpkin Pancake

Ingredients for one:
orange-tinted pancake
fruit cocktail
fruit-flavored syrup (or honey)

Utensils and supplies:
plastic container
small slotted spoon
disposable plate for each child
fork for each child
napkin for each child

Teacher preparation:
Use orange-tinted batter to make a pancake for each child. Place the fruit cocktail in the container; then place the spoon in the fruit. Arrange the ingredients, utensils, and supplies near the step-by-step recipe cards.

Beth Baranowski, Roselle Park, NJ

After the Recipe
Now that each child has nibbled on a pumpkin-themed snack, have him make this simple pumpkin craft! Help each youngster use green tempera paint to make a print of each hand. When the prints are dry, have students cut them out and then glue them to a personalized pumpkin cutout to resemble leaves. Finally, staple curling ribbon vine to the pumpkin!

Jo Ann B. Stock, Rainbow Preschool, Stockton, CA

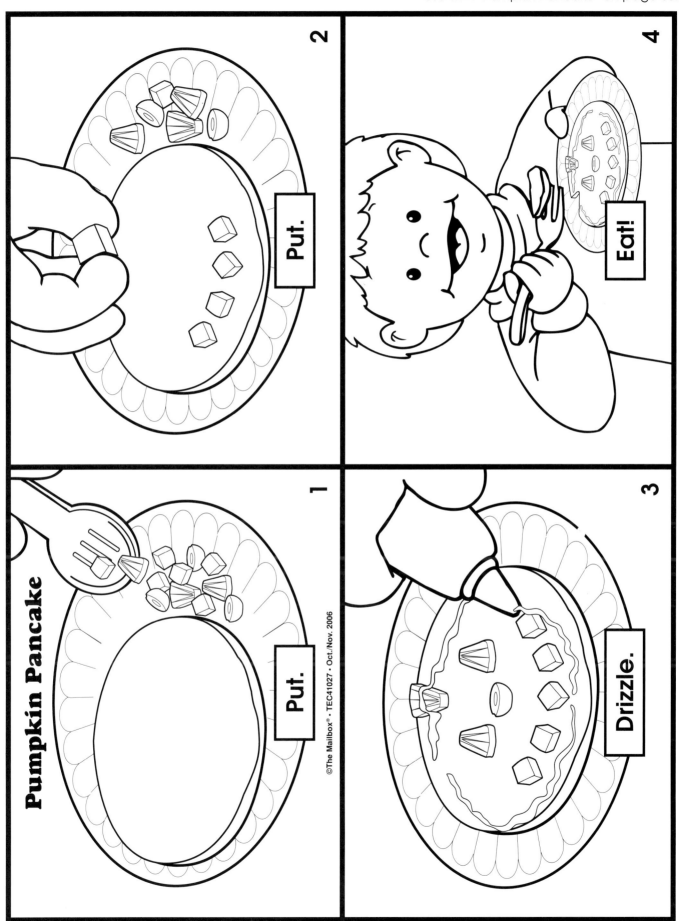

2

Put.

4

Eat!

Pumpkin Pancake

1

Put.

©The Mailbox® • TEC41027 • Oct./Nov. 2006

3

Drizzle.

KIDS IN THE KITCHEN

Serve up a batch of fun with a recipe that's just perfect for this chilly season! You may wish to show youngsters samples of quilts before they make their snacks. Then follow up the snack with the craft activity shown below!

To prepare for the snack:

- Collect the necessary ingredients and utensils using the lists on the recipe card below.
- Photocopy the step-by-step recipe cards on page 69.
- Color the cards; then cut them out and display them in your snack area.
- Follow the teacher preparation guidelines for the snack.

Sweet 'n' Savory Quilt

Ingredients for one:
4 square crackers
strawberry jam
2 banana slices
cheese spread
2 lunch meat strips

Utensils and supplies:
napkin for each child
plastic butter knife
teaspoon
2 plates

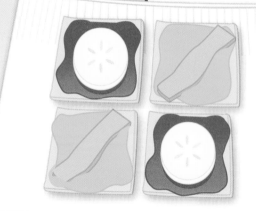

Teacher preparation:
Place the teaspoon in the container of jam. Place the butter knife in the cheese spread. Place the banana slices and lunch meat strips on separate plates. Arrange the ingredients, utensils, and supplies near the step-by-step recipe cards.

Lucia Kemp Henry, Fallon, NV

After the Recipe
Even the youngest of preschoolers will be successful with this simple quilt craft. Give each child a nine-inch square sheet of colorful construction paper. Encourage the youngster to glue fabric swatches to the paper. When the glue is dry, punch holes in the corners of each quilt block and then use yarn to connect them to make a quilt. Finally, hang this lovely quilt on a wall in your classroom.

Linda Lehmann, St. Charles Educational and Therapeutic Center, Aquebogue, NY

3
Put 2.

6
Eat!

2
Strawberry JAM
Plop.

5
Put 2.

Sweet 'n' Savory Quilt
1
Put 4.

4
CHEESE
Spread.

©The Mailbox® • TEC41028 • Dec./Jan. 2006–7

KIDS IN THE KITCHEN

Serve up a batch of fun with a recipe that's just perfect for St. Patrick's Day! Then follow up the tasty snack with the fine-motor activity shown below. It's worth its weight in gold!

To prepare for the snack:
- Collect the necessary ingredients and utensils using the lists on the recipe card below.
- Photocopy the step-by-step recipe cards on page 71.
- Color the cards; then cut them out and display them in your snack area.
- Follow the teacher preparation guidelines for the snack.

Gold Coins

Ingredients for one:
3 round crackers
3 banana slices
honey
green sugar crystals (lucky dust)

Utensils and supplies:
paper plate for each child

Teacher preparation:
Arrange the ingredients, utensils, and supplies near the step-by-step recipe cards.

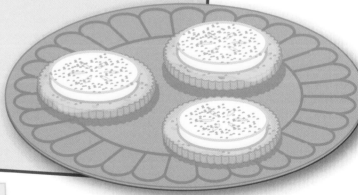

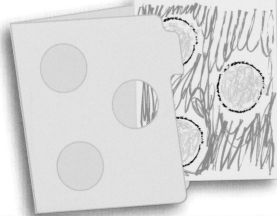

After the Recipe
Now that youngsters have eaten their gold coins, have them practice tracing skills to make more golden treasure! Cut circles in the front flap of a manila folder. Have a student slide a sheet of yellow paper into the folder and then trace each circle. Instruct him to remove the paper to see his gold coins. Then have him embellish his treasure as desired.

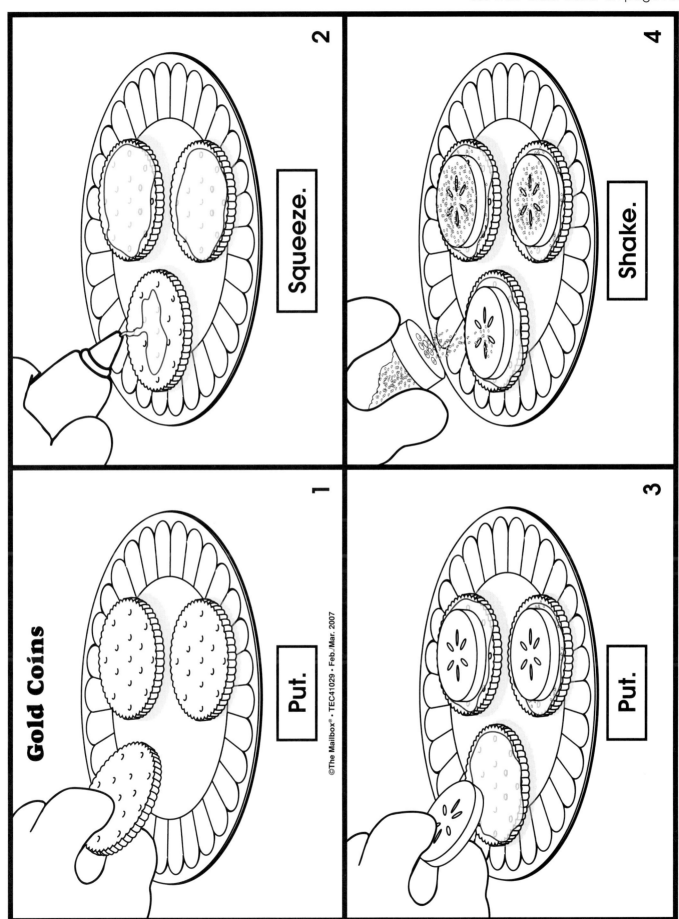

2

Squeeze.

4

Shake.

Gold Coins

Put.

1

Put.

3

©The Mailbox® • TEC41029 • Feb./Mar. 2007

KIDS IN THE KITCHEN

These pocket bread tacos are easy for little hands to grasp! That makes this recipe a fun preschool-friendly snack to add to your Cinco de Mayo celebration!

To prepare for the snack:

- Collect the necessary ingredients and utensils using the lists on the recipe card.
- Photocopy the step-by-step recipe cards on page 73.
- Color the cards; then cut them out and display them in your snack area.
- Follow the teacher preparation guidelines for the snack.

Tasty Veggie Tacos

Ingredients for one:
½ piece of pocket bread
shredded lettuce
diced tomatoes
mild salsa
shredded cheese

Utensils and supplies:
3 plastic containers
tongs
3 spoons
paper plate for each child
napkin for each child

Teacher preparation:
If desired, use the note provided on page 74 to request ingredients and supplies. Place the lettuce, tomatoes, and cheese in separate containers; then place the tongs and spoons in the appropriate ingredients. Arrange the ingredients, utensils, and supplies near the step-by-step recipe cards.

Sue Reppert, Widening World Pre-School, Mentor, OH

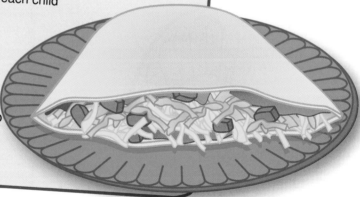

Today we made pocket bread tacos!

After the Recipe
Now that your little ones have eaten their tasty treat, they're ready to make this take-home booklet reviewing the experience! Make a paper pocket so that it resembles pocket bread; then label the pocket as shown. Help each youngster use a glue stick to secure paper cutouts in the pocket bread to resemble the ingredients in the recipe. Next, have each student color and cut out a copy of the recipe cards (page 73). Staple the cover and pages in order. Then encourage him to drop his recipe book into the pocket and take it home to share with his family.

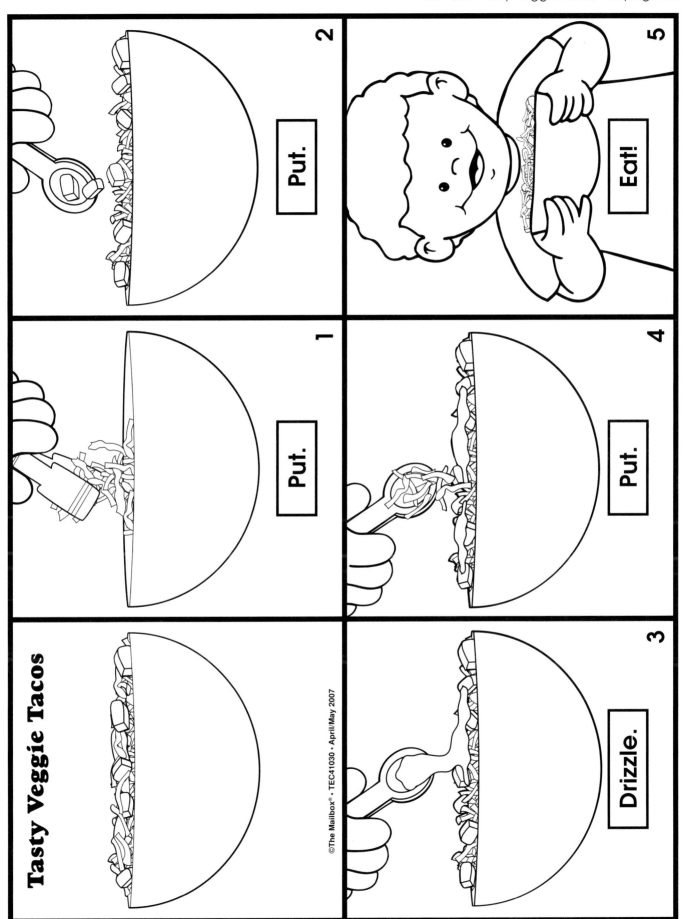

Tasty Veggie Tacos

1 — Put.

2 — Put.

3 — Drizzle.

4 — Put.

5 — Eat!

Dear Parent,
We are making Tasty Veggie Tacos soon. We would be grateful if you could help by providing the following ingredient(s):

_____

_____

_____

We need the ingredient(s) listed above by _____ .
                                              date
Please let me know if you are able to send the ingredient(s).
                              Thank you,

                        _____
                                  teacher

☐ Yes, I am able to send the ingredient(s).
☐ No, I am unable to send the ingredient(s) this time.

                        _____
                                parent signature

Dear Parent,
We are making Tasty Veggie Tacos soon. We would be grateful if you could help by providing the following ingredient(s):

_____

_____

_____

We need the ingredient(s) listed above by _____ .
                                              date
Please let me know if you are able to send the ingredient(s).
                              Thank you,

                        _____
                                  teacher

☐ Yes, I am able to send the ingredient(s).
☐ No, I am unable to send the ingredient(s) this time.

                        _____
                                parent signature

LEARNING CENTERS

Learning Centers

Looking at Letters
Literacy Center

Cut a supply of letters from advertisements and magazines. Place the letter cutouts in a container. Then place the container at a center along with a supply of construction paper and glue sticks. A child glues letter cutouts to a sheet of paper until he is satisfied with the appearance of his project. Then he examines his collage to find letters he is familiar with. Look! There's the letter *R!*

Carrie Whitney
TLC Learning Center
Cape Coral, FL

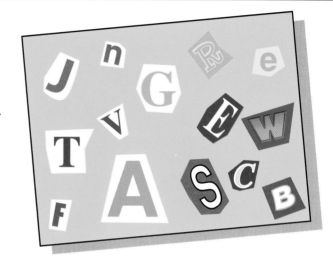

Perfect Pairs
Math Center

Little ones practice matching skills with magnets! In advance, gather several pairs of magnets, such as ones found at local businesses. Place the magnets at your math center along with a metal cookie sheet. A child chooses matching pairs of magnets and then places them side by side on the cookie sheet. When all the pairs have been found, he removes the magnets from the sheet and mixes them up. Now he's ready for another round!

Amy Aycock
Ballard County Preschool/Head Start
LaCenter, KY

Ready for Picking
Dramatic Play

Create loads of apple-picking fun with this realistic orchard! In advance, attach the hook side of a Velcro fastener to each of several plastic apples. Then make tree cutouts from bulletin board paper and laminate them for durability. Firmly secure the trees to a wall at a center. Next, mount the loop side of Velcro fasteners to the trees and attach the apples. Consider adding items such as a scale, baskets, and a pretend cash register to the center. Invite your youngsters to use desired props to pick and purchase apples.

Rachel Muchka
Storybook Learning Center
West Bend, WI

Lots of Lacing Cards
Fine-Motor Area

To prepare, cut the front panel from each of several empty food boxes, such as those used for cereal or cake mix. Hole-punch the edges of the resulting cards, or punch holes around a specific feature, such as a large letter. Cut several lengths of yarn and dip an end of each length in glue to prevent fraying. When the glue is dry, tie the remaining end of each length to a hole in a card. Then place the cards at a center. A student chooses a card and laces the yarn through the holes.

Bonnie Lanterman
St. Charles, MO

Combs, Brushes, and Curlers
Play Dough Center

Place a variety of hair care items—such as plastic rollers, picks, combs, brushes, and barrettes—at your play dough center. A youngster explores the impressions and textures he can make by pressing or dragging items over a piece of play dough. These items aren't just for hair care anymore!

adapted from an idea by Dorothy Stein
Christian Beginnings Preschool
Prince Frederick, MD

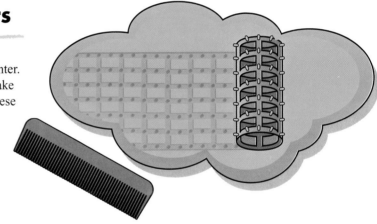

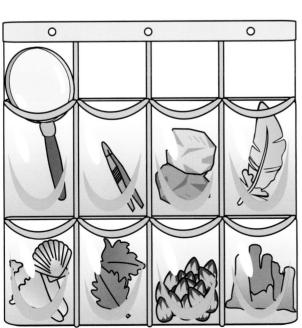

Shoe Pocket Science
Science Center

A shoe bag holds a variety of fascinating items at this center! Obtain a shoe bag with transparent pockets as shown. Then fill the pockets with items such as feathers, moss, seashells, seeds, sponges, large stones, magnifying glasses, and tweezers. A little one visits the center and uses the tools to investigate the items.

Susan Pufall
Red Cliff Early Childhood Center
Ashland, WI

Learning Centers

Square by Square
Literacy Center

To begin, make a mat by writing fall-themed words on a large sheet of construction paper, enclosing each letter in a box as shown. Label each word with a corresponding picture. Then cut and label matching letter tiles. Put the letter tiles in a resealable plastic bag and place the bag at a center along with the mat. A child visits the center and matches the letter tiles to the letters on the mat. Once the words are complete, have him look at the pictures to identify each word.

Karen E. McMillan
Pima Community College Child Development Center
Tucson, AZ

Lovely Leaves
Art Center

To prepare for these unique projects, attach to a tabletop several textured materials, such as corrugated cardboard, lace, wallpaper, and bubble wrap packaging material. Make a supply of leaf cutouts from white construction paper. Set the leaves on the table along with several unwrapped crayons. A child places her leaf cutout on top of one of the textured items. Then she rubs the side of an unwrapped crayon over the leaf. Encourage her to add a variety of different textures to each leaf she makes.

Vicki Brant
Ravenna, OH

Fresh Fall Fun
Sensory Center

Try this idea to bring some of the great outdoors inside. Fill a tub with fall leaves, Indian corn, and pinecones in various sizes. Tuck some color paddles in with the items, and invite youngsters to explore. Encourage them to view the items through the color paddles to change the items' appearance.

Sandy Barker
Children's World
St. Paul, MN

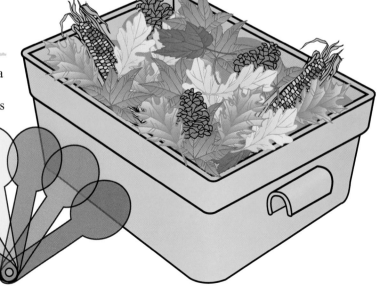

Pumpkins on a Perch
Math Center

To prepare, make five pumpkin cutouts from construction paper. Label half of each pumpkin with a number from 1 to 5. Draw a corresponding set of pumpkin seeds on the remaining half. Puzzle-cut each pumpkin down the middle and place the resulting pieces in a container at a center. Then tape a drawing of a fence, similar to the one shown, to a hard surface at the center. A youngster matches the corresponding pumpkin halves and then places each pumpkin on the fence.

adapted from an idea by Kimberly Wojcieszak
Peace Lutheran Preschool
Okeechobee, FL

Wonderful Webs
Fine-Motor Center

Little ones are bound to get caught up in this lacing activity! To prepare, hole-punch the edges of several round, plastic lids of various sizes. Cut several lengths of yarn and dip an end of each length in glue to prevent fraying. When the glue is dry, tie the remaining end of each length to a hole in a lid. Then place the lids at a center along with a supply of plastic spiders. A student chooses a lid and laces the yarn through the holes to create a web. Encourage her to lace a plastic spider ring or two onto her web to add to the fun!

Jeanene Watson
TLC Daycare
Fairfield, IL

A Good Impression
Play Dough Center

This center is sure to make a positive impression on your little ones! Place a variety of rubber stamps at a table along with a supply of colorful play dough. A youngster flattens a piece of play dough and then presses the stamps into the dough. The resulting impressions are sure to tickle your youngsters!

Nancy Foss
Wee Care
Galion, OH

Learning Centers

A Pretty Wreath
Flannelboard Center

Cut a large wreath shape from green felt and display it on a wall. Place a variety of felt shapes in a container near the wreath. A child chooses a shape and attaches it to the wreath. She continues in this manner until the wreath is decorated to her liking. Then she removes the shapes and places them back in the container for the next visitor.

Rebecca Cook
North Phoenix Baptist Preschool
Phoenix, AZ

So Shiny!
Art Center

Make a supply of shape cutouts from heavy-duty aluminum foil. Place the shapes at a center along with a block of foam, a supply of golf tees, and plastic toy hammers. Have a youngster place a shape on the foam block and use a hammer to tap a golf tee into the shape to make a hole. Have him remove the golf tee. Then encourage him to repeat the process until the desired effect is achieved. Help him tie a loop of ribbon to the shape to make an ornament as shown. Hang these sparkling ornaments near a sunny classroom window. How neat!

Charlet Estes
Highland Wee Care Learning Center
Highland, AR

Let It Snow
Fine-Motor Area

Whether there's snow outside or not, youngsters can create a winter wonderland indoors! Place quilt batting in a plastic tub. Then place the tub at a center along with several pairs of scissors. A little one cuts the batting or uses his fingers to pull the batting apart to make a flurry of snowflakes!

Denise Heiner
Tri City Christian School
Vista, CA

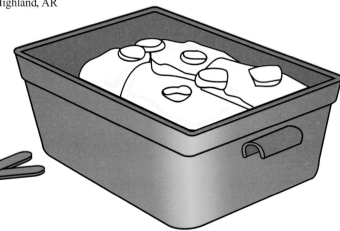

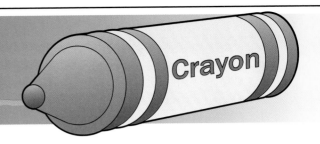

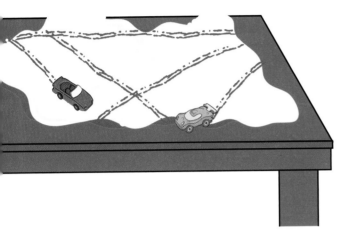

A Snowy Drive
Sensory Center

Invite your little ones to explore the slippery driving conditions of a snowy road. Squirt nonmentholated shaving cream (snow) onto a tabletop; then smooth the shaving cream for even coverage. Place a variety of small toy cars near the shaving cream. A youngster chooses a car and then "drives" it through the snow. What fun!

Kristen Hanson
Head Start Child Care
Hillsboro, ND

Mitten Match
Math Center

Youngsters practice matching skills with mittens! In advance, gather several pairs of mittens. Decorate a small box to resemble a washing machine. Then place both the mittens and washing machine in your math center. A child places the mittens in the washing machine, closes the lid, and shakes the box to "wash" the mittens. Then she removes the mittens from the machine and places matching pairs side by side. Now there's some good clean fun!

Susan Riehl
Ross Preschool
Fort Huron, MN

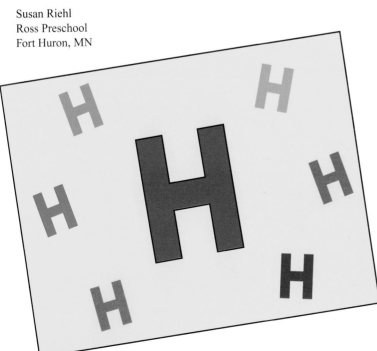

Lots of Letters
Literacy Center

Label a length of bulletin board paper with a desired letter and attach the paper to a tabletop. Place a container of colorful letter cutouts nearby, making sure that the focus letter is represented by several of the cutouts. A child chooses a letter from the container. If it matches the designated letter, he glues it to the paper. If it does not, he returns it to the container. He continues in this manner as time allows.

Danielle Wieging
Broadway Kids Place
Spencerville, OH

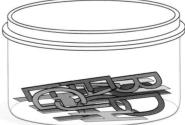

Learning Centers

Sort It Out
Science Center

Youngsters classify objects at this center! Transform a piece of poster board into a sorting mat similar to the one shown. Place the mat in your science center along with a variety of hard and soft items such as a wooden spoon, a block, a cotton ball, and a small stuffed animal. A little one visits the center and sorts each object onto the corresponding side of the sorting mat. A cotton ball is soft, but a wooden spoon is hard! For additional practice, have youngsters complete a copy of page 84.

Lois J. Ormiston
Moravian Academy
Bethlehem, PA

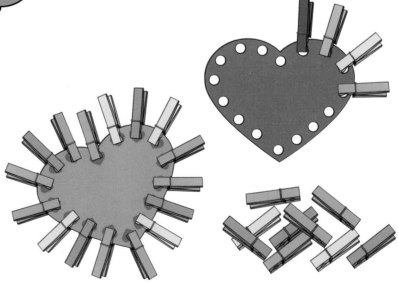

Shadow Matching
Math Center

To prepare, make two identical sets of seasonal shape cutouts. Cut one set from black construction paper (shadows) and the other set from colored construction paper. Secure the shadows to a wall at a center. Attach the loop side of a Velcro fastener to each shadow and the corresponding hook side to each of the other cutouts. A youngster visits the center and attaches each cutout to its matching shadow.

Michelle Beyerle
First Presbyterian Preschool
Anniston, AL

Clip the Clothespins
Fine-Motor Area

Attach sticky dots or stickers to the edges of several different tagboard cutouts as shown. Then place the cutouts at a center along with a supply of clothespins. A child chooses a cutout and clips a clothespin to each sticker. When he is finished, he removes the clothespins and repeats the process with additional cutouts as time allows.

Kathy Myles
Variety Child Learning Center
Syosset, NY

Personal Puzzles
Puzzle Center

For each child, brush glue over the back of a magazine picture; then attach the picture to a piece of construction paper. When the glue is dry, place the pictures at a center along with scissors and resealable plastic bags. A youngster chooses a picture and then puzzle-cuts the picture into a desired number of pieces. When he is finished cutting, he mixes up the pieces and assembles the puzzle. Then he places the pieces in a resealable plastic bag and takes the puzzle home to share with his family.

Melissa Rose
Early Childhood Alliance
Ft. Wayne, IN

The Hidden Letter
Literacy Center

Invite youngsters to uncover a buried treasure! Secretly attach a large laminated letter cutout to the bottom of your sand table (or a plastic tub). Then fill the table with sand, rice, or shaving cream. Place a set of alphabet cards nearby. A little one uses his hands to scoop the contents away from the letter. When he has determined which letter is buried, he shows you the corresponding alphabet card to confirm his answer.

Melissa Rose

Shaving Cream Swirl
Art Center

Cover a table with a vinyl tablecloth. Squirt a generous amount of shaving cream onto the table. A child squeezes dollops of colorful tempera paint onto the shaving cream; then she uses a paintbrush handle to briefly swirl the colors together. When a desired effect is achieved, she pats a tagboard cutout onto the colored shaving cream. She gently lifts the cutout and uses a rubber spatula to scrape off the excess shaving cream (with assistance as needed). When the project is dry, she mounts it on colorful construction paper.

Gina Walter
Kankakee Community College Child Development Center
Kankakee, IL

Hard or Soft?

Note to the teacher: Copy this page onto colored copy paper for each child. Encourage him to name the pictures on his sheet. Then have him press a large marshmallow into a shallow pan of white paint and make a print on each picture that shows an item that is soft.

MANAGEMENT TIPS
& TIMESAVERS

It's a Date!

Give the responsibility of dating work samples to your little ones! Gather a date stamp and a black ink pad. Then adjust the stamp to reflect the date and store the items in an accessible spot. Whenever each youngster completes a project, have her stamp the date on it before taking it home or placing it in her portfolio. *Angie Kutzer, Garrett Elementary, Mebane, NC*

SEP 05 2006

A Lovely Line

Help your little ones walk in a straight line with this simple prop. Gather several lengths of colorful yarn and make a thick braid. Then attach inexpensive shower curtain rings to the braid at regular intervals to make a class supply of handles. As you walk down the hall, hold an end of the braid and have each child grasp a handle. *Kim Reilly, Noah's Ark Child Care Center and Preschool, Zanesville, OH*

Mikayla
Arizona
Benji
Ethan
Lillian
Carter
Jar

Useful Binder Pouches

Gather a variety of binder pouches similar to those shown. Then slip in each pouch frequently used supplies, such as song cards, nametags, and phone number or address flash cards. Place all the pouches in a binder and you'll always know where all of those important items are stored! *Karen Ross, BHK L'anse Headstart, L'anse, MI*

Find the Spot!

For easy circle-time seating, glue each child's photograph to a personalized circle cutout and laminate the circles for durability. Place the circles on the floor in your large-group area. Then invite each student to have a seat on his spot! *Barb Good, Mt. Pleasant Children's Village, Monroe, OH*

Derek

Color-Coded Classes

If you teach multiple classes throughout the week, keep everything organized by color-coding each class! Simply designate a color for each class. Then use that color for important items such as nametags, cubby tags, notes to parents, and emergency cards. *Beth Knuth, St. Philip's Preschool, Rudolph, WI*

Management Tips & Timesavers

Riley's Day

What I learned...	What I did for fun...	What I ate...	Comments
counting to five cutting circles	played on the slide played in the sandbox	grilled cheese peas pears milk	Riley had a great day!

Quick Communication

Keep parents informed about happenings in their youngsters' day with this simple idea. Prepare a form similar to the one shown and copy to make a class supply. Each day, quickly jot notes on the form and send it home. Parents are sure to appreciate the daily communication. *Vicki Ault, Guiding Hand Preschool, Cheshire, OH*

The Quiet Train

To help little ones remember not to talk in the hallway, have them pretend to be a quiet train. As students walk down the hall in a line, have them whisper "Chugga, chugga, chugga, chugga, shhhh, shhhh." This simple tip keeps youngsters occupied while they walk. *Eileen Hume, Edu Care Children's Center, Midlothian, VA*

Portable Practice

Place materials for an independent activity in a personalized tub (or box) for each youngster. Consider tasks such as lacing, matching pictures, or cutting shapes. Store the tubs within student reach. When you find yourself with a few extra minutes, simply have each youngster complete the task in his tub. Periodically rotate the materials in students' tubs to keep interest high. *Katie Williams, Horace Mann Elementary, Springfield, MO*

Praiseworthy Pumpkin

Post a large orange pumpkin cutout. Store small black triangle cutouts near the pumpkin. Each time students exhibit positive behaviors, add a shape to the pumpkin. When the face is complete, reward little ones with a special privilege or a treat! *Chalene McGrath, Discovery Elementary, Brigham City, UT*

Restroom Sign

With this system, little ones will always know when the restroom is occupied! Attach the hook side of a Velcro fastener to your bathroom door; then attach another near the door. Adhere the loop side of a Velcro fastener to a laminated person cutout. Put the cutout on the Velcro fastener near the door. Before a youngster enters the restroom, she moves the cutout to the door. When she leaves the restroom, she places the cutout in its former location. *Sara Tidwell, Horizon Activities Center, Elyria, OH*

Management Tips & Timesavers

Terrific Transitions

Use this idea to transition youngsters to their next activity. Place several holiday cards on the floor. While youngsters cover their eyes, slip a star cutout in one of the cards. Then invite each youngster, in turn, to open a card. After each youngster's turn, he moves on to the next scheduled activity. When the star is found, hide it again in a different card and continue in the same way. *Danielle Roark, First United Methodist Preschool Ministries, Georgetown, KY*

Hallway Helper

Introduce a puppet to students and tell them that the puppet is going to watch to make sure they walk in a nice quiet line down the hall. As students walk, have the puppet look over your shoulder at your youngsters and "whisper" in your ear. When you reach your destination, share all of the wonderful praise the puppet shared with you! *Liana Mahoney, Beaver River Central School, Beaver Falls, NY*

A Festive Reward

Place a special treat in a lidded box; then wrap the lid and box separately. Puzzle-cut a holiday-related pattern and place the pieces near a bulletin board. When youngsters show positive behavior in the classroom, place a piece of the puzzle on the board. Then, when the picture is complete, open the gift and have youngsters share the treat. Repeat the process with other holiday-related patterns. *Chalene McGrath, Discovery Elementary, Brigham City, UT*

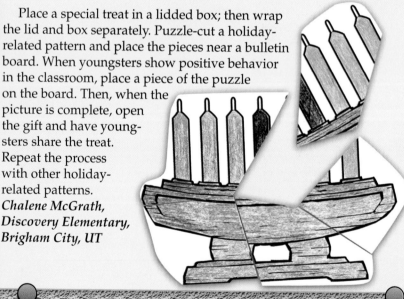

Snowboot Buddies

Have youngsters help each other get ready to go outdoors! When students arrive for the day, place pairs of snowboots together so that each youngster has a buddy. When students get ready to go outside, buddies can help each other put on scarves, mittens, boots, and jackets. *Meg Thaler, Scarsdale Congregational Church Nursery School, Scarsdale, NY*

The Rhyming Game

When you call on a youngster to help with a task, say a nonsense word that rhymes with the child's name. For example, you might say, "If your name sounds like Boshua, please help pass out the snack." Then Joshua would come forward to help. Youngsters are sure to giggle with delight! *Barbara Allen, Purcell Elementary, Purcell, OK*

Management Tips & Timesavers

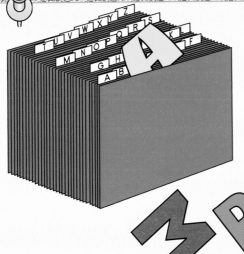

Letters on Demand

Here's an easy way to store bulletin board letter cutouts! Obtain an accordion-style organizer with letter tabs; then place each cutout in its corresponding compartment. The letters are easy to retrieve for your next bulletin board project! *Susan Riehl, Ross Preschool, Port Huron, MI*

Simply Tidy

Youngsters match symbols *and* clean up the room with this tip! Label each game or puzzle with a different symbol; then label the corresponding storage area with a matching symbol. Youngsters simply match the symbols to put the game in its correct location! *Wanda Reding, Greenbrier Elementary, Greenbrier, TN*

Storing Companion Pages

How can you keep track of the supplemental pages offered by The Mailbox Companion® site? Simply place the printed materials for each issue in an individual manila envelope and use a binder clip to attach the envelope to the magazine. The pages will be protected, and all of your resources will be in same place! *Marcia Helten, St. Mary Catholic School, Derby, KS*

Less Mess!

Place paint for projects in dog dishes! Dog dishes simply refuse to tip over when bumped or nudged, so the paint stays where it should. No more accidental spills! *Erin Killeen, Saint Therese School, Cresskill, NJ*

Who's Finished?

Which children have completed a project? It's easy to tell with this idea! Attach a self-adhesive magnet strip to the back of a personalized craft stick for each child. Place the sticks at your small-group project table. When a youngster completes the daily project, have him place his stick on a desired magnetic surface. Now it's easy to see who still needs to complete the project! *Dot Stein, Christian Beginnings Preschool, Prince Frederick, MD*

Learning Letters

To transform waiting time into learning time, attach letter cutouts to the wall next to your restroom. When children line up to use the restroom, each youngster stands next to a letter. Encourage each student to trace his letter with his finger and then name the letter while he is waiting his turn. *Aissa Dorsey, Palito Blanco Elementary, Ben Bolt, TX*

Themes at a Glance

To keep track of the themes in your resource books, make a copy of the table of contents in each book. Write the name of the appropriate book at the top of each copy and then store the copies alphabetically in a folder. When you're looking for a specific theme, you can immediately see which books will be the most helpful. *Lisa Carver, Capshaw Elementary, Cookeville, TN*

Puppet Helpers

Give each youngster a puppet during cleanup time; then encourage students to teach their puppets how to put away items to clean the room. Youngsters will love being the teachers, and you'll love how quickly the room looks clean and neat! *Christine Badey, Hamilton Avenue Early Childhood Center, Trenton, NJ*

Name That Painting!

Here's an easy way to label youngsters' artwork! Cut a variety of small shapes from construction paper scraps. When a child is finished painting a sheet of paper, place a personalized shape on the wet paint. The shape will stick, and the painting is identified! *Jean Gorham, Eastern Heights Little Lambs Preschool, St. Paul, MN*

Stay-Put Paper

Here's a tip just perfect for toddlers! To help papers stay in place when youngsters are drawing or coloring, place a small amount of nontoxic adhesive putty on the tabletop; then press the paper over the putty. Students can scribble vigorously, and the paper stays in place! *Deb McCarthy, Kiddie City Family Childcare, Holden, MA*

SCIENCE EXPLORATIONS

Science

Mix It Up!
When little ones mix liquids, they're sure to see some fascinating results!

STEP 1

The juice might make the water look purple!

Gather a small group of youngsters and present one of the jars of water. Then show students the grape juice and ask them what they think will happen if the juice is poured into the water.

STEP 2

It doesn't look like water anymore.

Invite a child to pour the juice into the water. Have the students observe the mixture for a minute; then encourage a child to gently stir the mixture with a spoon. Prompt children to discuss what they see.

STEP 5

Ask students to suggest ways they could get the oil to mix throughout the water, such as stirring it or placing a lid on the jar and shaking it. Have students test some of their theories, leading them to realize that in each case the oil eventually spreads above the water as before.

STEP 6

Place the two jars side by side and compare them. Did the juice and water stay mixed, or did the juice spread at the top like the oil? Finally, explain that some things mix together very well, like the juice and the water, while other things separate, like the oil and the water.

Explorations

To explore mixing liquids, you will need the following:
2 lidded plastic jars, partially filled with water
cup of grape juice
cup of cooking oil
mixing spoon
optional recording sheet on page 102

STEP 3

Set the juice and water mixture aside. Then present the remaining jar of water and the cooking oil. Repeat the process, asking the students to describe what they think will happen when the oil is poured into the jar of water.

STEP 4

It's staying on the top!

Encourage a student to pour the oil into the water. Then have youngsters discuss their observations.

Did You Know?

Youngsters may be surprised to find out that oil is used frequently during cooking, and it can often be difficult to remove the residue it leaves behind on pots and pans. Dish soap breaks down the oil so that water can wash it away!

What Now?

Help students place food coloring in a two-liter bottle partially filled with water. Add cooking oil to the mixture; then secure the cap and reinforce it with heavy-duty tape. Encourage youngsters to shake and swirl the mixture, noting how the oil separates from the colored water.

Science

Good Vibrations

What's that sound? Why, it's your youngsters expressing delight over this fun vibration investigation!

idea contributed by Carolyn B. Taylor, Lincoln Head Start,
Salt Lake City, UT

STEP 1

It's moving.

Gather a small group of students. Play a recording of slow music. Give each youngster the opportunity to touch the speakers of the portable stereo as the music plays. Then invite each child to describe what she feels.

STEP 2

It makes my hand feel buzzy!

Next, play a recording of upbeat music. Repeat the process, inviting each child to touch the speaker and then discuss what she feels.

STEP 5

Play the recording of upbeat music and have students continue to watch the salt. Ask youngsters to compare the salt's current movement with its movement during the slow music.

STEP 6

?

Will other items move when you put them on the waxed paper? Have youngsters experiment with items such as sugar, crumpled paper, or a small toy.

Explorations

To explore vibrations, you will need the following:
portable stereo
waxed paper
recordings of slow and upbeat music
salt
tape

Lightly tape the piece of waxed paper to the speaker. Then shake salt onto the waxed paper. Ask youngsters to predict what will happen to the salt when you turn on the music.

The salt is bouncing a little.

Play the recording of slow music once again and have the students carefully observe the salt. Prompt them to describe what they see.

This is Why

Sounds are caused by things that shake or vibrate. A strummed guitar, a flying hummingbird, and a person's voice are all vibrations that we hear as sound. In this experiment, the cones in the stereo speakers vibrate, allowing us to hear the music. These vibrations make the salt jump.

HMMMM!

What Now?

Invite youngsters to explore other objects that vibrate and thus produce sound. Have each student place her hand on her throat as she sings or talks. You may also wish to provide musical instruments for little ones to investigate.

BITTY BOP

BOP

Science

Melting Away

With this nifty investigation, youngsters explore the best way to melt an ice cube!

idea contributed by Suzanne Moore, Tucson, AZ

STEP 1

It's cold and wet!

Gather a small group of youngsters and present an ice cube. Invite each youngster to observe the ice cube and describe it. Then encourage each child to touch the ice cube and discuss how it feels.

STEP 2

?

Ask youngsters to explain what will happen if the ice cube sits out in the warm room for a long time. Lead students to conclude that the ice cube will melt and leave a puddle of water on the plate.

STEP 5

I was right!

Were youngsters surprised by the outcome of the experiment? Invite students to revisit their predictions.

STEP 6

We could put blankets on the ice cube.

Invite youngsters to suggest other ways to make the ice melt quickly. If desired, encourage youngsters to test their suggestions to see whether they are effective.

Explorations

To explore melting, you will need the following:
ice cubes
plastic plate
clear container of warm water
clear container of cold water

STEP 3

"It will melt fastest in the warm water."

Explain to students that they are going to try to find a way to melt the ice cube faster than it would melt sitting on the plate. Present a container of warm water and a second container of cold water. Ask youngsters whether they think the ice cube will melt fastest in the warm water, in the cold water, or on the plate.

STEP 4

Have youngsters place a fresh ice cube on the plate, a second ice cube in the warm water, and a third in the cold water. Invite the students to watch carefully to see which ice cube melts the fastest.

Did You Know?

When one cup of snow melts, it results in only about one-fourth cup of water!

What Now?

Now that the ice cube on the plate has melted, what will happen to the water that's left? Invite youngsters to share their predictions. Then have students observe the water over the next few days. When the water completely disappears, explain that they can no longer see the water on the plate because it is now in the air.

Science

A Beautiful Rainbow!
Youngsters make a rainbow right in the classroom with this vibrant exploration!

idea contributed by Tabitha Bohannon
The Growing Tree Learning Center
Cookeville, TN

STEP 1

I saw a rainbow over my house!

Gather a small group of children. Ask youngsters whether they have ever seen a rainbow; encourage them to describe their experiences.

STEP 2

Explain that rainbows are seen outside when sunlight shines through raindrops. Tell students that they can make a rainbow in the classroom using a pan of water, sunlight, and a mirror.

STEP 5

I see red!

Give each child an opportunity to manipulate the mirror to form a rainbow. Encourage youngsters to identify the colors they see in the rainbow on the wall.

STEP 6

Give each student a simple rainbow pattern. Then help him color the rainbow so that it matches the one he saw on the wall.

Explorations

To explore rainbows, you will need the following:
small mirror
sunlight
pan partially filled with water
rainbow patterns

STEP 3

"Maybe you hold the mirror above the water!"

Have students predict what you might do with the props to make a rainbow. Then invite youngsters to test their suggestions.

STEP 4

After several youngsters experiment with the mirror, help a child partially submerge the mirror and then turn it to face the sunlight. Have the youngster adjust the angle of the mirror until a wavy rainbow appears on a wall in your classroom. (The rainbow will be difficult to see immediately if the water is moving.)

This Is Why

When a rainbow is made in nature, sunlight travels through a raindrop, which causes the sunlight to bend. When sunlight bends, it is separated into the colors of the spectrum.

What Now?

Give youngsters other opportunities to see rainbows! Attach a nozzle with a mist option to a hose. Then take youngsters outside on a sunny day and spray the hose into the air. Little ones will see a lovely rainbow!

Science

Splendid Stems
Youngsters learn about plant stems with this nifty exploration!

STEP 1

It's bumpy!

Gather a small group of youngsters and show them a stalk of celery. Help students identify the stem and leaves of the celery. Then tell them that the stem is the part we eat. Invite each child to explore the celery stalk and comment on what he sees.

STEP 2

Lead students to notice the small holes visible at the bottom of the stalk. Ask students to predict what the purpose of these holes might be. After each young-ster has had an opportunity to guess, explain that plants need water and that water enters the holes and travels up the stem.

STEP 5

?

Have students use the information they learned in the experiment to help them predict the answer to the following question: What will happen when a stalk of celery is placed in a container with colored water? After students share their predictions, tint a container of water and then have a child place a new stalk of celery in the water.

STEP 6

The leaves are blue!

After a few days, have youngsters closely observe the stalk of celery. They will be delighted to discover that the leaves are discolored due to the food coloring.

Explorations

To explore stems, you will need the following:
3 celery stalks, freshly cut and with leaves
3 containers
food coloring
water

STEP 3

Place one celery stalk in a container of water; then place a second stalk in an empty container. Have students predict what will happen to the two celery stalks.

STEP 4

Plants need water to stay alive.

After a few days, have students compare the stalks. Help them conclude that the stalk in the water looks and feels less wilted than the one without water. Ask students to explain why they think this is so.

Did You Know?

Almost all plants have stems! The exceptions are liverworts, hornworts, and mosses.

What Now?

Explore the stems of other plants in a similar way. Place a white carnation or wild carrot (also known as Queen Anne's lace) in tinted water. The water will rise up the stem and color the flowers. How lovely!

Name _____

Mix It Up!

1. We mixed  and  .

water   juice

It looked like [jar] .

2. We mixed [jar] and [cup] .

water   oil

It looked like [jar] .

Note to the teacher: Use with "Mix It Up" on page 92.

OUR READERS WRITE

A Loving Message

After a read-aloud of *The Kissing Hand* by Audrey Penn, I send a note home with each youngster, similar to the one shown, along with a sheet of construction paper and an index card. When the parents send to school the items requested in the note, I place a heart sticker in the middle of each hand cutout. Then I attach the items from each family to a sheet of construction paper. After placing each sheet in a page protector, I put all the sheets in a binder to make a class book.

Tina Grenier, Great Beginnings, Plainville, CT

Dear Joshua,
I know you will have a terrific time in preschool. I can't wait to hear about all the fun things you've done today!
I love you, Mom

Dear Parent,
Please trace your hand on the sheet of construction paper and then cut out the tracing. Write a brief encouraging note to your preschooler on the index card. Then send the hand cutout and card back to school with your child along with a family picture.

Thanks so much!
Ms. Grenier

Window Dressing

To dress up my windows, I attach colorful bulletin board border around the window frames. I like to change the border with the seasons. This way the border's decorations reflect what youngsters see through the windows!

Anita Edlund, Cokesbury Children's Center, Knoxville, TN

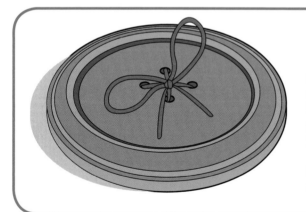

Lunch-Lid Tying

My youngsters bring their own lunches to school, and the small meals in microwavable containers are very popular. I like to wash and save the lids for tying practice. I lace yarn through the holes in each lid and then place them in a basket. Each youngster can remove a lid, tie the yarn into a bow, and then take the lid home!

Melissa Bustamante, Melissa's Preschool, Buda, TX
Angela Lenker, Bright Beginnings, Limerick, PA

Ten Little Fingers

For this fun counting craft, I program construction paper, as shown, for each child. Then I have each student glue a green circle and a brown rectangle cutout to her paper to resemble a tree. Next, I encourage students to dip all ten fingertips into a shallow container of red paint and then press them on the tree. When the paint is dry, they can count ten little apples on their trees!

Linda Knutson, Blooming Prairie Elementary, Blooming Prairie, MN

Ashley

I have ten fingers. Count them with me.
They make ten apples on my tree!

High Five Award

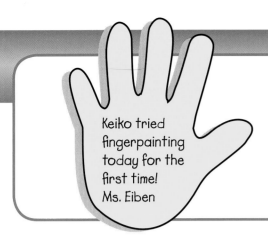

Keiko tried fingerpainting today for the first time! Ms. Eiben

Whenever my youngsters have a good day or accomplish a milestone, I give them a high five and a special hand cutout to take home. The cutout is labeled with the child's name and the reason she's being given the high five award. My youngsters and their parents really enjoy these tangible reminders of youngsters' successes.

Karen Eiben, The Learning House, La Salle, IL

Personalized Placemats

During the first week of school, I send home a large personalized sheet of construction paper and a note encouraging parents to attach family photos to the paper. When the resulting placemats are brought back to school, I laminate them for durability. Youngsters love to discuss the pictures with their classmates during snacktime!

Tammy LaMothe-Toland
Suffolk, VA

Messy Matters

I send home the poem shown to remind parents to send in a change of clothing for their children. The poem helps explain the need for extra clothing and the gentle reminder makes parents smile.

Barbara-Jean Toth, London Bridge Child Care, East Greenwich, RI

A Message From Your Preschooler
During our day, we learn and play.
Sometimes we get messy, and that's okay.
Please send extra clothes we can keep on hand
So if I paint or play in the sand
And make a mess on the clothes I wear
Then I'll have extra clothes to spare!

Simple Stencils

To make sturdy stencils, I cut vinyl placemats into squares and then die-cut the squares using different shapes. I place both the stencils and the shape cutouts in our art center. They are long-lasting and quite popular with my students!

Erika Prieto, Converse, TX

Trisha Adams
August 25

Creative Cupcakes

At the beginning of the year, I have each youngster decorate a cupcake cutout similar to the one shown. Then I write the appropriate name and birthdate on each cupcake and set them aside for safekeeping. During calendar time each morning, I announce who has a birthday to celebrate that day; then I reveal the corresponding cupcakes and attach them to the board!

Diana Kraft, Growing Vines Playschool, Arusha, Tanzania

Props for Play

These pleasing props make our dramatic-play kitchen area extra special! I place colorful paper shreds in clean plastic containers, such as red shreds in a ketchup bottle, yellow shreds in a mustard jar, and purple shreds in a dishwashing-liquid bottle. I seal the tops with hot glue before placing them in our center. These props really have pizzazz!

Susan Hamme, Mechanicsville Baptist Church Child Care Center, Mechanicsville, VA

Supersize Blocks

I use 12-pack soda boxes to make large, sturdy blocks. Simply rinse out the empty soda cans and place them back in the box. Tape the box closed with heavy-duty tape and then cover it with decorative Con-Tact covering. The resulting blocks are colorful and fun for little hands.

Cathy Consford, Buda Primary Early Learning Center, Buda, TX

A Classroom Patch

It's very difficult for our special needs class to take a field trip to a pumpkin patch, so we bring the pumpkin patch to our youngsters! We run butcher paper through a paper shredder and place the shreds in a corner of our room to resemble straw. Then we nestle a variety of donated pumpkins among the shreds. For extra fun, enhance the patch with a scarecrow and bunches of Indian corn. If enough pumpkins are donated, have each child take a pumpkin home.

Diane Kovac and Pam Macchioni, Capital Area Intermediate Unit #15 Summerdale, PA

Super Snack Holders

Cereal, small crackers, and cookies often roll around when placed on a napkin or plate. I've solved this problem for my youngsters by serving small snacks in coffee filters! The filters are the perfect size for small treats, and the sloped sides keep the food in place.

Anne Arceneaux, Ward Elementary, Jennings, LA

Play Dough With Pizzazz!

To make play dough extra special for the back-to-school season, I add red glitter and sparkly apple-shaped confetti! This is a fun way to add flair to play dough for any special theme or season.

Marsha Feffer, Bentley Early Childhood Center, Salem, MA

A Pat on the Back

To recognize teachers in our school for the magnificent work they do, I provide access to a bag of Hershey's Hugs candy and copies of a form similar to the one shown. Whenever a teacher notices a coworker doing something that deserves recognition, she fills out a form and places it in the coworker's mailbox along with a piece of candy. This has been a terrific morale booster at our center!

Kimberly Treamer, Hearts and Hands Children Center, Mt. Horeb, WI

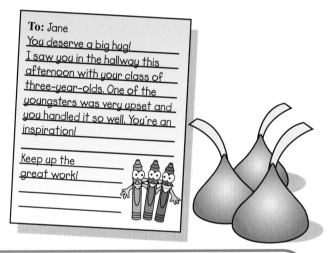

To: Jane
You deserve a big hug!
I saw you in the hallway this afternoon with your class of three-year-olds. One of the youngsters was very upset and you handled it so well. You're an inspiration!

Keep up the great work!

Dramatic-Play Makeover!

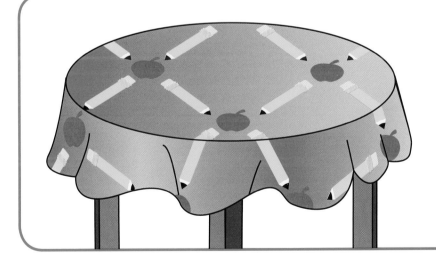

Give your dramatic-play center an attractive boost every few months by placing a different decorative tablecloth on your play table. I change mine to coordinate with the seasons and our classroom themes!

Susan Ottman, Susanna Wesley Preschool, Topeka, KS

Reluctant Painters

In the past, I've had students who are reluctant to try fingerpainting. It often helps them if I draw a shape or design on the paper first so they have something to fill in with the paint. In time, they become comfortable touching the paint and create pictures on their own!

Karen Eiben, The Learning House Preschool, La Salle, IL

It's a Spinner!

Don't throw away the circular plastic cases that hold blank compact discs—recycle them into spinners! I trace a CD on poster board; then I cut out the circle and decorate it for the desired activity. I cut a hole in the circle to fit over the center tube in the case. Then I slide it over the tube along with a jumbo paper clip to use as a spinner. To protect the spinner while in storage, I fit the plastic cover over the case!

Melisa Horsfield, Flying Colors Preschool, Ft. Payne, AL

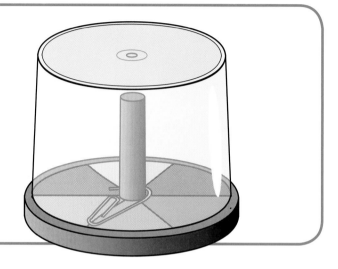

Handy Hair

Whenever I have leftover construction paper scraps in brown, black, red, and yellow, I put them through my paper shredder. The shreds make terrific hair for self-portrait projects!

Denise Heiner, Tri City Christian School, Vista, CA

1 large black rectangle
1 medium black rectangle
2 small black rectangles
2 tiny white rectangles
2 tiny orange rectangles
2 teensy-weensy black rectangles
1 FLAPPING FLUTTERING BAT!

A Shapely Halloween

This adorable bat is made completely of rectangles! For each child, I cut one long rectangle for the wings; then I make smaller rectangles for the body, teeth, ears, eyes, and pupils. I help students recognize each shape as a rectangle. Then I instruct them to accordion-fold the large rectangle and glue the pieces together to make the bat. I like to display these cute crafts with a sheet of poster board labeled as shown.

Angie Kutzer, Garrett Elementary, Mebane, NC

Hats Off to Thanksgiving!

These simple Pilgrim hats go over big at our classroom feasts! For each child, I trace a basic hat shape on black construction paper. I have each child cut out his hat; then I encourage him to glue a precut brown band and yellow buckle to the cutout. I staple a black headband to the hat and then size it to fit the child's head.

Beth Kordus, Little Learners Nursery School, West Allis, WI

Take-Home Envelopes

My youngsters enjoy taking home our class-made books. To make sure the books are returned promptly, I program a special take-home manila envelope with the following message: "Please share this with your child and return it to school tomorrow." Then I slip the book in the envelope and send it home with a child.

Stephanie Kramer, Horrall Elementary, San Mateo, CA

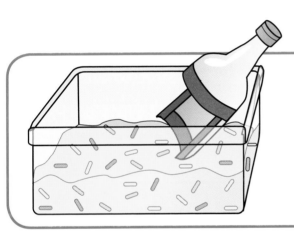

Splendid Scoops

I've discovered a simple way to make scoops for our sand table! I take a clean plastic salad-dressing bottle and cut off the bottom and a portion of one side as shown. I tape the edges and then put the resulting scoop in our sand table (or sensory tub).

Krista Schmidt, Community Care, Inc., Beaver Dam, WI

Handprints Made Easy

To simplify handprint projects, I place a large sponge in a container and then squirt paint on the sponge. A youngster simply presses a hand on the sponge and then makes a print on her project!

Martha Berry, Main Street Methodist Preschool, Kernersville, NC

The Box Monster

This class project is really popular with my students. I hot-glue several boxes together; then students paint the boxes. When the paint is dry, students cut features from construction paper and tape them to the boxes to resemble a monster. The result is simply adorable!

Kathy Rollins, Children's Creative Corner, Springfield, MA

Our Readers Write

Santa Socks

To make these cute ornaments, I have each student stuff paper into the foot portion of a small white sock. Then I use a rubber band to secure the end of the sock. Next, I fold the top portion of the sock and cuff it to resemble a cap. The child paints the cap red. After the paint is dry, he uses a marker to add a mouth and then glues cotton batting over the mouth to make a beard. I hot-glue craft items to the sock to make other features. Then I add a yarn loop to use as a hanger. These ornaments always turn out to be so cute!

Edith "CC" Heinsohn, Leeway School, Sayville, NY

Winter Wear

We love to go outside to play during the winter months, but often my youngsters aren't sent to school with appropriate winter wear. To solve this problem, we have designated certain days as Outdoor Play Days on which we begin the school day outside. This way parents make sure their youngsters are bundled up because they drop them off in our outdoor play area!

Andrea Henderson, Jefferson Brethren Preschool, Goshen, IN

Hoop Activities

Whenever we have a few extra minutes at the end of class, we do hoop activities. I place several plastic hoops on the floor and then place different items—such as lacing cards, matching activities, or blocks—in each one. I assign two or three youngsters to each hoop, and they play with the items. Then, after a few minutes, I have the youngsters put down the items and rotate to a new hoop!

Susan Luengen, Makalapa Elementary, Honolulu, HI

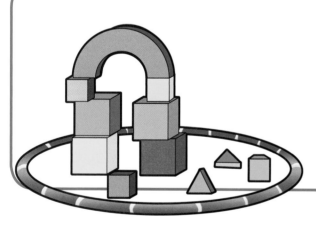

Tagalongs

To add a learning element to my youngsters' nametags, I safety-pin a different attachment to each one as shown. Each attachment, which I call a tagalong, reflects a letter, number, shape, or color we've studied. Throughout the day, I have each youngster identify her own tagalong as well as some of her classmates' tagalongs. After a few weeks, I change each child's nametag to reflect new information.

Carole Watkins, Holy Family School, Crown Point, IN

110

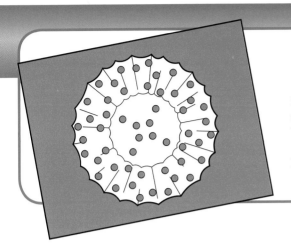

Simple Snowflake

My youngsters feel so successful after making these simple snow-flakes. For each child, I fold a coffee filter into quarters. Then I have each youngster use a craft punch to punch holes in the folded filter. When he opens up the filter, it looks like a lacy snowflake!

Karen Tubbs, Malad Headstart, Malad, ID

Sticky Board

Students can be in charge of displaying their own artwork with this bulletin board. I spray a length of bulletin board paper (or a vinyl tablecloth) with 3M Spray Mount adhesive according to the directions on the can. Then I attach the paper to a bulletin board. Youngsters can add desired artwork to the board by simply pressing it to the tacky surface of the paper! I respray the paper every month so that we have a continuous display area.

Mandi King, Thomas G. Scott Elementary, Forsyth, GA

Handmade Ornament Holder

These holiday gifts are always popular with my youngsters and their families. I have each of my students decorate a shoebox with pictures cut from holiday wrapping paper. I add a personalized sign to each box. Then I have youngsters brush two coats of Mod Podge sealant over the box. When it's dry, send the project home with instructions telling families to store their child's handmade ornaments in the box.

Karen Eiben, Lasalle, IL

Sort It Out

This sorting activity is also very helpful! I have my youngsters sort sheets of paper from my multicolored construction paper packages. This way my students practice sorting by color and my construction paper is separated to use with various craft projects.

Rachel Lawrence, Weatherford Christian School, Weatherford, TX

Flannelboard Fun

When there isn't a particular story or activity in my flannelboard center, I place youngsters' photos on the flannelboard. Simply laminate the photos; then ready them for flannelboard use and place them in the center. My students love to manipulate their classmates' pictures by placing them on the flannelboard. I've done similar activities by inviting parents to send in family photos or photos of pets. The center always gets rave reviews!

Sharon Swenson, Staples, MN

Our Readers Write

Simple Drying Racks

Use pizza boxes to make this simple drying rack for art projects! Ask a local pizzeria to donate several large, unused pizza boxes. I cut off one end from each box and then tape the boxes in a stack as shown. Then I cover the back and sides of the resulting drying rack with Con-Tact covering. The sturdy boxes are perfect for messy painting projects!

Cathy Consford, Buda Primary Early Learning Center, Buda, TX

Super Snack

My preschoolers enjoy making quesadillas for our Cinco de Mayo unit! I simply place two large tortillas on each of two cookie sheets. My youngsters help me spoon shredded cheese on the tortillas and top each one with another tortilla. I bake the resulting quesadillas in a 325° oven for about ten minutes. After they have cooled slightly, I cut them into wedges with a pizza cutter. My youngsters love topping the snacks with lettuce, tomatoes, and salsa!

Michelle Frati, Gentle Hearts Preschool, Center Moriches, NY

Sweet Scents

My little ones make these lovely potpourri holders for Mother's Day gifts. I collect an empty microwave cup along with its lid for each child. I clean the cups thoroughly and remove the labels. Next, I invite each youngster to decorate his cup with stickers, glitter, and self-adhesive foam shapes. Then I have each child place a scoop of potpourri in the container and secure the lid. My youngsters' moms always enjoy this sweet-smelling gift.

Stacie Scalisi, Capital District Beginnings, Troy, NY

Door Decor

This simple display really spruces up my classroom door! I cut a flowerpot shape from brown tagboard. Then I attach the flowerpot to my door with tape, making sure to leave the top of the pot open. Finally, I tuck some colorful artificial flowers in the pot. Instant springtime!

Isobel Livingstone, Rahway, NJ

Spring Wheelbarrow

My youngsters love to plant flowers in these cute wheelbarrows! To create them, I hot-glue poster board circles and craft sticks to snack-size plastic containers, such as those from Pringles potato crisps. Then I have each youngster place a scoop of potting soil in his wheelbarrow. I help each child plant flower seeds in the soil, and pretty soon we have lovely flowers sprouting from these adorable wheelbarrows!

Nancy DeHaven, Shady Grove UMC Preschool, Glen Allen, VA

Placemat Floaters

Whenever I find vinyl placemats with cute animals (or characters), I buy a bunch! I cut out the animals and then place them in my water table. My youngsters are always enthralled with these colorful floating cutouts!

Nancy Morgan, Care-a-Lot In Home Daycare and Preschool, Bremerton, WA

Delightful Doilies

One of our preschool program requirements is to provide an attractive classroom environment for our youngsters. To make our plant area more inviting, I attach paper doilies to the tabletop. I place Con-Tact covering over the doilies; then I place a plant on each doily. This simple idea makes our plant area look more cozy and homey.

Angela Lenker, Montgomery Early Learning Center/Head Start, Pottstown, PA

Mirror Magic

To add excitement to the mirrors in our housekeeping area, I tape child-size clothing cutouts to them. Youngsters can stand in front of a mirror and it appears as if they are wearing the clothing! This always makes my little ones giggle!

Charity Jantzon, Kid Kollege Preschool, Billings, MT

Creative Faces

Collect the plastic facial features used in a variety of different toys. Then place the features at a table with some play dough on a tray. My youngsters just love to place the features on the play dough to make fun and creative faces. This has always been a big hit at my play dough center.

Karen Briley, Nacogdoches, TX

Our Readers Write

Wish-You-Well Frames

These simple frames make special preschool keepsakes. For each youngster, I purchase a small, acrylic double frame. In one side, I place a photo of the child. In the remaining frame, I place a personalized version of the poem shown. This heartfelt gift has always been a big hit!

Michelle Rodman, Trinity Baptist Church Mother's Day Out
Amarillo, TX

Just a little note to say
That I enjoyed every day
I spent with Maggie
And her friends.
I wish her well
As this year ends.
—Ms. Rodman
Trinity School, 2007

Magic Dust

When a student has a boo-boo that needs some tender care but not a bandage, I sprinkle invisible magic dust on it! I find it's a great way to acknowledge the child is hurt so he can get on with his activity.

Jen Finnerty, Walnut Grove Elementary, Council Bluffs, IA

Growing Veggies

Here's a fun way to get little ones to eat their veggies! I make several holes for drainage in the bottom of a small plastic swimming pool and then fill the pool with topsoil. In it, I plant vegetable plants and seeds. The youngsters help me water and tend to the plants. Then we harvest the veggies when they're ripe and use them to make salads or toppings for a class pizza. I find that children are eager to try the vegetables because they helped grow them!

Allison Crawford, Sunshine Day Care, Iowa City, IA

Marker Painting

I recycle dried-out markers by having my students dip them in water and paint with them. They make beautiful pictures that have an appearance similar to watercolor paintings. Now markers that would have been discarded get a second chance!

Chrissy Papnick, Bright Horizons Family Solutions, Oakbrook, IL

STORYTIME

Storytime

Bark, George
Written and Illustrated by Jules Feiffer

George, a small dog, does not bark as he should. Instead, he meows, quacks, oinks, and moos! Find out how a trip to the vet solves George's problem in this delightful read-aloud.

ideas contributed by Suzanne Moore
Tucson, AZ

Before You Read

Help youngsters tune in to animal sounds with this little ditty. Color and cut out a copy of the animal cards on page 124. Invite a student to choose a card and identify the animal. Then lead youngsters in singing the song below for the chosen animal. Continue in the same way for each remaining card. Next, explain that the book you're about to read includes different animals and the sounds that they make. Then have students settle in for this amusing read-aloud.

(sung to the tune of "The Wheels on the Bus")

When [cows] say hello they [moo] to you,
[Moo] to you, [moo] to you.
When [cows] say hello they [moo] to you.
That's what they do.

Meow.

After You Read

Youngsters reenact part of the story with this follow-up activity. Invite two volunteers to play the parts of George and his mother. (If desired, invite youngsters to don simple costumes, such as a dog ear headband to resemble George and a red scarf to resemble his mother.) Place nearby a copy of the animal cards on page 124. Instruct George to select a card. Then prompt his mom to say, "Bark, George!" Encourage George to make the sound of the animal on his card. Have the remaining students identify the animal that makes that sound. Then select new volunteers for another round!

There's an Alligator Under My Bed

Written and illustrated by Mercer Mayer
When a little boy's parents can't see the alligator lurking under his bed, he decides to take matters into his own hands. See how this young hero soothes students' nighttime fears as he successfully lures the pesky alligator away from his room.

ideas contributed by Roxanne LaBell Dearman
Charlotte, NC

Before You Read

In advance, hide an alligator cutout under a desk or table. During circle time, call students' attention to the creature and ask them to identify what it might be, leading them to conclude that it's an alligator. Then ask them what they would do if it were a real alligator. After each child has had an opportunity to share his thoughts, invite little ones to listen to the story to find out what one little boy did when he found an alligator under his bed.

After You Read

This story innovation prompts each youngster to write about an animal lurking under his bed. To begin, have each student draw an animal of his choice on a paper programmed as shown. Then help him glue one edge of a felt square (the bed's blanket) to the paper to create a flap. To complete the page, write the name of his animal in the blank. If desired, gather the pages into a class book titled "There's an Animal Under My Bed!"

There used to be a ___lion___ under my bed. When it was time to go to sleep, I had to be very careful!

117

Storytime

I Know an Old Lady Who Swallowed a Pie

Written by Alison Jackson
Illustrated by Judith Byron Schachner
This little old lady looks sweet and harmless, but neither turkey nor cake is safe from her ravenous feeding frenzy! Youngsters are sure to chime in as you read aloud this delightful Thanksgiving Day tale.

ideas contributed by Roxanne LaBell Dearman
Charlotte, NC

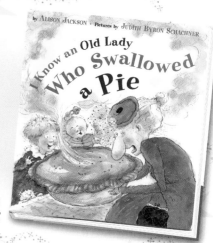

Before You Read

Have little ones name foods a family might eat during a Thanksgiving Day meal. Encourage each youngster to draw his favorite holiday food on a paper plate. Label the plate with the food's name. If desired, arrange the completed plates on a table to resemble a feast. As students settle in for this read-aloud, call attention to the old lady on the front cover of the book. Challenge youngsters to see if this little old lady eats any of their Thanksgiving favorites!

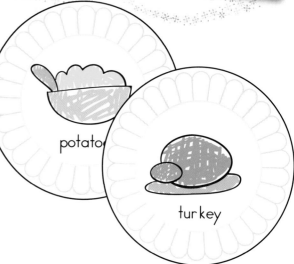

potato

turkey

After You Read

Actively engage students with this retelling activity. To prepare, decorate a small tissue box to resemble an old lady. Then color and cut out a copy of the story cards on page 125. Help youngsters use the cards and the book's illustrations to determine the story sequence. Then lead a group retelling of the story, asking individual volunteers to "feed" the old lady the corresponding card as the food is introduced. Culminate the ending of the story by hoisting the lady into the air like a float and having youngsters parade around the room!

The Jacket I Wear in the Snow

Written by Shirley Neitzel
Illustrated by Nancy Winslow Parker
From her green jacket to her wrinkled socks, this young child is bundled up against the harsh winter weather. It's too bad all those itchy, bunchy layers are so uncomfortable! This rebus story filled with repetitive text is sure to captivate your preschoolers.

ideas contributed by Suzanne Moore
Tucson, AZ

Before You Read

With this prereading activity, youngsters are sure to conclude that playing in the snow requires warm clothing! Sit with students in a circle and encourage them to suggest several different kinds of winter apparel. For each item mentioned, lead little ones in an enthusiastic verse of the song below, substituting the underlined words with the item's name. After several rounds, explain that the storytime selection for the day is about a youngster who piles on many of these familiar items to play outside in the snow.

(sung to the tune of "Mary Wore Her Red Dress")

I would wear a [jacket], a [jacket], a [jacket].
I would wear a [jacket] to play in the snow.

After You Read

Youngsters contribute to a class rebus book with this follow-up activity. To prepare, cut out several copies of the clothing cards on page 124. Program a sheet of construction paper, as shown, for each student. To begin, invite each youngster to select a card. Have him color the card and glue it to the prepared paper to complete the sentence. Next, encourage him to draw himself wearing the item in a snowy scene. Bind the completed pages in a book and place it in your reading corner.

Storytime

Hattie and the Fox

Written by Mem Fox
Illustrated by Patricia Mullins

When a nose pokes through some nearby bushes, Hattie the hen alerts her uninterested farm friends. As the hidden animal slowly reveals itself, Hattie becomes increasingly alarmed, but her friends continue to disregard the situation—until Hattie declares that the animal is a fox!

Before You Read

Show youngsters only the front cover of the book and explain that in the story, Hattie, a hen, sees a nose poking out from some bushes. Ask youngsters to predict what kind of creature the nose might be attached to. Write down the students' suggestions. Then have youngsters settle in for this entertaining read-aloud, encouraging them to keep their suggestions in mind to see whether anyone guessed the correct animal.

Maybe it's a dog!

"Wow!" said the goose.

"I'm scared!" said the pig.

"Hello!" said the sheep.

"Neigh!" said the horse.

"Uh-oh!" said the cow.

After You Read

The animals in the story repeat the same words whenever Hattie mentions the creature lurking in the bushes. Invite students to suggest different words each animal might say. Write the new quotations on a sheet of chart paper. Then reread the story, inserting the student-generated words whenever appropriate. These animals certainly have a lot to say!

Silly Sally

Written and illustrated by Audrey Wood
When Silly Sally goes to town, she walks backward and upside down! On the way she meets a bunch of dancing, singing, and sleeping characters who join in the fun. Your little ones are sure to adore this giggle-inducing rhyming extravaganza!

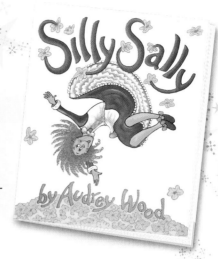

Before You Read

Play an upbeat recording of music and have youngsters walk around the room. Stop the music and ask them to suggest and then demonstrate silly ways they could walk, such as walking sideways or walking while flapping their arms. Play the music again and encourage youngsters to walk around the room in a silly way. Then gather students in your storytime area. Explain that the book you're about to read is about a character named Silly Sally—and she walks backward and upside down! No doubt little ones will be eager to see Silly Sally in action.

After You Read

Your little ones can be silly just like Sally! Take a photograph of each youngster posing with her arms in the air and her palms flat. Laminate the photographs and attach them to jumbo craft sticks as shown. To begin, have youngsters build a town out of blocks. Then invite youngsters to take turns walking their puppets to town while they repeat the first sentence in the story, altering it to add their own names. Silly Janna went to town, walking backwards, upside down!

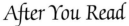

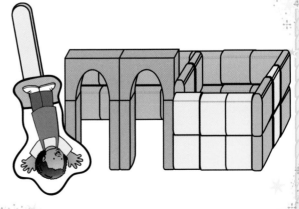

Storytime

Growing Vegetable Soup

Written and illustrated by Lois Ehlert
A child and father lead youngsters through the steps of making vegetable soup from planting all the way to the cooking pot! To enhance the story, Lois Ehlert has included labels with her bright attention-grabbing illustrations.

ideas contributed by Ada Goren
Winston-Salem, NC

Growing Vegetable Soup
Written and illustrated by Lois Ehlert

I like corn in my soup!

Before You Read

Draw a large pot on a sheet of chart paper. Encourage little ones to name the ingredients they would put in the pot to make vegetable soup. Write or draw their responses on the paper. As students settle in for this colorful read-aloud, challenge them to see whether any of the ingredients in the story match the ingredients listed on the chart paper.

After You Read

Place real or plastic vegetables next to a large soup pot. Provide access to a ladle. Invite a youngster to select a vegetable from the collection and identify it. Then encourage the volunteer to drop the ingredient in the pot and pretend to stir the soup as you lead youngsters in chanting the rhyme shown, substituting the appropriate veggie name where indicated. Continue in the same way with the remaining vegetables.

Put the [corn] in our soup pot.
Let it simmer till it's hot.
[Corn] is oh so good for you;
Stir until the soup is through.

122

Old Black Fly

Written by Jim Aylesworth
Illustrated by Stephen Gammell
*An old black fly leaves a trail of disaster
as he whizzes through the house and the
letters of the alphabet!*

*ideas contributed by Ada Goren
Winston-Salem, NC*

Before You Read

Prepare your own version of an annoying fly by gluing a fly
cutout (patterns on page 126) to a ruler or wooden dowel rod.
As students sing the alphabet song, "fly" the pesky critter around
the room, making buzzing sounds and tapping little ones on their
shoulders. Then have youngsters tell how the fly bothered them
during the song. Finally, invite youngsters to settle in for a read-
aloud that involves the alphabet and another pesky fly.

After You Read

The splatter-paint illustrations in this book
are sure to inspire your little artists! In advance,
make a fly cutout (patterns on page 126) for
each child. Also, die-cut a letter for each child
that matches the first letter in her name. To
begin, have a youngster dip a paintbrush into
tempera paint and then flick the brush over a
sheet of construction paper to create a splattered
effect. Have her repeat the process with several
colors of paint and then drag the paintbrush over
the paper to make streaks reminiscent of those
in the book's illustrations. Finally, have her color
her fly and then glue it to her paper along with
her letter.

Animal Cards
Use with "Before You Read" and "After You Read" on page 116.

TEC41028

TEC41028

TEC41028

TEC41028

Winter Clothing Cards
Use with "After You Read" on page 119.

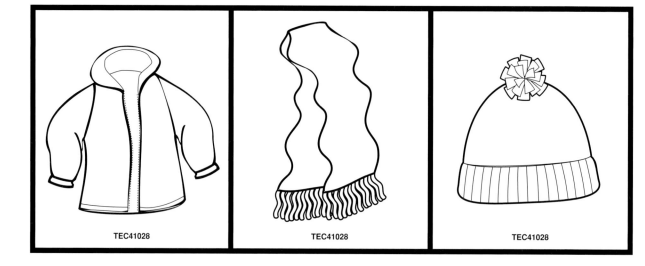

TEC41028

TEC41028

TEC41028

TEC41027

TEC41027

TEC41027

TEC41027

TEC41027

TEC41027

TEC41027

TEC41027

TEC41027

Fly Patterns
Use with "Before You Read" and "After You Read" on page 123.

SONGS & SUCH

SONGS & SUCH

Finding Friends

When youngsters go into their preschool, they find oodles of friends! Display a student's name card and help youngsters identify the name and the corresponding child. Then lead children in singing the song below, inserting the child's name when indicated. Youngsters are sure to enjoy several rounds of this getting-acquainted song and game.

(sung to the tune of
"The Bear Went Over the Mountain")

We went into the preschool. We went into the preschool.
We went into the preschool to see who we could see.
We found a friend named [Jack]. We found a friend named [Jack].
When we went into the preschool, we found a friend named [Jack].

Cindy Quigley
Corning Christian Academy
Corning, NY

Sneaky Mr. Worm

Youngsters practice number skills with an action chant about a sneaky little worm! Lead students in performing the chant five times, decreasing the number in the first line by one each time.

[Five] shiny apples hanging from a tree

Hold up five fingers (apples).

Teased Mr. Worm, "No, you won't get me!"

Move hand from side to side.

Along comes Mr. Worm as sneaky as can be.

Wiggle pointer finger on other hand.

CRUNCH!

Wrap pointer finger around an apple.

He eats one apple—munch, munch, munch!

Fold down one finger.

Jean Prickett
Shining Star Preschool
Mildford, MA

Quiet, Little Children

Here's a song that's just perfect for helping little ones leave the classroom in a quiet line. Simply lead students in singing the song before guiding your line of youngsters out the door.

(sung to the tune of "Hush, Little Baby")

Quiet, little children, don't say a word.
We're leaving our room, and we shouldn't be heard.
With hands at our sides, we do not talk.
Stay in our line as we start to walk.

Yvonne Kelting
Hobe Sound Child Care Center
Hobe Sound, FL

Wiggles!

When youngsters are full of wiggles, lead them in this delightful song. They're sure to be wiggle free in no time!

(sung to the tune of "Shoo Fly")

Wiggle your happy toes.
Wiggle your happy nose.
Wiggle your fingers too.
Then wiggle yourself like wiggle worms do.

Reach down and touch your knees.
Reach up and touch the trees.
Tap, tap your happy feet.
Then turn around and take a seat.

Suzanne Moore
Tucson, AZ

SONGS & SUCH

Autumn Is Here

Spotlight unique fall events with a cute little action poem!

Acorns drop—plop, plop, plop!

Colored leaves in the breeze.
Pumpkins bright, what a sight.

Autumn's here—give a cheer!

Drop to the floor; pat it with your hands.
Twirl like a leaf.
Hold arms out to resemble a round pumpkin.
Jump up and down in excitement.

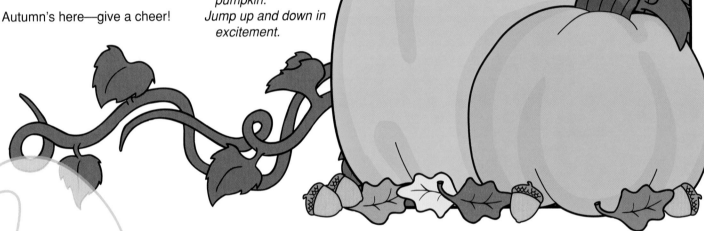

Happy Halloween!

This rollicking song is sure to be a fall festival favorite!

(sung to the tune of "Do Your Ears Hang Low?")

Do you love Halloween?
When you dress up to be seen,
You can be a furry cat
Or a silly flying bat.
You can walk down your street,
Knock on doors, say "trick-or-treat."
Do you love Halloween?

Lauri Nolan
Tots-N-Us Nursery and Day Care
Hopewell Junction, NY

It's Thanksgiving Day!

No doubt youngsters will be thankful for this appetizing Thanksgiving Day song!

(sung to the tune of "Over the River and Through the Wood")

Thanksgiving Day has arrived again.
It's fun to celebrate.
The turkey is baking; the pies are too.
Oh, we can hardly wait!
The table is ready. It looks so nice
And pretty for this day.
Our guests should be here very soon.
Yes, they are on their way!

Deborah Garmon
Groton, CT

Fire Truck Tune

Incorporate this jaunty little song into your fire safety study.

(sung to the tune of "The Wheels on the Bus")

The wheels on the fire truck go around,	*Roll hands over each other.*
Go around, go around.	
The wheels on the fire truck go around.	
They're here to help.	*Shake pointer finger.*

Continue with the following:

The lights on the fire truck go blink, blink.	*Open and shut hands.*
The siren on the fire truck goes woo, woo.	*Move finger in a circular motion.*
The firefighters on board bump along.	*Bump up and down.*
The firefighters put the fire out.	*Pretend to spray fire hose.*

Debbie Lamphere
Vaughan-Steffensrud School
Chisholm, MN

SONGS & SUCH

A Sitting Song

This giggle-inducing song will encourage little ones to take a seat in a timely fashion!

(sung to the tune of "Short'nin' Bread")

Everybody have a seat, have a seat, have a seat.
Everybody have a seat on the floor.
Everybody have a seat, have a seat, have a seat.
Everybody have a seat on the floor.
Not on the ceiling, not on the door!
Everybody have a seat on the floor.

Deb Menze
Debby's Giggles and Wiggles Childcare
Mora, MN

Thank you!

Thanks for Today

At the end of the day, have students join in this rhyme to thank each other and you for a fabulous day at preschool!

Thanks for today and our time to play.
Thanks for our friends and the weather.
Thanks for the books and the happy looks.
We're happy to have been here together.

Barby Brilliant
El Dorado Hills, CA

Travelin' Turkey

Your little ones will be all smiles for this splendidly silly Thanksgiving song! Give each youngster a turkey cutout. Then lead students in singing the song as they place the turkey on each body part described.

(sung to the tune of "If You're Happy and You Know It")

There's a turkey on my [nose], on my [nose].
There's a turkey on my [nose], on my [nose].
Oh, I wonder if he'll stay or
If he'll choose to go away.
There's a turkey on my [nose], on my [nose].

Continue with the following: head, foot, ear, hand, knee, leg, back

Denise Dobbins
Elyria YMCA Preschool
Elyria, OH

Shoe-Tie Time

Help little ones wait patiently to have their shoes tied by leading them in singing this little ditty!

(sung to the tune of "Shoo Fly")

Shoe tie, don't bother me.
Shoe tie, don't bother me.
Shoe tie, don't bother me.
For I can wait so patiently.

Barbara Borich
Westport Road Baptist Child Care Center
Louisville, KY

SONGS & SUCH

What to Wear?

What kinds of clothing items are appropriate for winter wear? This song identifies several cozy options! Lead students in singing the song. Then have them repeat the song three times, substituting the suggested items shown and having them stomp their feet, pat their heads, and pretend to zip their coats as appropriate.

*(sung to the tune of
"She'll Be Comin' Round the Mountain")*

I'll be wearing [two warm mittens] when it snows. *(clap, clap)*
I'll be wearing [two warm mittens] when it snows. *(clap, clap)*
I'll be wearing [two warm mittens].
I'll be wearing [two warm mittens].
I'll be wearing [two warm mittens] when it snows. *(clap, clap)*

Additional verses: *two warm boots (stomp), one warm hat (pat), one warm jacket (zip)*

LeeAnn Collins
Sunshine House Preschool
Lansing, MI

Twinkling Evergreen

Colorfully decorated trees are an important part of a holiday celebration! Gather youngsters around your classroom holiday tree and then lead them in an enthusiastic rendition of the song below!

(sung to the tune of "Twinkle, Twinkle, Little Star")

Twinkle, twinkle, evergreen,
Prettiest we've ever seen.
Ornaments and presents too,
Some for me and some for you.
Twinkle, twinkle, evergreen,
Prettiest we've ever seen!

Stacy Washburn
McCluer North Child Development Center
Florissant, MO

Kwanzaa Candle Tune

This simple Kwanzaa tune spotlights the colors of the candles in a kinara! Make a simple kinara cutout as shown. Then point to the candles as you lead little ones in singing the song.

(sung to the tune of "Ten Little Indians")

One little, two little, three red candles,
One little, two little, three green candles,
One black candle sitting in the middle,
All lit up for Kwanzaa!

Ada Goren
Winston-Salem, NC

Falling Snow

When it's too cold and wet for outdoor play, help youngsters get rid of the wiggles with this cute song!

(sung to the tune of "When the Saints Go Marching In")

Oh, when the snow
Begins to fall,
I'll build a snowman round and tall.
Oh, how I love the cold, cold weather
When the snow begins to fall.

Move fingers to resemble falling snow.
Continue moving fingers.
Move hands upward from floor.
Hug self.
Move fingers to resemble falling snow.

And then I'll lie
Down in the snow
And move my arms and legs just so.

Sit on the floor.
Lie on the floor.
Move arms and legs to make a snow angel.

Oh, how I love to make snow angels
When the snow begins to fall.

Continue moving arms and legs.
Continue moving arms and legs.

Suzanne Moore
Tucson, AZ

SONGS & SUCH

A Valentine Song

Here's a sweet little Valentine's Day song students are sure to love!

(sung to the tune of "I'm a Little Teapot")

Here's a little card made just for you!
It's made with paper, glitter, and glue.
Inside, there's a message: "Please Be Mine!"
What a perfect valentine!

adapted from an idea by Sandra Rosen
Fascination Station
Latrobe, PA

Splish, Splash, Splat!

To keep students from tracking mud into the school, have youngsters repeat this catchy little chant.

Splish, splash, splat!
Playing outside—I like that!
Splish, splash, splat!
Wipe your feet on the mat!

Janet Boyce
King's Kids
Hutchinson, MN

Five Little Shamrocks

You'll hear oodles of giggles when you use youngster's names in this adorable St. Patrick's Day chant! In advance, make five shamrock cutouts and attach them to a wall at a child's eye level. Lead students in reciting the chant, replacing the names in the rhyme with names of youngsters in your classroom. As each child's name is called, have him remove a shamrock from the wall. Finally, remove the last shamrock yourself. What fun!

Five little shamrocks growing near my door,
[David] picked a shamrock, and now there are four.
Four little shamrocks under a tree,
[Mia] picked a shamrock, and now there are three.
Three little shamrocks in the morning dew,
[Connor] picked a shamrock, and now there are two.
Two little shamrocks growing in the sun,
[Kira] picked a shamrock, and now there is one.
One little shamrock standing all alone,
I picked that shamrock and took it home!

Amy LaPiccirella
Northeast Park Preschool
St. Petersburg, FL

Scrub, Scrub, Scrub!

Have little ones recite this chant as they wash their hands!

Front and back and in between,
Wash your hands till they're superclean.
Scrub and scrub those germs away,
And you will have a healthy day!

Gwen Marra
Learning Ship Preschool
Sioux Center, IA

SONGS & SUCH

Spring Is Here!

This snazzy little song will have youngsters eagerly looking for signs of spring!

(sung to the tune of "Up on the Housetop")

Up in the treetops, I see leaves.
They are forming on the trees.
There's lots of rain and it's getting warm.
Beautiful blossoms begin to form.
Yay! Yay! Yay!
Let's shout hooray!
Yay! Yay! Yay!
Spring's here today!
Winter is over—now it's clear.
We are excited that spring is here!

Susan Flener
Children's Circle Second Presbyterian Church
Indianapolis, IN

What's the Weather?

Add zip to your daily weather discussion with this rhyme! Choose a youngster to be the weatherperson; then lead students in the chant shown, changing the title from *Mr.* to *Ms.* if needed. When youngsters are finished with the chant, encourage the weatherperson to share what he knows about the current weather.

Hey, Mr. Weatherperson, what do you see?
Take a look out the window and then tell me.
Hey, Mr. Weatherperson, what do you know?
Is there sun or rain or wind or snow?
Hey, Mr. Weatherperson, what do you say?
Just what kind of weather are we having today?

Leslie Tisdale
Lakewood Presbyterian Church Nursery School
Lakewood, OH

Who's the Lucky One?

All your little ones are lucky when they sing this bouncy tune! Make a tagboard rainbow cutout similar to the one shown. Hold the rainbow over a youngsters' head and lead the students in singing the song, encouraging them to sing the chosen youngster's name in the first, second, and fourth lines. Continue in the same way, choosing different children for subsequent verses.

(sung to the tune of "The Farmer in the Dell")

A rainbow over [Sam].
A rainbow over [Sam].
Hi-ho, the lucky one,
A rainbow over [Sam].

Kelly Ash
Waukesha Head Start
Waukesha, WI

Springtime!

Spring is here! That means it's time to sing this toe-tapping tune!

(sung to the tune of "Do Your Ears Hang Low?")

Oh, you know it's spring
When the robins start to sing.
Then the flowers grow,
And you see the melting snow.
Know what else I've seen?
Everything is turning green!
Yes, we know it's spring!

Deborah Garmon
Groton, CT

SONGS & SUCH

Beautiful Butterfly

No doubt your little ones will giggle with glee when they sing this silly little ditty! If desired, have youngsters make a simple butterfly finger puppet. Then encourage them to move their puppets as they sing the song.

(sung to the tune of "O Christmas Tree")

Oh butterfly, oh butterfly,
Your wings are all aflutter.
Oh butterfly, oh butterfly,
Which part of you is butter?
There is no butter, I can see,
On this small critter wild and free.
Oh butterfly, oh butterfly,
Your wings are all aflutter.

Vicki Padgett
Arlington Baptist Church Preschool
Charlotte, NC

BUTTER

Plant Parts

This action song is sure to help little ones recognize the parts of a flower! As you lead youngsters in singing the song, encourage them to move their bodies to resemble the different flower parts mentioned.

(sung to the tune of "Head, Shoulders, Knees, and Toes")

Flowers, leaves, stems, and roots (stems and roots).
Flowers, leaves, stems, and roots (stems and roots).
Please don't sneeze; there's pollen in the breeze!
Flowers, leaves, stems, and roots (stems and roots).

Jodi G. Zeis
Dinwiddie County Schools
Dinwiddie, VA

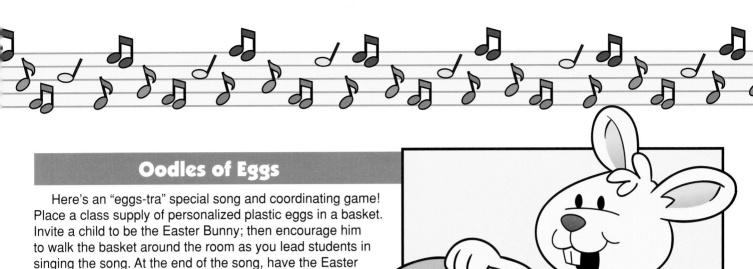

Oodles of Eggs

Here's an "eggs-tra" special song and coordinating game! Place a class supply of personalized plastic eggs in a basket. Invite a child to be the Easter Bunny; then encourage him to walk the basket around the room as you lead students in singing the song. At the end of the song, have the Easter Bunny remove an egg from the basket. Help him read the name on the egg and then give it to the appropriate youngster. Play several rounds of this fun game!

(sung to the tune of "My Bonnie Lies Over the Ocean")

The bunny is hopping to my house.
How heavy his basket must be.
He has lots of eggs and I'm hoping
An Easter egg's in there for me!
Please have, please have
An Easter egg in there for me, for me!
Please have, please have
An Easter egg in there for me!

Karen Amatrudo
The Learning Village
Madison, CT

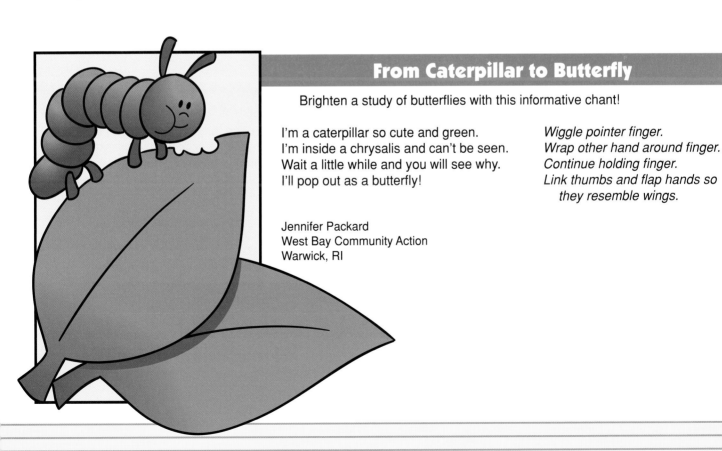

From Caterpillar to Butterfly

Brighten a study of butterflies with this informative chant!

I'm a caterpillar so cute and green.
I'm inside a chrysalis and can't be seen.
Wait a little while and you will see why.
I'll pop out as a butterfly!

Wiggle pointer finger.
Wrap other hand around finger.
Continue holding finger.
*Link thumbs and flap hands so
 they resemble wings.*

Jennifer Packard
West Bay Community Action
Warwick, RI

SONGS & SUCH

Living in the USA

This song is just perfect for a Fourth of July celebration and it's easy enough for even your youngest students to sing! If desired, have youngsters shake tambourines and jingle-bell bracelets to add percussion to the sing-along.

(sung to the tune of "London Bridge")

We live in the USA, USA, USA.
We live in the USA!
Hooray, freedom!

Gail Marsh
Pacific, MO

Buzzing Bumblebee!

The buzzing little bee featured in this song sure is happy to fly around your preschoolers! Have each child make a simple bumblebee stick puppet. Then lead students in singing the song as they move their bees to correspond to the lyrics.

(sung to the tune of "Jingle Bells")

Bumblebee, bumblebee, buzzing round my nose.
Bumblebee, bumblebee, buzzing round my toes,
Round my legs, round my arms, even my elbows!
Bumblebee, bumblebee—it buzzes as it goes!

Sandy Barker
Early Childhood Family Education
Cottage Grove, MN

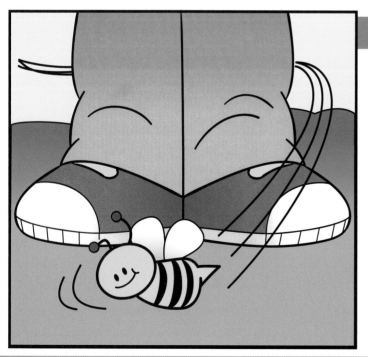

BOOK UNITS

Wemberly Worried

Written and Illustrated by Kevin Henkes

Wemberly worries about everything, from her stuffed bunny toy to the disturbing crack in the living room wall. And when it's time for school to begin, Wemberly has a whole new set of worries. This popular storytime selection helps youngsters see that there's often nothing to worry about at all!

ideas contributed by Ada Goren, Winston-Salem, NC

What Does It Mean?
Identifying emotions

Help students understand what the word *worried* means with this prereading activity. Display in your classroom a happy face, a sad face, and a worried face. Explain these three emotions, emphasizing that someone who is worried feels upset about something that he thinks might happen. Next, read aloud one of the suggested sentences below. Encourage a child to decide how he would feel in that situation and then to point to the corresponding face. Continue in the same way for each suggestion. Then have little ones settle in for a read-aloud about Wemberly, a chronically worried little mouse.

Suggested sentences:
You spilled your juice, and you wonder whether your mom will be mad. *(worried)*
You got a new toy! *(happy)*
Your brother ripped your favorite book. *(sad)*
You hear a strange noise at night, and you wonder what it could be. *(worried)*

Petal Project
Developing home-school connections

When Wemberly is worried, she rubs the ears of her beloved bunny toy, Petal. With this activity, youngsters make their very own Petal to share with their families! Have each child glue a copy of one of the book notes on page 146 to the back of a small yellow disposable plate. Help him glue a pink circle cutout to the front of the plate as shown. Then use a permanent marker to draw Petal's features. Next, have each child color two tagboard ear cutouts (patterns on page 147) as shown. For soft, touchable ears, instruct him to glue a matching piece of felt to each one. Finally, direct him to glue the ears to the plate. What a cute way to let families know about this storytime selection!

Go Away, Worries!

Writing

Wemberly certainly has a lot of worries! It's too bad she doesn't have a worry box like the one described in this simple idea. Decorate a box and detachable lid, and label it as shown. To begin, gather youngsters around and explain that sometimes you get worried just as Wemberly does. Tell students one of your worries as you write it down on a strip of paper. Next, fold the paper, place it in the box, and say, "Go away, worries!" Throughout the next few days, encourage youngsters to share their worries with you and then place their dictated worries in the box. Go away, worries!

Go Away, Worries!

What if Mom isn't here soon?

Shake, Shake, Shake!

Participating in an interactive read-aloud

The word *worried* is used repeatedly throughout the story. Have students emphasize the word even more with this interactive rereading. Give each child a "worry shaker" (a bean shaker or other simple instrument). Then read aloud the story, emphasizing the word *worried* each time it's read and having youngsters back up the word with a quick shake of their instruments. Your youngsters won't feel a bit of worry during the marvelous musical rereading!

Comparing Classrooms

Making comparisons

Wemberly's classroom has a lot of intriguing items to play with. No doubt some of those items are similar to ones in your classroom! Revisit with students the pages in the book that show Wemberly's classroom. Encourage youngsters to name items they see as you write their words on a sheet of chart paper. Help students identify any items that are found both in Wemberly's classroom and their own classroom. Then invite them to name items found in their classroom that are not seen in the classroom in the book. We have a sand table in our room!

balls
puppet stage
slide
toy dinosaur
musical instruments
toy car
blocks

145

This is Petal
from the story
Wemberly Worried
by Kevin Henkes.

Ask me to show you
what Wemberly does
to Petal's ears when
she is worried.

TEC41026

This is Petal
from the story
Wemberly Worried
by Kevin Henkes.

Ask me to show you
what Wemberly does
to Petal's ears when
she is worried.

TEC41026

This is Petal
from the story
Wemberly Worried
by Kevin Henkes.

Ask me to show you
what Wemberly does
to Petal's ears when
she is worried.

TEC41026

This is Petal
from the story
Wemberly Worried
by Kevin Henkes.

Ask me to show you
what Wemberly does
to Petal's ears when
she is worried.

TEC41026

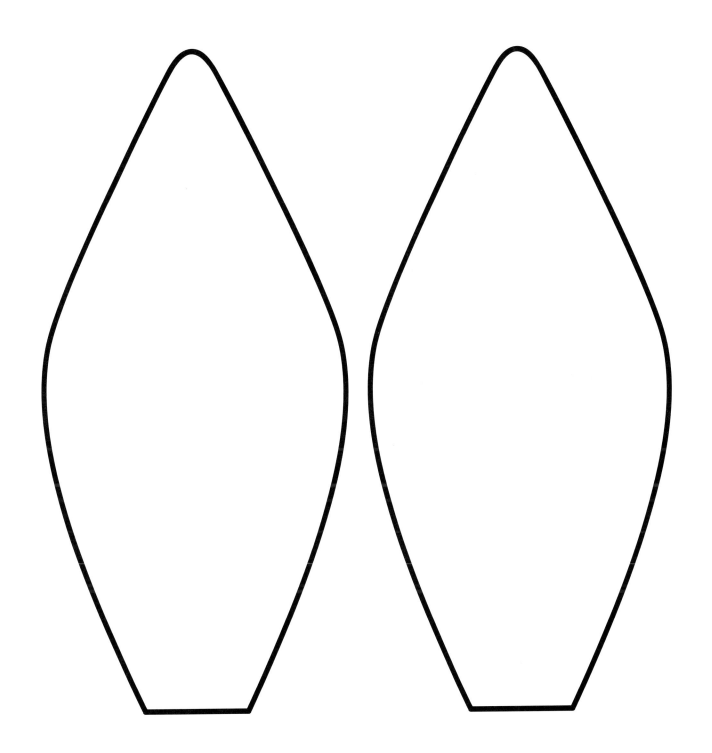

Owl Moon

Written by Jane Yolen
Illustrated by John Schoenherr

A father and daughter walk through the snowy woods. They're going owling—searching for the great horned owl. Throughout their walk, the father calls "Whoo-whoo-whoo!" Suddenly a magnificent owl appears on a branch before them. This gentle, mesmerizing tale is an exquisite choice for storytime.

Walking in the Woods
Building prior knowledge

Take youngsters on an imaginary walk through the woods with this prereading activity. To begin, explain to youngsters that they are going to pretend to go for a walk in the woods. Tell them that it's nighttime and there is snow on the ground, so they will have to dress warmly. Have youngsters pantomime putting on boots, a coat, a scarf, a hat, and mittens. Once they are bundled up, lead them around the room, encouraging them to be quiet as they walk. Stop students throughout the walk and ask them what animals they might see in the woods. When students are back in your large-group area, encourage them to remove all of their pretend outerwear. Then have students settle in for a reading of *Owl Moon*, a story about a very special nighttime walk.

Owl Art
Using a variety of art media

This artsy scene is reminiscent of the book's illustrations. Have each student rub blue chalk and white chalk over a 12" x 18" sheet of black construction paper. Invite him to use the chalk to add snow to the bottom of the page; then have him glue a white moon cutout near the top of the page. Encourage him to brush a crumpled piece of paper towel over the paper to smear the chalk. As a child holds his paper over a tray, spoon thinned black tempera paint on the paper, allowing it to run to make a tree trunk. Spoon more paint along the trunk, having the child tilt and move the paper as desired to make branches. When the paint is dry, have each student add a small owl cutout to his scene (pattern on page 150, reduced in size). If desired, display these lovely projects on a board titled "Under an Owl Moon."

Let's Go Owling!
Investigating living things

When little ones go owling in the classroom, they find oodles of owl information! Cut out five brown construction paper copies of the owl pattern on page 150. Write a different provided fact on each owl. Then display the owls in different locations around your room. To begin, dim the lights to simulate nighttime. Give a youngster a flashlight and invite her to use it to find an owl in the room. (Encourage classmates to be very quiet during this process so they don't scare the owls away.) When she locates an owl, read the fact aloud. Then repeat the process for each remaining owl.

Debbie Bartsch
Gloria Dei Preschool
Crestview Hills, KY

Owl Facts

Many owls eat small animals like mice and rats.
Owls have sharp claws called *talons*.
Many owls go out at nighttime.
An owl is a type of bird.
An owl's call sounds like "Whoo, whoo, whoo!"

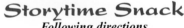

Many owls go out at nighttime.

Storytime Snack
Following directions

Spotlight this classic story with a tasty and simple snack! Have each child place a pretzel on a napkin. Encourage her to place yellow M&M's Minis candies in different sections of the pretzel to make owl eyes. Then encourage her to place a triangular cheese slice below the pretzel to resemble a beak. Invite students to make three or four of these owls and then nibble on their snack.

Debbie Bartsch

"Whoooo" Else Is There?
Developing observation skills

Is the owl the only creature out in the forest? No, but youngsters will have to use keen observation skills to find other hidden animals! To begin, give each child a crayon and a copy of page 151. Encourage students to identify each animal on the paper. Next, take children on an animal search. Flip through the book, encouraging youngsters to study each page carefully to find the animals. As youngsters see each animal, have them color its twin on the paper. They might even find a few extra critters that are very carefully concealed!

Owl Pattern

Use with "Owl Art" on page 148 and "Let's Go Owling!" on page 149.

TEC41028

Note to the teacher: Use with "'Whoooo' Else Is There?" on page 149.

Green Eggs and Ham

Written and Illustrated by Dr. Seuss

Do you like green eggs and ham? When Sam poses this question, it triggers a series of outlandish events designed to tempt the main character to try this colorful cuisine. Little ones are sure to learn a lesson from this whimsical rhyming tale: You won't know whether you like it until you try it!

ideas contributed by Elizabeth Cook, St. Louis, MO

Do You Like It?
Activating prior knowledge

Get youngsters excited about the story with this prereading activity! Have each child draw a happy face on one side of a construction paper circle and a sad face on the remaining side. Name a common food and ask each child to display the happy face if he likes the food and the sad face if he does not. Continue in this manner with several different foods, ending the activity by saying, "Green eggs and ham." After youngsters express their opinions about this uncommon food, explain that the character in the book you're about to read believes that he does not like green eggs and ham. Finally, have little ones settle in for this classic story.

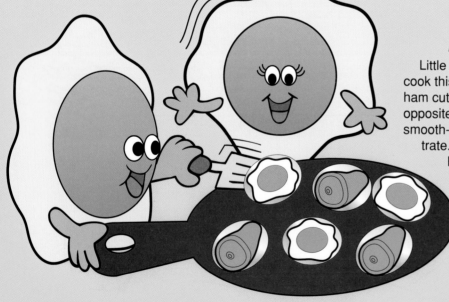

Flipping Food
Developing hand-eye coordination

Little ones can pretend to be Sam when they cook this imaginary food! Make pairs of egg and ham cutouts. Attach each pair of egg cutouts to opposite sides of a juice-can lid. (Be sure to use the smooth-edged lids used for frozen juice concentrate.) Repeat the process with the ham cutouts. Place a poster board frying pan on the floor; then place the lids on the frying pan. Provide access to a spatula and a paper plate. Encourage a child to use the spatula to flip the eggs and ham so they will cook evenly. When she determines that the eggs and ham are ready, she uses the spatula to transfer them to the plate.

152

Ham and Eggs to Go!
Developing home-school connections

This take-home project is a sure way to get little ones talking about the story with their families! For each child, pour a small amount of thinned light green paint on a colored paper plate. Have her tilt the plate back and forth to make an egg white. After the paint has dried, invite each child to glue green pom-pom yolks and a green paper ham cutout to her plate. Encourage her to take her plate home and retell the story to a family member.

Train? Boat? Plane?
Making connections between spoken and written words

Sam names a variety of places in which to try green eggs and ham. Use this idea to have youngsters share where they would like to eat a desired food. Have each child cut out a picture of a favorite food from a grocery store circular. After she glues the picture to the center of a paper plate, ask her to name a fun place where she would like to eat this tasty food. Then write her response on her plate in the format shown. Display the completed projects with the title "Would You Eat Them Here or There?"

I would eat hot dogs in a tree.

Where's the Chicken?
Using position words

Those green eggs must have come from a green chicken! In advance, make an oversize brown paper nest cutout and place it in a traffic-free area. Embellish the nest with green craft feathers. Next, make a green chicken cutout and post the chicken in your room. To begin, explain that the green chicken wants to lay more green eggs but can't find her nest. Have youngsters scan the room for the chicken. When a child finds the chicken, prompt her to explain where it's located using position words. For example, she might say, "The chicken is below the bulletin board." Then have her place the chicken on the nest. Repeat the activity several times throughout your book study. If desired, add green egg cutouts to the nest, increasing their number each day to keep interest high.

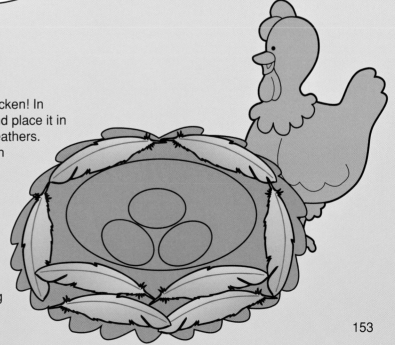

Would You? Could You?
Matching rhyming pictures

In advance, program two sentence strips as shown and place them in a pocket chart. Also color and cut out a copy of the picture cards on page 155 and place the cards below the strips. Revisit several rhyming words in the text. Then place a critter picture card at the end of the first sentence strip and lead youngsters in reading the sentence aloud. Invite a youngster to find the rhyming picture and place it at the end of the second sentence strip. After helping students read aloud both sentences, remove the cards and repeat the activity with the remaining rhyming pairs.

The Green Café
Dramatic play

Fold and label a large sheet of poster board as shown to resemble an oversize menu. Invite each child to think of a unique green food item, such as green spaghetti and meatballs, green pizza, or a green grilled cheese sandwich. Then encourage him to draw the food, cut it out, and attach it to the menu. Label each child's picture. Place the completed menu at your dramatic play center along with a variety of restaurant-themed items. When students visit the center, they take on the roles of customers, cooks, and servers at the Green Café!

A Second Helping
Revisiting the story

Get youngsters involved in a second reading of the story! Gather a small group of youngsters and give each child a green bingo dauber and a 12" x 18" sheet of white construction paper. Read aloud the story. Each time a child hears the phrase *green eggs and ham,* prompt him to stamp the dauber on his paper. After the story, have each child count the circles on his paper. When the paint is dry, invite him to draw an egg white around each green circle to make green eggs. There are 11 green eggs!

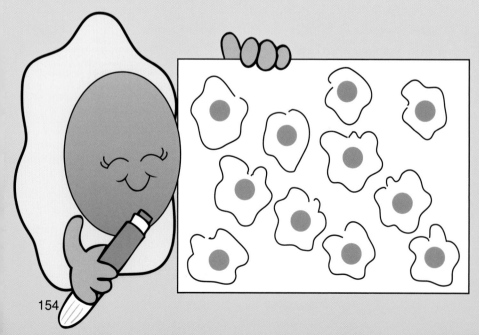

TEC41029

TEC41029

TEC41029

TEC41029

TEC41029

TEC41029

TEC41029

TEC41029

The Little Red Hen

In this classic tale, the Little Red Hen labors to make a loaf of bread. Although none of her animal friends are eager to help her during the process, they are more than happy to assist in eating the results! Use your favorite version of this traditional story for the following fun learning opportunities!

What's in the Bag?
Predicting

Get youngsters excited about the book with a mysterious bag full of props! Place in a paper grocery bag the following items: a loaf of bread, a red craft feather, a bag of flour, and a bowl and mixing spoon. Present the bag and explain that the items in the bag are clues to the story you're about to read. Have youngsters help you pull the items out one at a time, taking students' suggestions about the contents of the story after each object is removed. When the bag is empty, reveal the book and congratulate students on their well thought-out guesses. Then have little ones settle in for this classic tale.

Eileen Reese
Troy Nursery School
Qu'appelle, Saskatchewan, Canada

Little Red Hands
Expressing an opinion

Was it right for the Little Red Hen to eat all of the bread herself? No doubt your little ones will be eager to share their opinions using this handy chart. Have each child make a red handprint on a sheet of paper. When the paint is dry, help her use a marker to make an eye, a wing, feet, and a beak on her print as shown. Then encourage her to cut out the resulting hen. Have youngsters gather around a simple chart labeled as shown. Then invite each child to tape her hen to the chart to show whether she thinks the Little Red Hen did the right thing. Finally, discuss the completed chart.

Suzanne Moore
Tucson, AZ

Was it right for the Little Red Hen to eat all the bread herself?

Yes	No

Servin' Up Sequencing
Sequencing events in the story

Have each child color and cut out a copy of the cards on page 158; then encourage her to place them in order on a bread-loaf cutout. When the cards are ordered correctly, instruct her to glue the cards in place. Next, invite each youngster to drizzle glue on the top of the loaf and then sprinkle oatmeal over the glue to make a nice crunchy crust. What a fun way to serve up sequencing practice!

Suzanne Moore
Tucson, AZ

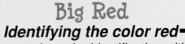

Big Red
Identifying the color red

Little ones practice color identification with the star of the story! Make a simple red hen cutout from bulletin board paper. Place the hen at a table along with a supply of glue and a container full of craft items and scraps, such as ribbon pieces, pom-poms, and tissue paper squares. Make sure that several of the craft items are red. A visiting child searches through the container and finds an item that is red; then she glues it to the hen. She continues in the same way, adding other red items to this big red hen.

April Hamrick
Mother's Day Out at Second Baptist Church
Conway, AR

Little Gray Mouse
Creating a story innovation

Color and cut out a tagboard copy of the mouse pattern on page 159; then transform the cutout into a stick puppet. Obtain a loaf of bread and butter. When youngsters are quite familiar with the story, bring out the puppet and tell students that they will help tell the story of the Little Gray Mouse. Give the puppet to a child. Then use the original story as a guide to narrate this new version. Prompt the child to move the puppet along with the actions, and have each remaining student add to the retelling by saying "Not I" and "I will" when appropriate. Finally, alter the ending to explain that the mouse is very polite and will share his bread; then have each youngster snack on a slice of bread with butter!

Jill Howard
First Foot Forward
Staten Island, NY

Suzanne Moore

157

Mix.

TEC41027

1

Plop.

TEC41027

2

Bake.

TEC41027

3

Yum!

TEC41027

4

TEC41027

Jack and the Beanstalk

In this classic tale, Jack is faced with the tough decision to either sell the family cow or trade her for some magic beans. His decision leads to some dangerous yet prosperous adventures! Read aloud your favorite version of this traditional tale and then guide youngsters through the following fun learning opportunities!

Fee, Fie, Foe, Fun!
Developing phonological awareness

Get ready for some giant-size giggles and grins! Label a sentence strip "Fee, Fie, Foe, Fum!" and then place the strip in a pocket chart. Make four identical letter cards for each of four different consonants. Place the card sets in matching piles nearby. Lead children in reciting the words on the sentence strip, encouraging them to stomp and use their best giant voices. Then have a child pick a set of cards and slide each one over the *F* in each word. Lead the group in reciting the new phrase in the same manner as before. Continue in the same way with each set of cards.

Janet Boyce
Cokato, MN

Go, Jack, Go!
Cooperating to play a game

Review the story with youngsters with a toe-tapping song and puppet props! Have each child color and cut out a copy of the patterns on page 162. Then have him tape each cutout to a craft stick to make a set of puppets. Lead students in singing the song below, encouraging them to hold up each puppet when appropriate.

(sung to the tune of "The Farmer in the Dell")

The beans began to grow.
They grew up from the ground.
When Jack climbed up the stalk,
What do you think he found?

Jack found [some gold].
Jack found [some gold].
Way high up in the sky,
Jack found [some gold].

Additional verses:
a hen, a harp

Janet Boyce

Castle in the Clouds
Creating a three-dimensional sculpture

Cut cardboard tubes into various sizes. Have each child paste or tape several tubes to a cardboard base to make a castle. Once the paste is dry, encourage youngsters to paint their castles and glue cotton batting clouds around the base. If desired, invite each student to dictate words to make a sign and then have her attach the sign to her project. Encourage little ones to use their castles to retell the story or to create a story of their own!

String Bean Snap
Developing fine-motor skills

A beanstalk that size is sure to grow a huge bunch of beans! Place a supply of fresh string beans at a table along with a wastebasket and a cooking pot. Explain that Jack's beanstalk has grown a bumper crop of beans! Then invite youngsters to visit the center. While there, a child snaps the ends off of the beans and discards them. Then he snaps each bean into sections and places the sections in the pot. When all the beans are prepared, cook them with some butter and seasonings and serve them up for a tasty garden treat!

Janet Boyce
Cokato, MN

Imagine That!
Making a connection between spoken and written words

After reading the story, make a beanstalk from construction paper and attach it to a wall. (Or plant pole beans with the children to grow a classroom beanstalk of your own!) Then encourage youngsters to imagine what they might find in the giant's castle if they were able to climb the beanstalk. Record children's dictations and post them near the beanstalk for all to see!

Brigitte Dade
Helping Hands Preschool
Medina, OH

161

TEC41030

TEC41030

TEC41030

Laying Golden Eggs

Note to the teacher: Have youngsters trace the dotted lines. Then instruct them to glue gold glitter onto the eggs.

163

To Market, to Market

Written by Anne Miranda
Illustrated by Janet Stevens

When a woman brings home a variety of animals from the store, she finds that they make chaos in her house. This zany tale begins like the traditional rhyme, but silly twists and a crowd of critters give it an amusingly frisky spin!

ideas contributed by Lucia Kemp Henry, Fallon, NV

Off to Market!
Promoting interest in a story

Set the stage for storytime and get children excited with this prereading activity! Prepare for a pretend shopping spree by arranging an inviting display of plush animals on a table or a shelf. To begin, give a child a paper grocery bag. As she views the merchandise on display, lead the remaining students in reciting the first two lines of the rhyme shown. Next, encourage her to put a critter in the bag as you lead the group in reciting the remaining two lines of the rhyme. After the child returns the critter to the display, have her give the bag to a classmate. Continue until everyone has had a chance to "shop" and then explain that the character in the story you are about to read also buys some unusual critters at the store. Then invite little ones to settle in as you read this comic tale.

[Child's name] is off to the market
For eggs, milk, and bacon.
Instead [she] buys a great big [animal name]!
What a silly choice [she's] makin'!

Which One's First?
Sequencing

Ready a copy of the critter cards on page 166 for flannelboard use. Place the cards and a paper lunch bag near the flannelboard. Help volunteers place the critter cards on the flannelboard in the order the animals appear in the story. (Refer to the book's illustrations as needed.) Encourage little ones to make corresponding animal sounds or movements each time a card is placed on the board. After all the cards have been sequenced, reread the story. As you read, invite volunteers to remove each card as the animal pictured appears in the story and place the card in the bag.

Critters à la Carte
Dictating information to complete a sentence

The peculiar grocery list of the shopper in this story is sure to inspire little ones to imagine what they would buy! To begin, have each child place a copy of the shopping cart pattern on page 167 on a piece of plastic canvas. Have her make a crayon rubbing of the canvas to give the cart texture. Then help her cut out the cart and glue it to a sheet of paper programmed as shown. Next, encourage her to draw an animal of her choice above the cart. Finally, write the child's response to the prompt.

I'd buy a purple elephant to take home.
Jordan

Todd

Good Grocer

Soup Lover's Delight!
Expressing oneself through arts and crafts

After a wild morning of shopping, the woman in the story makes soup for all the critters. Teach students to recognize some of her soup ingredients with this cute craft! Give each child a 9" x 12" sheet of construction paper folded in half. Have her unfold the paper and color one half brown. Instruct each child to color and cut out a copy of the soup ingredient patterns on page 168. After she is finished, have her glue some of the soup ingredients and a grocery bag handle and logo to her paper as shown. What a "soup-er" idea!

Better Buying Options
Generating rhyming words

Had the shopper in the story known her purchases would be so unruly, she might have decided to buy different items! Write the rhyme shown on chart paper. Place a copy of the critter cards on page 166 in a small shopping bag. Begin by inviting a volunteer to pick a card from the bag. After the class names the critter, have the student attach the card to the second line of the rhyme. Next, read the rhyme and help a volunteer complete the last phrase with a word that rhymes with the picture. (Accept nonsense words for rhyming reinforcement.) Write the word on an index card and then attach it to the final line. Finally, lead the group in reciting the completed rhyme. Remove the cards and then repeat the process.

To market, to market
To buy a big ____.
But then I decided
I wanted a coat ____.

Critter Cards

Use with "Which One's First?" on page 164 and "Better Buying Options" on page 165.

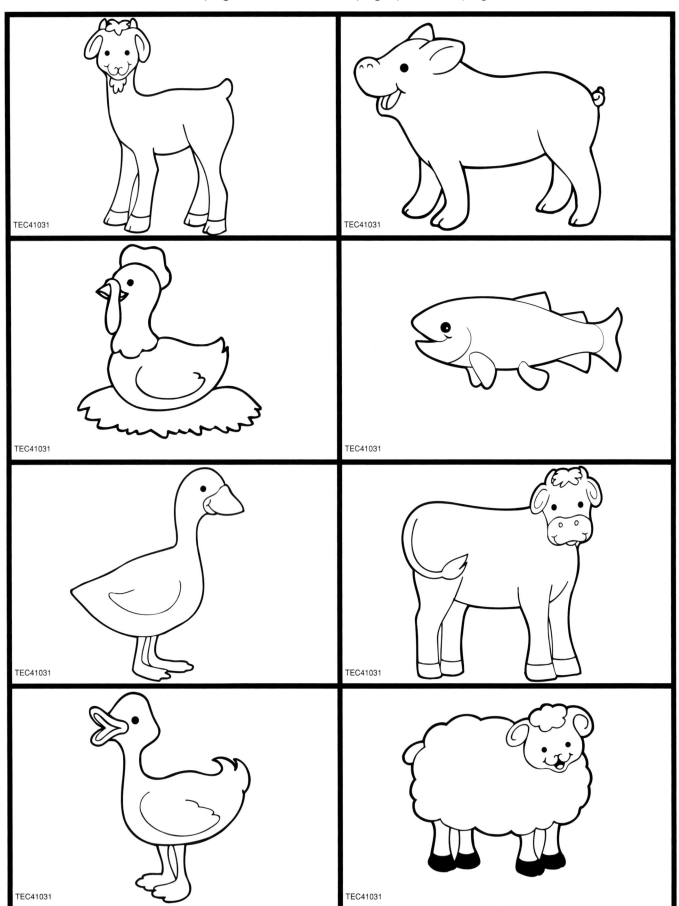

TEC41031

TEC41031

TEC41031

TEC41031

TEC41031

TEC41031

TEC41031

TEC41031

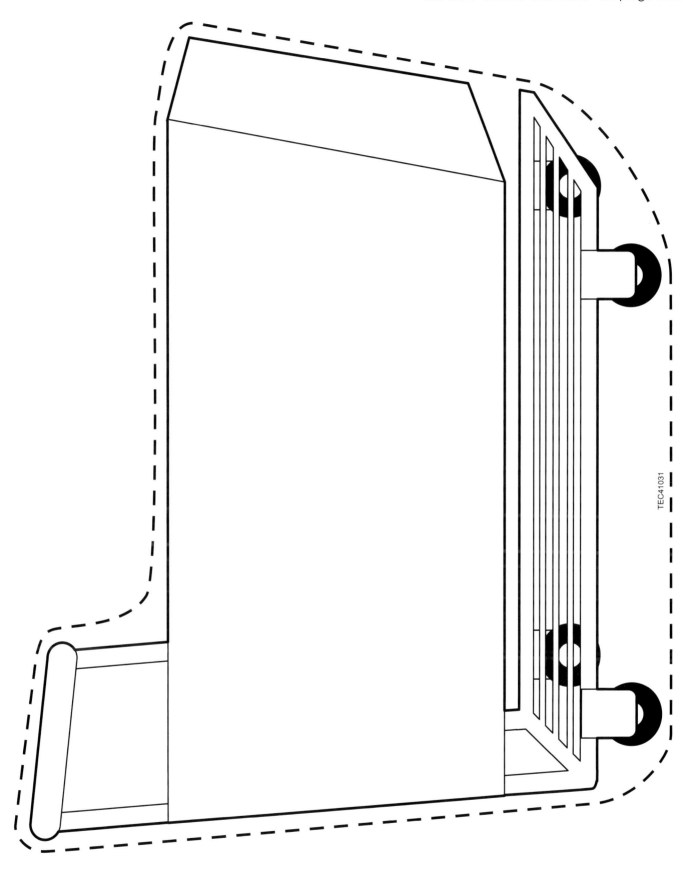

TEC41031

Soup Ingredient Patterns

Use with "Soup Lover's Delight" on page 165.

TEC41031

TEC41031

TEC41031

TEC41031

Brown Rice

TEC41031

TEC41031

CENTER UNITS

Lots of LADYBUG Centers

Go ahead and linger over these ladybug centers. You're sure to spot plenty of just-right learning opportunities!

ideas contributed by Lucia Kemp Henry, Fallon, NV

Fine-Motor Area
Lunch for a Ladybug
Developing fine-motor skills

Little ones pretend to be ladybugs preparing plates of appetizing insects! Place at a center a paper plate, two spring-style clothespins, and several leaf cutouts. Put green pom-poms on the leaf cutouts to resemble aphids (small insects that are a favorite food of most ladybugs). Before students visit the center, explain that ladybugs use their tiny claws to pick up aphids to eat. When a youngster visits the center, he pretends to be a ladybug and holds on to a clothespin claw with each hand. Then he picks up the aphids and places them on the plate. Now that's a lunch fit for a ladybug!

Art Center
A Perfect Home
Contributing to a class display

Since ladybugs are often found on trees and plants, why not have youngsters create a fitting display? On a length of bulletin board paper, draw a simple scene with trees, leaves, and flowers. Tape the paper to a wall at students' eye level. Place near the mural the following supplies: red construction paper, black construction paper strips and hole-punched dots, scissors, glue, and black crayons. If desired, post pictures or photographs of ladybugs nearby. A youngster cuts out red paper ladybugs and glues on black spots and legs. After he embellishes his bug as desired, he attaches it to the mural.

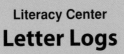

Literacy Center

Letter Logs

Recognizing one's first initial

These literate ladybugs form letters when they rest on logs! For each child, round the corners of a light brown construction paper rectangle and add details to resemble a log. Then print the first letter of each student's name on a separate prepared log. Place the prepared logs, a red ink pad, and black fine-tip markers at a center. A child finds a log with the first letter of his name. Then he makes red fingerprints over the letter. Finally, he uses a marker to add dots to the prints to resemble ladybugs.

Math Center

Bugs on Blossoms

Counting

Great big daisies make super resting spots for ladybugs! To make a daisy, cut out and discard triangular sections from the rim of a paper plate as shown. Make four more daisies in the same manner. Color the middle of each daisy yellow. Then program each one with a different numeral and matching dot set from one to five. Place the daisies and 15 red pompoms (ladybugs) at a center. A child places the corresponding number of ladybugs on each daisy.

Games Center

Ladybug Lotto

Developing visual discrimination skills

Everyone's a winner with this lotto game! Make two red construction paper copies of the gameboard on page 173. Place the gameboards, a large die, and a supply of game markers at a center. Two youngsters visit the center. One child tosses the die and covers the matching ladybug with a game marker. Then his partner repeats the process. The youngsters continue tossing the die in this manner until they both have all of their ladybugs covered.

Gross-Motor Area
Fly Away
Developing gross-motor skills

Ladybug, ladybug, fly away home—to this crafty hollow log! Cover a cylindrical container (such as an empty, clean ice-cream container) with brown paper and add details to resemble a hollow log. Place the log and a supply of large red pom-poms (ladybugs) in an open area of the classroom. A youngster visits the center and tosses the ladybugs into the log from a variety of distances.

Flannelboard Center
Not Just Red!
Identifying colors

Explain to youngsters that not all ladybugs are red. They can be many colors, including orange, yellow, gray, black, blue, and pink. Make a ladybug cutout in each color named above; then ready them for flannelboard use. Cut out six felt leaves and attach them to your flannelboard. Then hide the ladybugs nearby. A child finds a ladybug, names its color, and places it on a leaf. She continues in the same manner for each remaining bug.

Puzzle Center
Build a Bug
Developing spatial skills

The supersize ladybug at this center needs its spots! Make an extra large ladybug from bulletin board paper, omitting the spots. Puzzle-cut each of several black paper circles (spots) into two pieces. Place the puzzle pieces and the ladybug at a center. A student reassembles each spot and places it on the ladybug.

Note to the teacher: Use with "Ladybug Lotto" on page 171.

A Fabulous Feast of Centers!

Turkey, potatoes, and pumpkins, oh my! It's Thanksgiving time again, so serve up the following centers to honor this unique American holiday. Little ones are sure to want second helpings!

ideas contributed by Ada Goren, Winston-Salem, NC

Myricle is thankful for having good food to eat.

Writing Center
A Thankfulness Wreath

Making a connection between spoken and written language

Find out what your little ones are thankful for this Thanksgiving with a festive wreath! Make a class supply of simple fruit and vegetable patterns (see page 177). Place the cutouts at a center along with a large poster board wreath. Arrange for an adult to be stationed at the center. A center visitor names something she is thankful for, while the adult writes her response on a chosen cutout. Then the child glues her cutout to the wreath. After all youngsters have visited the center, add a raffia bow and display the wreath for all to see!

Math Center
Family Time

Developing one-to-one correspondence

Thanksgiving is the perfect time for families to gather and have a fabulous meal! Cut out several copies of the people patterns on page 178. Glue cutouts to several strips of construction paper to make simple patterns; then place the strips at a center along with the remaining people cutouts. A youngster chooses a strip and then places the corresponding people below the strip to duplicate the pattern. He then removes the people and repeats the process with a different strip.

174

Literacy Center
Pleasing Pie
Clapping syllables

Little ones decide who shares a pumpkin pie by clapping syllables. Color and cut out a copy of the animal cards on page 179. Make a simple orange construction paper pie. (If desired, attach the pie to an aluminum tin for a three-dimensional effect.) Then place the pie and cards at a center. Explain that only animals whose names have one clap can share this Thanksgiving pie. A visiting child chooses a card and claps the animal name. If the name has one clap, as the word *pie* does, then she places the card on the pie. If the name has more than one clap, she sets the card aside. Challenge each student to find the two critters that won't be eating this tasty pie.

Play Dough Center
Potato Mash
Developing fine-motor skills

Little ones mix up a batch of homemade mashed potatoes for an imaginary Thanksgiving feast! Place the following items at a table: empty spice shakers, white play dough, yellow play dough, a mixing bowl, mixing spoons, and potato mashers. A child forms potatoes with the white dough and places them in the mixing bowl with some yellow play dough butter. He adds imaginary spices as desired and then uses the masher to make mashed potatoes. Looks good enough to eat!

Water Table
Turkey Soup
Sorting

What do you do with leftover Thanksgiving turkey? Why, make turkey soup, of course! Die-cut brown turkey shapes from craft foam. Also cut from craft foam orange circles (carrots), white squares (potatoes), and green strips (beans). Store each ingredient in a separate container; then place the containers near your water table along with a plastic bowl, a wooden spoon, and a ladle. A youngster adds a desired amount of each ingredient to the water (broth). Then he mixes the soup with the spoon and uses the ladle to serve himself a bowl. Finally, he pours the soup back into the water table and then sorts the ingredients back into the containers.

175

Just Like Squanto
Engaging in pretend play

When little ones visit this center, they plant corn the way Native Americans did hundreds of years ago! Prior to students visiting the center, explain that a Native American named Squanto had a trick for making corn grow tall and healthy. He planted the corn seed with fish. To prepare the center, place near your sand table craft foam fish cutouts, scoops, shovels, and a supply of corn seed. A youngster plants the seeds and the fish in the sand, just as Squanto did!

Art Center
Oodles of Indian Corn
Using art media

A child uses a sponge to dab orange, red, and purple tempera paint onto a square of bubble wrap. She presses a sheet of yellow construction paper over the paint and then removes it. She revisits the center when the paint is dry and cuts a corncob shape from the paper. Then she fringe-cuts strips of a grocery bag and glues them to the corn to resemble husks. These ears of corn look lovely decorating the classroom.

Bonnie Walker, Future Generations, Newhall, CA

Gross-Motor Area
Load the *Mayflower*
Developing gross-motor skills

Your preschool pilgrims work together to load supplies onto a mock *Mayflower!* Label a large tub or box with the name *Mayflower.* Tape a paper mast to a yardstick and attach the yardstick to the inside edge of the tub. Place a supply of soft blocks (supplies) several feet away from the ship. Explain that the Pilgrims went on a long trip and had to take many supplies. They loaded their supplies onto a ship called the *Mayflower.* When two students visit the center, one child sits near the blocks and his partner sits near the ship. Then the student nearest the blocks tosses one block to his partner, and the partner places the block in the ship. Students continue in the same way to load the remaining supplies onto the ship.

©The Mailbox

©The Mailbox

©The Mailbox

©The Mailbox

People Patterns

Use with "Family Time" on page 174.

TEC41027

TEC41027

TEC41027

TEC41027

TEC41027

TEC41027

TEC41027

TEC41027

TEC41027

TEC41027

TEC41027

TEC41027

St. Patrick's Day Centers!

Your little leprechauns will feel lucky indeed when you introduce them to these enchanting center activities!

ideas by Ada Goren, Winston-Salem, NC

Fine-Motor Area
Rainbow Snip

Developing fine-motor skills

These rainbow strips can be used for a variety of crafts. Draw parallel lines on 12" x 18" sheets of colorful construction paper. Place the paper at a center along with scissors and a container. Have youngsters visit the center and give their fine-motor skills a workout by cutting apart the strips and placing them in the container. Use these strips for a nifty St. Patrick's Day craft, such as the rainbow headband shown.

Games Center
Leprechaun Lotto

Identifying symbols

Customize this simple center with symbols that suit your little ones' skill levels. Program a copy of the gameboard on page 183 with desired symbols; then make a class supply. Place the gameboards in a center along with yellow bingo daubers. Gather a small group of youngsters and give each child a gameboard. Name one of the symbols. Have each child press the bingo dauber over the corresponding symbol to resemble a gold coin. When all of the symbols are covered, encourage each youngster to stand up and dance a lucky leprechaun jig!

Play Dough Center
Great Gobs of Gold
Developing fine-motor skills

Invite your preschoolers to the Leprechaun Mint, where leprechauns make their money! Make an oversize black pot cutout like the one shown. (If desired, enlarge the pot pattern on page 185.) Tape the pot to a tabletop. Then provide access to St. Patrick's Day–related stamps and a supply of yellow play dough mixed with gold glitter. A youngster shapes the sparkly play dough into small disks, stamps the disks to create official leprechaun coins, and then places them on the pot.

Literacy Center
Hide-and-Seek Shamrocks
Matching letters

Attach a supply of light green shamrock cutouts to a length of green bulletin board paper. Label each shamrock with a different letter. Then make a matching set of loose shamrocks. Place the paper on the floor in a center and hide the loose shamrocks in the center area. A youngster searches for a hidden shamrock. When he finds one, he places it on the matching shamrock on the paper. When all of the letters have been matched, your little leprechaun hides the letters again for the next child.

Gotcha!

If I caught a leprechaun,

I would ask him to play on the swing set with me.

Writing Center
Gotcha!
Dictating information to complete a sentence

What would your little ones do if they caught a leprechaun? They'll be eager to tell you at this writing center! Make a class supply of the leprechaun patterns on page 184. Have each child color and cut out a leprechaun. Then take a photograph of each child holding her captured leprechaun. Next, instruct the child to visit your writing center and attach her photo to a page programmed as shown. Encourage the youngster to explain what she would do if she caught a leprechaun. Write her words and then attach a speech bubble that says, "Gotcha!" to complete the page.

Math Center
Equal Amounts

Making equal sets

Lenny and Leo Leprechaun want the same amount of gold. Youngsters can help spread the leprechaun's wealth evenly with this tasty activity! Make a copy of the gameboard on page 184. Label each leprechaun as shown; then make a copy for each child. Place the papers at a center. Also place at the center a cup of eight Ritz Bitz crackers (gold coins) for each child. A student takes a copy of the gameboard and a cup of gold coins. She places the gold coins on the leprechauns, arranging them until each leprechaun has the same number. Then she nibbles on the gold coins!

Lenny   Leo

Art Center
Sparkling Shamrocks

Mixing primary colors

Make a white construction paper shamrock for each child. Cut out the shamrocks and fold each one in half vertically. Place the shamrocks at the center along with green glitter, paintbrushes, and yellow and blue tempera paint. A youngster unfolds a shamrock and then paints one half of the shamrock yellow and the remaining half blue, making sure the paint is brushed on fairly thick. She refolds the shamrock and presses down firmly, smoothing the paper from the fold outward several times. She unfolds the shamrock again to observe the magical color transformation! Then she adds a sprinkle of green glitter to the wet paint to finish off this magical masterpiece.

Science Center
Attracted to Gold

Exploring magnets

Searching for leprechaun gold is easy with the help of some magnets! Collect a supply of smooth-edged metal lids (gold coins) from cans of frozen juice concentrate. Attach black paper to a soup pot, as shown, to resemble a leprechaun's pot of gold. Tint batches of uncooked rice rainbow colors. Place the rice in the pot; then bury the coins in the rice. A youngster uses a magnetic wand to retrieve the coins from the rice.

TEC41029

Note to the teacher: Use with "Leprechaun Lotto" on page 180.

184

©The Mailbox® • TEC41029 • Feb./Mar. 2007

Note to the teacher: Use with "Lounging Leprechauns" on page 25, "Gotcha!" on page 181, and "Equal Amounts" on page 182.

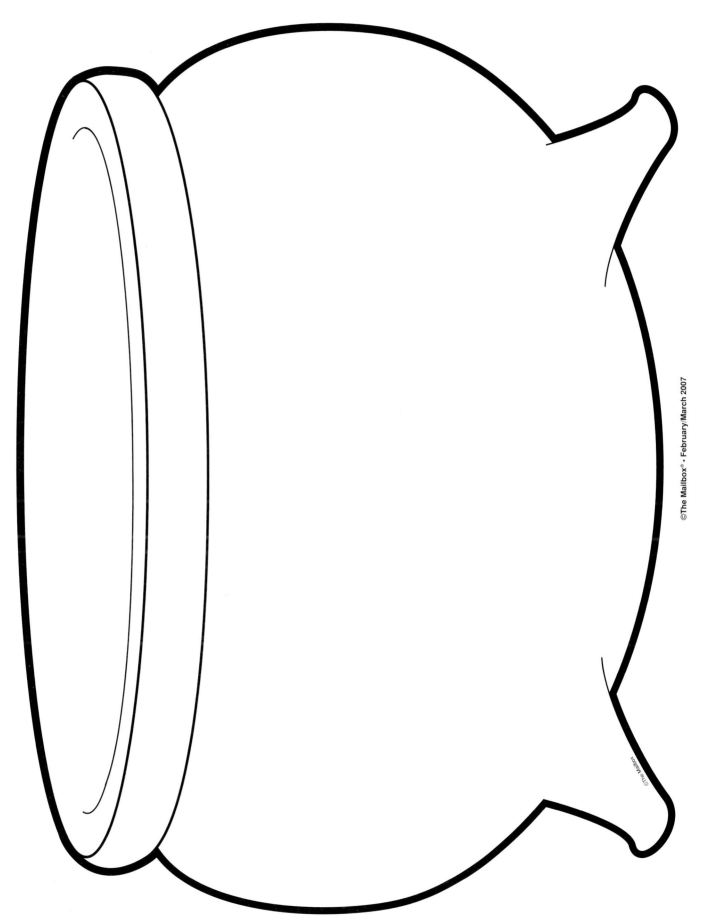

Buzzin' Bee Centers!

No doubt little ones will make a beeline to these adorable center activities!

Literacy Center
Bees on *B*s

Here's a honey of an idea that has little ones recognizing the letter *B!* Make several yellow construction paper bee cutouts (see the small patterns on page 188). Then label a large beehive cutout (enlarge the pattern on page 191) with a variety of different letters, making sure that many of them are *B*s. Attach the hive to a tabletop. Then place the bee cutouts nearby. A youngster visits the center and places a bee on each *B*.

Suzanne Moore, Tucson, AZ

Gross-Motor Area
Buzzin' Around

Attach yellow and black crepe paper streamers to several elastic hair bands. Then place the resulting movement props at a center. Play a recording of Nikolai Rimsky-Korsakov's "The Flight of the Bumblebee" or another fast-paced musical selection. Invite students to slip a hair band over each wrist and then move to the music!

Cindy Wetzig, Bethany Lutheran Preschool, Fairview Heights, IL

Math Center
Honeycomb Match

Youngsters develop spatial awareness with this simple idea! Cut out several copies of the honeycomb pattern on page 189 and then use Con-Tact paper to attach the honeycomb to a tabletop as shown. Decorate the table with several bee cutouts (see the small patterns on page 188). Then place a supply of yellow hexagonal pattern blocks at the table. A youngster visits the center and places pattern blocks on sections of the honeycomb. Now this honeycomb is filled up with yummy yellow honey!

Rachel Frey, Roots and Wings, Thousand Oaks, CA

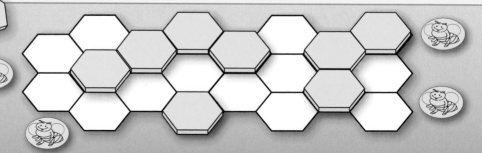

Writing Center
"Un-bee-lievable" Sights!

To prepare for this supervised center, make a copy of the writing sheet on page 190 for each child. Place the sheets at the center, along with a black permanent marker, crayons, and a supply of yellow sticky dots. Invite a child to the center and have him attach a sticky dot to his paper. Encourage him to use the marker to add details to the dot to make a bee. Next, prompt the youngster to choose a crayon and color the flowers on his sheet. After he identifies the color, write the color name in the blank on his paper. Then read the words back to the child. What a lovely sight!

Suzanne Moore, Tucson, AZ

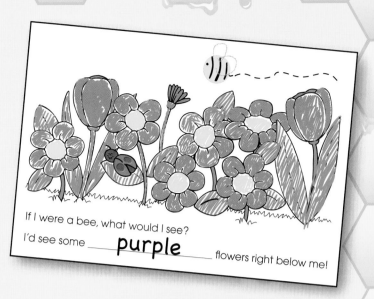

If I were a bee, what would I see?
I'd see some ___**purple**___ flowers right below me!

Science Center
Pollen Pickup

Youngsters may be surprised to find out that bees go from flower to flower gathering pollen on their legs. Cut out a class supply of the large bee pattern on page 188. Tape a disposable bowl to a tabletop and add gold glitter (pollen) to the bowl. Tape petal cutouts around the bowl. Then place the prepared bee cutouts nearby, along with a container of glue, a paintbrush, and crayons. A youngster colors a bee as desired; then she brushes glue on its legs. She "flies" the bee onto the center of the flower. As it "flies" away, she observes the pollen clinging to its legs. If desired, she repeats the process with another bee.

Art Center
Honeycomb Prints

In advance, secure a piece of bubble wrap to a protected tabletop. Place white construction paper nearby, along with copies of the small bee patterns on page 188. A child uses a paint roller to spread yellow tempera paint onto the bubble wrap. Then she presses a sheet of paper over the bubble wrap. After she removes the sheet and lets the paint dry, she colors and glues bees to the finished honeycomb. Simple and cute!

187

Small Bee Patterns
Use with "Bees on *B*s" and "Honeycomb Match" on page 186 and "Honeycomb Prints" on page 187.

Large Bee Pattern
Use with "Pollen Pickup" on page 187.

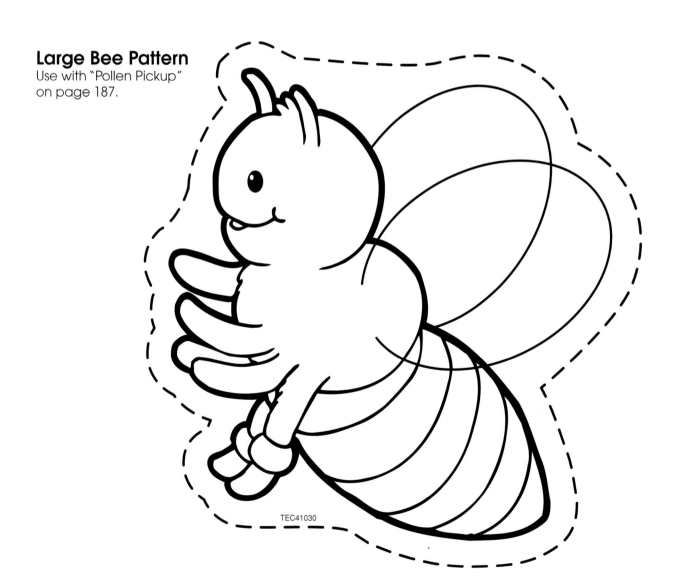

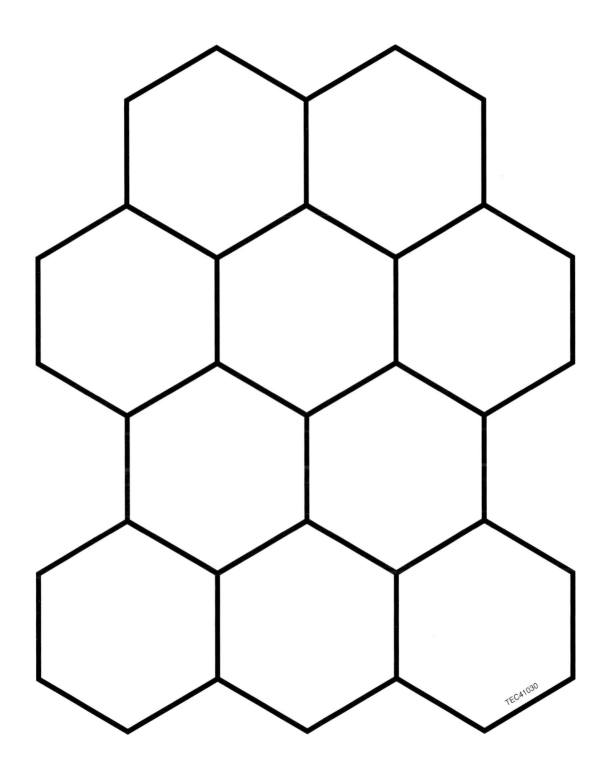

TEC41030

If I were a bee, what would I see?

I'd see some _____ flowers right below me!

©The Mailbox® · TEC41030 · April/May 2007

Note to the teacher: Use with " 'Un-bee-lievable' Sights!" on page 187.

©The Mailbox

Center Time at the Farmers' Market

When little ones visit these centers, they're sure to find bushels of learning opportunities!

ideas contributed by Ada Goren, Winston-Salem, NC

I milk the cows.

I plant some seeds.

I pick lots of corn.

Writing Center
What Does the Farmer Say?
Making connections between spoken and written words

It takes a hardworking farmer to be successful at a farmers' market! Discuss the different jobs and chores that a farmer might do on his or her farm. Post a large farmer cutout on a wall at your writing center. Place a supply of speech bubble cutouts at the center. When a child visits the center, ask her to dictate something a farmer might say, and write her response on a speech bubble. Post the speech bubbles around the farmer. What a busy job!

Annette C. Sheldon, Riverview School, Denville, NJ

Math Center
Weighing In
Comparing weights

Invite your preschoolers to weigh produce, just like they may do at a real farmers' market! Gather a variety of fruits and vegetables and place them at a center along with a balance scale. A visiting youngster chooses two different items and places them on opposite ends of the scale. She takes note of which item is heavier. Then she repeats the process with other fruits and vegetables.

Dramatic Play Center
What's for Sale?
Engaging in dramatic play

Set up a pretend farmers' market right in your classroom! Stock your dramatic play area with a variety of real or plastic fruits and vegetables as well as plastic jam and honey jars. Set out paper grocery bags, a toy cash register, a variety of writing utensils, and a supply of display signs (pattern on page 195). Invite little ones to set up shop and make signs to showcase what's for sale. Prompt them to display the signs at the center, and then let the shopping and selling begin!

Games Center
Plenty to Purchase
Building visual memory skills

For this partner center, arrange several real or plastic produce items on a tray. Place the tray at a center. One youngster (the guesser) turns away from the tray and covers her eyes while the other child (the hider) secretly removes one item from the tray. When the hider asks, "What did I buy at the farmers' market?" the guesser turns around and examines the tray to determine the missing item. Once she correctly identifies the missing item, youngsters switch roles and play again.

Art Center
Potato Bug Prints
Developing fine-motor skills

When farmers find pesky potato bugs in their plants, they know their stall at the upcoming market might be low on potatoes! At your art center, place a class supply of large green leaf cutouts. Also provide potato halves and a shallow tray of bright yellow paint. A child dips a halved potato in the paint and makes several prints on a leaf. Then, when the prints are dry, she uses a marker to add black stripes, six legs, and two antennae to complete the bugs.

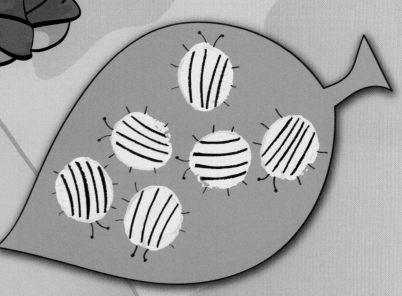

Deborah Ryan
Early Head Start
Milwaukie, OR

Science Center
Up Close!
Making observations

Little ones explore the insides and outsides of many farm-fresh foods at this center! Obtain several pairs of fruits and vegetables. Cut one item of each pair in half and leave the other intact. Place the produce at a center along with plastic magnifying glasses. Invite a child to look, touch, and smell each item to make observations. Encourage her to use a magnifying glass to take a closer look at the inside and outside of each item. If desired, have students dictate their observations. Then write their words on blank cards and post the cards at the center.

Farmers' Market Mix

Take 1 .

Take 2 .

Take 3 .

Take 4 .

Dip

Eat!

Snack Center
Market Mix
Following directions

Here's a healthy snack made with items easily found at a farmers' market! Gather for each child one broccoli floret, two celery sticks, three cucumber slices, and four carrot sticks. Place the vegetables in separate containers. Place a spoon in a container of vegetable dip. Then place the food items at a table along with paper plates and napkins. Gather a small group of youngsters at the center and give each child a copy of page 196. Help each child follow his directions to make a plate of veggies and dip for his snack.

Play Dough Center
Pickles for Sale!
Developing fine-motor skills

Explain to students that farmers' markets often have other items besides fresh fruits and vege-tables for sale. For example, farmers may sell baked goods, jams, and even pickles! Use the recipe shown to make a batch of pickle dough. Then place the dough along with some plastic jars at a center. A youngster rolls the dough into a pickle shape and places it in a jar. She repeats the process until her jar is full of pickles!

Dee Hulsey
Atonement Preschool
Glendale, AZ

Pickle Dough

Ingredients:

4 c. flour   4 c. dill pickle juice

1 c. salt   1 tbsp. oil

1 tbsp. cream of tartar   1 tbsp. green food coloring

How to Make:

Combine the flour, salt, and cream of tartar in a large bowl. Pour pickle juice, oil, and food coloring in a saucepan and bring it to a low boil. Pour the liquid mixture in the bowl with the flour mixture. Stir until cool enough to touch; then knead well.

Fresh

Produce

TEC41031

Farmers' Market Mix

Take 1 ![broccoli].

Take 2 ![celery].

Take 3 ![cucumber slices].

Take 4 ![carrots].

Dip 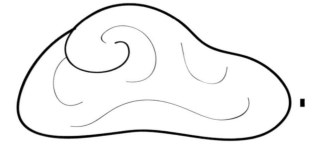.

Eat!

Note to the teacher: Use with "Market Mix" on page 194.

LITERACY UNITS

Let's Play With Sounds!

Hearing click-clacking claws and curious growls? No worries—it's just these adorable monsters here to help little ones build phonological awareness skills!

ideas contributed by Lucia Kemp Henry, Fallon, NV

What's to Eat?
Manipulating phonemes

To prepare for this whole-group activity, cut pictures of food from magazines. Also cut out several colorful copies of the monster pattern on page 201. Place the monsters on your floor in a row and place the food cutouts nearby. Have students sit in a circle around the cutouts. Tell youngsters that the monsters are very hungry; then name the food a particular monster wants, changing the initial sound in the food name. For example, you might say, "The green monster would like to have some 'dananas.'" Have youngsters identify the food that the monster wants; then encourage a child to place the appropriate cutout on the monster. Continue in the same way with the remaining food items.

Cute Suit
Reciting a rhyming poem

Give each child a copy of page 201. Lead students in reciting the provided poem several times, prompting them to supply the final word in each rhyming couplet. Next, provide access to crayons, tissue paper squares, and a bowl of glue with paintbrushes. Have little ones use the supplies to give their monsters cute furry suits!

Little Monster looks so cute
In his fuzzy, furry suit.
Should his fur be long and green?
Messy? Curly? Short and clean?
Should his fur be pink and blue?
What does he look like to you?

Odd Monster Out
Identifying nonrhyming words
One little monster in this cuddly trio has to go! Cut out one copy of the cards on page 202 and six colorful copies of the monster on page 201; then color the cards and glue a different card to each monster. Gather a small group of youngsters and present three monsters, making sure that two of the monsters show pictures whose names rhyme. Lead students in reciting the chant shown. Then help students identify the picture whose name doesn't rhyme with the remaining two. When the monster is identified, have a youngster remove it from the group. Continue in the same way with other monster combinations.

Three little monsters standing in a row.
Two can stay, but one must go!

How Many Words?
Segmenting a sentence into words
Gather a small group of youngsters. Give each child a napkin with Bugles corn snacks (teeth) and a monster face cutout similar to the one shown. Say a simple sentence, such as "The monster is furry." Repeat the sentence and pause after each word, encouraging the child to place one tooth on his monster for each word he hears. When the students are finished, have them count the teeth on their monsters. After several rounds of this activity, have little ones nibble on their snacks!

Beginning and End
Combining segmented words
Cut out two copies of the monster pattern on page 201; then mount each one on a paint stirrer to make stick puppets. Hold one puppet in each hand. Then introduce the monster on your right as "Beginning" and the monster on your left as "End." Explain that Beginning only knows how to say the beginning of words and End only knows how to say the end of words. Tell students that it's very difficult to understand what they are saying and you could use their help. Have Beginning say "pre" and End say "school;" then prompt students to put the fragments together to say the word *preschool*. Continue in the same way with other common words, such as *pumpkin, carpet, monster, footprint,* and *candy*.

A Monster Melody
Singing a rhyming song

Little ones are sure to be delighted with this toe-tapping song. Lead students in singing the song, beginning by singing the chorus and then repeating the chorus again between each verse. Encourage youngsters to sing the rhyming words with extra gusto and to add actions to the performance by stomping their feet, displaying their pointy claws, and showing their gorgeous green teeth!

(sung to the tune of "Alouette")

Chorus
I'm a monster. I'm a silly monster.
I'm a monster. I'm sure you'll agree.

Verses
I can stomp my hairy feet,
Scaring people that I meet.
Hairy feet, that I meet,
Oh!

I can wave my pointy claws.
You will see them on my paws.
Pointy claws, on my paws,
Oh!

My teeth are the color green.
I am sure they're nice and clean.
Color green, nice and clean,
Oh!

Sandy Rothstein
On Our Way Learning Center
Far Rockaway, NY

Cluttered Cave
Identifying rhyming pairs

This monster saves a lot of things inside his cave! In advance, color and cut out a copy of pages 201 and 202. Trim a small box to resemble a cave. Set the monster aside and place the cards inside the cave. After gathering a small group of youngsters around the cave, lead them in reciting the rhyme shown. Have a child peek in the cave; then help him quietly remove two cards with rhyming names. As you repeat the process with each remaining child, pause briefly and say with great drama that you hear the monster coming. Prompt youngsters to be extremely quiet as you "walk" the monster cutout in front of the cave and then back to his previous location. When each child has found a rhyming pair, have them quietly place the cards back in the cave.

Little monster likes to save
Many things inside his cave.
While he's gone, we'll take a peek.
Rhyming words are what we seek.

Monster Pattern
Use with "What's to Eat?" and "Cute Suit" on page 198, "Odd Monster Out" and
"Beginning and End" on page 199, and "Cluttered Cave" on page 200.

TEC41027

Rhyming Picture Cards

Use with "Odd Monster Out" on page 199 and "Cluttered Cave" on page 200.

TEC41027

TEC41027

TEC41027

TEC41027

TEC41027

TEC41027

TEC41027

TEC41027

A Cozy Collection of Writing Ideas

Here's a selection of activities to help little ones warm up to writing! With helpful tips, ideas on dictated writing, and ways to zip up your writing center, there are sure to be several ideas just perfect for your little authors.

Daily News

Youngsters dictate information to add to your classroom's daily news! During center time, call a student over to a table and ask him if he has any news he would like to share. As the child shares any desired information, write his words on a sheet of chart paper. Continue in the same way with other youngsters. Then, later in the day, read aloud the daily news to the class. Repeat the activity several times each month, calling on different young-sters to share their news each time.

Sharon K. Swenson
Hazel Lake Montessori
Staples, MN

Daily News

Mom and I are going to the store today.
                                        Juan
I like my cat.
                                        Ella
I saw Grandma this morning.
                                        Lee
I had pancakes for breakfast!
                                        Jordan

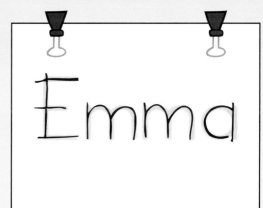

Emma

Name-Writing Success!

When little ones are ready to practice writing their names, this tip will help them succeed! Use an extra thick black marker to write each child's name on a separate sheet of copy paper; then laminate the papers for durability. Help a child clip a blank sheet of copy paper on top of the laminated sheet. Her name will show through the paper and she can easily trace it with a marker or chubby crayon. Ah, success!

Beth Lemke, Highland Headstart, Coon Rapids, MN

Super Center Additions

Spice up your writing center by incorporating one or more of the suggestions below. You may wish to rotate center additions to keep interest level high.

• Little ones can roam and write with the addition of clipboards to your writing center! Use a string to attach a writing utensil to each of several clipboards. Then clip a piece of paper to each board. A youngster can roam around the room, writing letters or words he sees!

• Laminate several pieces of environmental print and place them at the center along with dry-erase markers. Youngsters can use the markers to trace letters on the labels, or they can use other available writing utensils to write familiar favorites on provided paper.

• Flash card sets come in many different themes, such as animals, shapes, letters, and colors. Place different sets of flash cards at your writing center on a rotating basis. If desired, you can also use die-cuts to make unique sets of flash cards. Youngsters will enjoy flipping through the cards as well as attempting to write the words they see.

Amber Baker, Learn a Lot Christian Preschool, Moorseville, IN; Monica Grimm, Wasatch Presbyterian Preschool, Salt Lake City, UT; Twilla Lamm, Jenks, OK; Lynne Lenchak, Avon, OH

Here's a quick tip! If youngsters have a difficult time gripping pencils or crayons, invite them to write with a short piece of chubby crayon. Little fingers can't help but grip these the correct way and children often transfer that hold to other writing utensils!

Jennifer Cochran, Morgan County Primary School, Madison, GA

Writing and Rebus Poems

In advance, use the picture cards on page 206 to make a rebus poem poster similar to the one shown. Encourage youngsters to help you chant the poem as you follow the words with your finger. Next, place copies of the picture cards on page 206 at a table along with large pieces of paper and crayons. Invite students to use the pictures to make their own writing. What a fun way to be successful at writing!

Kimberly Corzine, Learning Tree East, Elgin, IL
Louise Frankel, Family Development Day Care, Plainfield, NJ

[Santa], [Santa], works all day to pack his big red Christmas [sleigh].

[Santa], [Santa], with his [Mrs. Claus], empties toys from all his shelves.

[Santa], [Santa], dressed in red, waits for all to go to [bed].

[Santa], [Santa], gives out toys to all the little [girls] and [boys].

Splendid Speech Bubbles

To prepare, cut pictures of people from magazines, making sure you have at least one for each child. Make a copy of the speech bubble pattern on page 207 for each youngster. Invite him to choose a picture and decide what that person might say. Write his words on a speech bubble; then encourage him to cut out the speech bubble and glue it to a sheet of construction paper along with the corresponding magazine picture. If desired, place copies of the speech bubble and additional magazine pictures at your writing center for continued practice.

Renee Parker, Selinsgrove Area School, Selinsgrove, PA

Sign In!

A center sign-in sheet is an appealing way to have youngsters practice writing their names! In advance, set up an engaging center for youngsters to visit. Then place a clipboard with a sign-in sheet near the center. Tell students that they have to sign in before they can visit the center. This handy little sheet encourages youngsters to visit the area and helps them practice writing their names.

Ella Stroupe
Williams Trace Children's Day Out
Sugar Land, TX

Ladder Stories

In advance, draw a simple picture on a sheet of paper, such as the one shown. Then write the first line of a story underneath the drawing. Gather a small group of youngsters and read aloud the story starter. Ask a student what might happen next. Write the student's words on a sentence strip and then personalize the strip. Continue in the same way, having each remaining youngster contribute a sentence to the story. Then attach the picture and strips to a sheet of chart paper and display it in the room.

Karen Abel
Immaculate Conception School
Spotswood, NJ

205

Picture Cards

Use with "Writing and Rebus Poems" on page 204.

TEC41028

TEC41028

TEC41028

TEC41028

TEC41028

TEC41028

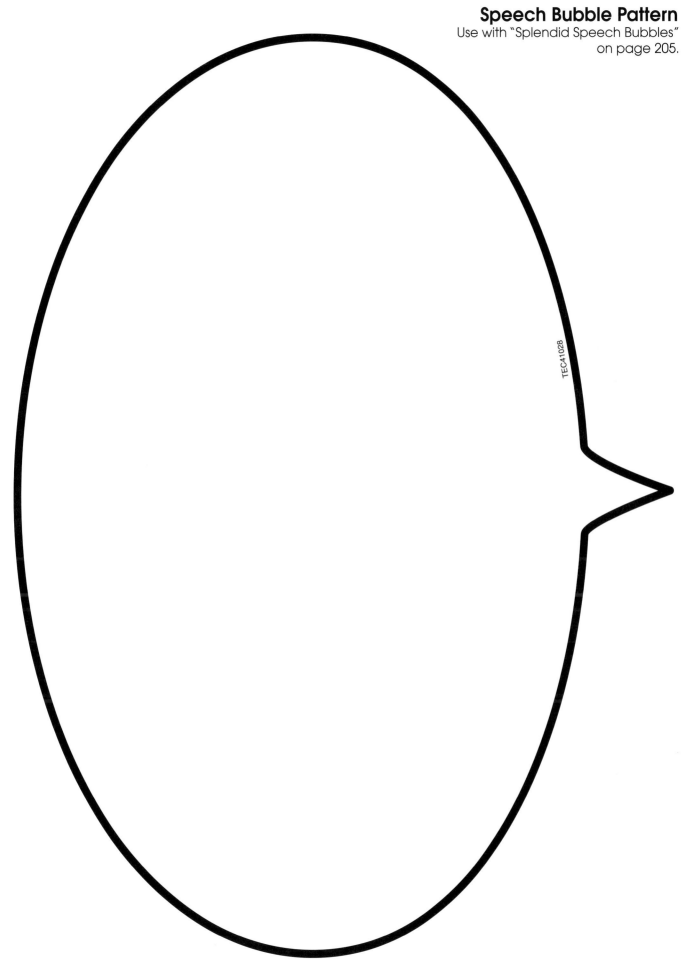

TEC41028

A Sweet Selection of Letter Activities

Here's a batch of letter name and sound activities that are just perfect for preschoolers and are frosted with fun!

Freshly Baked Letters

This twist on a familiar chant is a fun way to review letter names! Before reciting the chant, give each child a copy of the cake pattern on page 212 programmed with the first letter of his name. Invite each student, in turn, to name his letter. Encourage one child to hold up his cake. Then lead students in the rhyme shown, inserting the child's letter and name where indicated and encouraging youngsters to pat their legs to the beat of the chant. Continue in the same manner for each remaining child. To complete the activity, invite each youngster to ice his cake by tracing over the letter with colored glue.

Aileen Ellis
Parkview Preschool
Nampa, ID

Pat-a-cake, pat-a-cake,
Baker's man!
Bake us a letter
As fast as you can.

Roll it and pat it
And mark it with a [P].
Then put it in the oven
For [Peter] and me!

Name-O

For this small-group game, give each student a supply of O-shaped cereal pieces and a tagboard strip programmed with her name. (Consider grouping students by the number of letters in their names.) Place a set of letter cards in a bag. To play, remove a card and help children announce the letter name. Each child searches her card for a matching letter. If she finds the letter, she covers it with a cereal piece each time it occurs in her name. Play continues until a child covers all of her letters and announces, "Name-O!" After verifying her letters, celebrate by inviting all of the group members to eat a few pieces of cereal. Then have students clear their cards and play again!

Karen Saner, Burns Elementary, Burns, KS

Search and Circle

Nursery rhymes make this take-home activity extra fun! Choose a nursery rhyme that features a letter youngsters have previously studied. Make a copy of the nursery rhyme, slip it in a large resealable plastic bag, and tape it in place. Place in the bag a letter card and a wipe-off marker. Then give the bag to a child to take home. The child reads the poem with a family member and circles all of the letters that match the letter on the card. After she returns the bag and shares her work with you, wipe off the bag and then prepare it for a different student.

Vickie Osborne, Atkins Elementary, Atkins, VA

Marvelous Letter M!

M&M's candy pieces are the inspiration for this taste bud–tempting center! Place at a center the following items: a supersize cookie cutout, a supply of small colorful paper circles, glue, and an ink pad with a letter *M* stamp. When a child visits the center, she stamps an *M* on a small circle while saying, "/m/." Then she glues the resulting candy to the cookie. She continues stamping and gluing as time allows. After each student has had an opportunity to add candy to the cookie, display it for all to see!

Maryann Bennett
North Phoenix Baptist Preschool
Phoenix, AZ

Feed the Dog

These cute canines are hungry for letters! Decorate the underside of a paper plate to create a dog as shown. Staple the rim of the plate to the rim of a second plate, leaving a section open near the dog's mouth. Also staple a paper tongue to the second plate. Make several copies of the bone pattern on page 213 and label each bone with a different letter. Cut out the bones and place them on the floor; then gather youngsters around the bones. Invite a child to choose a bone and hold it up for all to see. Have students name the letter on the bone. Then press the plates inward as shown to open the dog's mouth, and have the student "feed" the bone to the dog. Play several rounds of this nifty activity!

Bonnie Moore
Lighthouse Christian Academy, Cumberland, MD

The Letter Bus

Youngsters sing letter sounds with this catchy rendition of a familiar song! Enlarge, color, cut out, and laminate a copy of the school bus pattern on page 213.
Have a student lightly tape a letter card to the bus; then
lead youngsters in singing the song shown. Repeat this
rollicking tune several times with different cards!

(sung to the tune of "The Wheels on the Bus")

The *[D]* on the bus says, "[/d/, /d/, /d/],
[/d/, /d/, /d/, /d/, /d/, /d/]."
The *[D]* on the bus says, "[/d/, /d/, /d/]"
All the way to school!

Pam Colby
Pam's Puddle Jumpers Family Daycare
Minneapolis, MN

Where Is It?

The search is on with this quick daily activity! Each day before students arrive,
remove a letter from your classroom alphabet display and place it somewhere in
the room. After all students have arrived for the day, explain, with great drama,
that a letter is missing from the alphabet! Help students determine the name of
the missing letter. Then invite your young detectives to look around the classroom
and locate the letter. When the letter is found, have a student place the letter back
where it belongs.

Sally Avila-Garcia, Shepherd of the Valley Preschool and Kindergarten
Hacienda Heights, CA

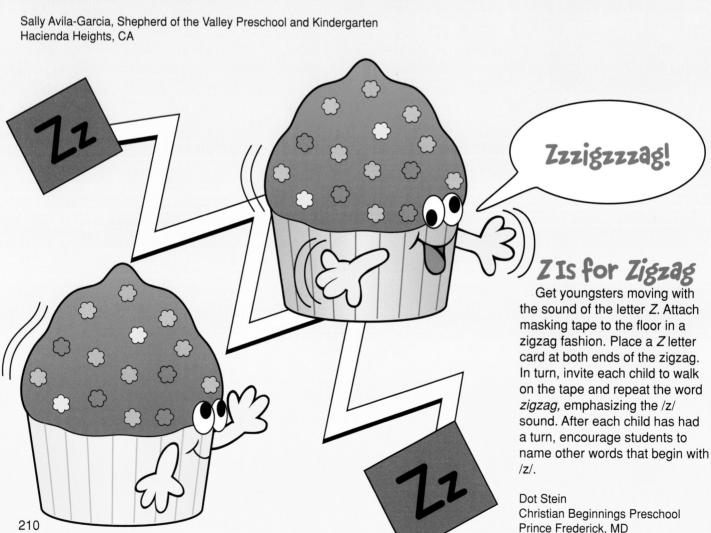

Zzzigzzzag!

Z Is for Zigzag

Get youngsters moving with
the sound of the letter *Z*. Attach
masking tape to the floor in a
zigzag fashion. Place a *Z* letter
card at both ends of the zigzag.
In turn, invite each child to walk
on the tape and repeat the word
zigzag, emphasizing the /z/
sound. After each child has had
a turn, encourage students to
name other words that begin with
/z/.

Dot Stein
Christian Beginnings Preschool
Prince Frederick, MD

Alphabet Soup

Serve up letter practice that is just right for your preschoolers! Place a set of foam alphabet letters in a large pot. Add enough water to the pot so that the letters float. Lead students in reciting the poem shown while a student uses a ladle to stir the "soup." Then have him scoop up a letter and show it to the class. Ask youngsters to name the letter and its corresponding sound. Place the letter back in the pot and repeat the activity until each child has had a turn to stir the soup.

Yummy, yummy soup
Really hits the spot.
It's filled with floating letters
And it's piping hot!

adapted from an idea by Adrianne Hobbs
Mooresville, NC

The Letter Jar

Here's a letter activity that doubles as a home-school connection! Draw a simple jar shape on a sheet of paper; then label the lid with a desired letter. Copy the paper to make a class supply. Send home a copy of the jar and a note to parents like the one shown. On the day the jars are returned to school, invite each child to share her work.

Jaime Cunningham
Leaps and Bounds Nursery School
Horseheads, NY

Dear Parent,
Please help your youngster place items in this jar that begin with the letter T. To do this, your child can draw pictures on the jar and you can label them, or you can help your youngster glue pictures from magazines or store circulars to the jar. Please send the jar to school with your child by April 20.

Thank you,
Ms. Cunningham

Simple Assessment

Here's a quick and easy way to assess students' letter knowledge. On a metal cookie sheet, place several magnetic letters that are familiar to your youngsters. During center time, gather this mobile assessment tool and walk over to a specific youngster. Name a letter and instruct the student to locate the letter on the cookie sheet. Continue in the same manner with the remaining letters. Write comments about the assessment on sticky notes and attach them to the back of the cookie sheet. This is also a fabulous way to assess color and number knowledge!

Jennae Snow, Snow Preschool, St. George, UT

Bone Pattern
Use with "Feed the Dog" on page 209.

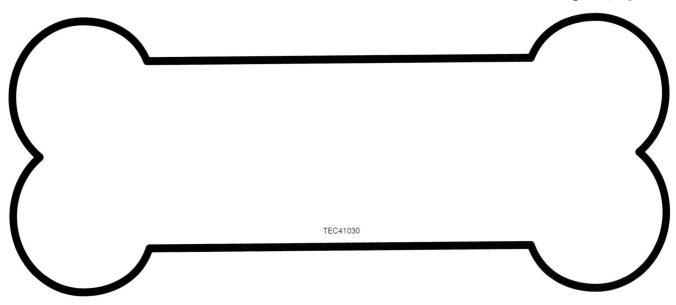

TEC41030

School Bus Pattern
Use with "The Letter Bus"
on page 210.

TEC41030

Fabulous Fairy Tales

Little ones will have a ball with this selection of activities that are just perfect for demonstrating comprehension of well-known fairy tales!

ideas contributed by Lucia Kemp Henry, Fallon, NV

A Book Full of Props

Encourage students to share their knowledge of popular fairy tales with this unique prop! In advance, obtain a large cereal box and cut along three edges of the box front as shown. Decorate the box so it resembles a book. Place several objects in the box that relate to different fairy tales (see the suggestions shown). After read-alouds of the chosen stories, display the box and then pull out one of the props, such as the plastic bag filled with bread crumbs. Pass the bag around for youngsters to examine. Then say, "Once upon a time in a fairy tale, there were some bread crumbs. Who can tell us something about this fairy tale?" Encourage students to share information about the story. Continue in the same way with the remaining props.

Story prop suggestions:
Cinderella, high-heel shoe
Goldilocks and the Three Bears, small colorful bowl
Hansel and Gretel, bread crumbs in a resealable plastic bag
Jack and the Beanstalk, dry beans in a resealable plastic bag
The Princess and the Pea, peas in a pod or a small can of peas
The Three Little Pigs, straw in a resealable plastic bag

The Magic Wand

Help students identify the characters in a story with this nifty circle-time idea! In advance, decorate a dowel rod so it resembles a magic wand. Color and cut out a copy of the fairy-tale cards on page 217. Write the corresponding story name on the back of each card. Then place the cards facedown in your circle-time area. Gather students around the cards; then give one child the wand. Prompt him to tap the wand on one of the cards. After you name the story, help the child identify one or more characters in the story. Then have him flip the card over to show the picture. Continue in the same way with different youngsters until all the cards have been chosen.

Pigs' New Digs

Youngsters show their understanding of the fairy tale *The Three Little Pigs* with an engaging take-home project! After a read-aloud of the story, send home a note with youngsters requesting that students make new homes for the pigs that lost their houses. When students bring the projects to school, ask youngsters to explain what happened to the houses of straw and sticks. Next, invite each child to describe the new home he has made for the pigs. Finally, encourage youngsters to stand back and huff and puff on the houses just like the wolf did. No doubt these sturdy homes won't blow away like the pigs' previous dwellings!

Arleen Cummings
Four Seasons Child Care
West Amherst, NY

A Tasty Retelling

After a read-aloud of *Goldilocks and the Three Bears,* give each child a copy of page 218 and three bear-shaped graham cracker snacks. Prompt students to retell the story to you, moving their bears from picture to picture to show how they found the bowls of porridge, the chairs, and, finally, Goldilocks herself lying in bed. When they are finished with the retelling, encourage youngsters to nibble on the three bears and color the page!

Kish Harris
Sacred Heart School
Danville, VA

Cottage Living

Youngsters recall fairy-tale characters who live in cottages with this adorable idea! To begin, help youngsters understand that a cottage is a small house. Share illustrations of cottages from several books. Then prompt youngsters to recall fairy tales you've read aloud in class that have characters who live in cottages, such as Hansel and Gretel, the three bears, and the dwarfs in *Snow White and the Seven Dwarfs*. Next, have each child draw on a cutout copy of page 219 a picture of her favorite cottage dweller. After she colors the cottage, have her glue brown paper shreds to the cottage's roof so it resembles a thatched roof. Finally, program a strip of paper with the question shown and then record the child's answer on the strip and attach it to her cottage. If desired, mount the cottages on a wall with the title "Once Upon a Cozy Cottage."

Who lives here? Hansel and Gretel live here.

Fairy Tale Troublemakers

A fairy tale wouldn't be complete without a giant, witch, or other troublemaker! Have students recall different trouble-makers they have encountered in fairy tales you've read aloud in class. Next, cut out several copies of the fairy tale cards on page 217. Have each child glue a card to a sheet of paper programmed as shown. Invite him to identify the character or characters in the picture and the character that caused trouble in the story. Write the child's words in the spaces provided. Finally, have each child draw the story's villain on his paper.

Tower Tale

Here's a perfect prop to aid in the retelling of *Rapunzel.* After a read-aloud of *Rapunzel,* place a sheet of white poster board in a center along with a shallow pan of gray paint and a small rectangular sponge. Have youngsters use the sponge to make prints on the poster board so the poster board resembles a wall. When the paint is dry, cut a square from the poster board to make a window. Then roll the poster board and secure the ends in place. Put the resulting tower in a center along with a copy of the book and Rapunzel, prince, and witch stick puppets similar to those shown. Youngsters visit the center and use the props to retell and extend the story.

A Century Snooze

Youngsters reflect on the story *Sleeping Beauty* with this class book. After a read-aloud of the story, ask youngsters to explain what happened to the people in the castle after Sleeping Beauty pricked her finger. Lead youngsters to conclude that everyone in the castle immediately fell asleep. Periodically throughout the school day, say, "Sleep!" and encourage youngsters to pretend they are asleep as if they were in the castle. As youngsters pretend to sleep, take a photograph of each youngster. Also, take a photograph of your whole class wide awake. Have each child glue his photo to a paper programmed as shown and then write his name on the paper. Attach the class photo to a page labeled with the words shown. Then bind the pages together behind a cover. This book is sure to be popular at your reading center!

adapted from an idea by Camille Cooper
Emporia State University Center for Early Childhood Education
Emporia, KS

Use with "The Magic Wand" on page 214 and "Fairy-Tale Troublemakers" on page 216.

TEC41031

TEC41031

TEC41031

TEC41031

TEC41031

TEC41031

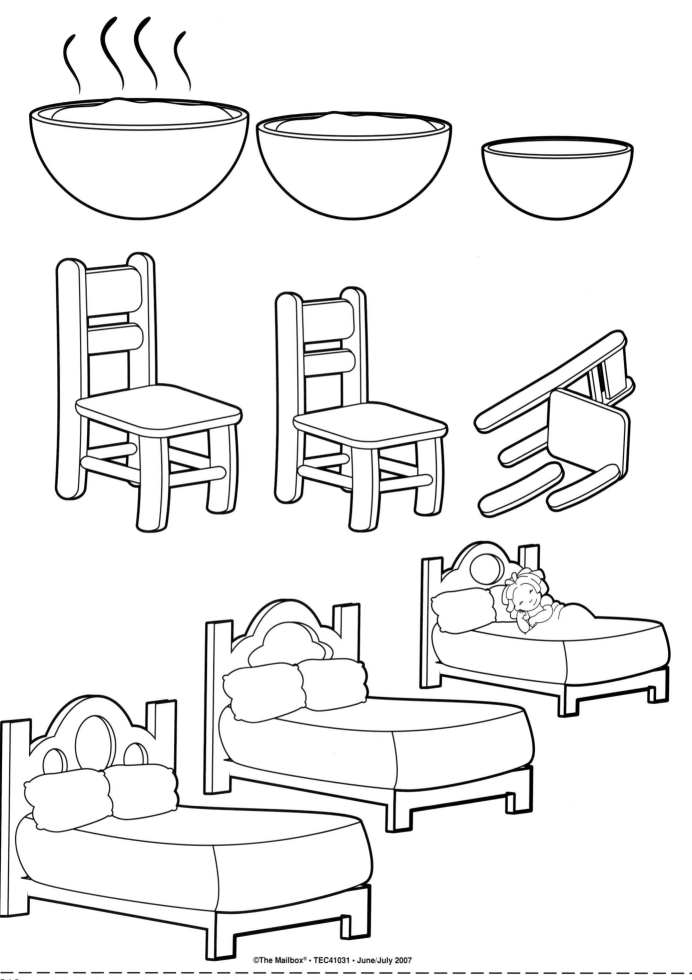

Note to the teacher: Use with "A Tasty Retelling" on page 215.

TEC41031

Speaking and Listening

Spotlight listening and speaking skills with this appetizing collection of ideas. You're sure to savor the results!

ideas contributed by Roxanne LaBell Dearman
Western NC Early Intervention Program for Children Who Are Deaf or Hard of Hearing, Charlotte, NC

Pat the Dough

Speaking to contribute to a game

Even your shyest little chefs are sure to be eager to speak during this game! To begin, have youngsters recite the chant shown as they pretend to pat pizza dough. After the final line of the chant, choose a child to name a topping he would like on his pizza. Have him sprinkle the pretend topping over his crust. Then repeat the rhyme and ask a new child to name a topping. When each youngster has had a turn, have students pretend to place their pizzas in an oven. Then when they're finished, encourage students to gobble their pizzas up with great gusto!

Pat the dough, pat the dough
To make a pizza pie!
What kind of topping
Would you like to try?

Question of the Day

Speaking clearly, using appropriate eye contact

Highlight speaking etiquette with this quick activity! Make several copies of your class list and write a different question at the top of each one. You might consider asking questions such as the following: What is your favorite color? What is your favorite food? or How can you help your family? When you have a few minutes of extra time, grab a question sheet. Ask each student the question and encourage him to speak clearly and look at you while giving his answer. Then write his answer next to his name. After sharing the results with your youngsters, post the finished sheets on a parent message board or add them to your weekly newsletter!

What is your favorite color?	
Anne Rogers	blue
Lee Wong	purple
Lucas Johnson	red
Emma Freeport	pink
D'Jaun Steckler	blue

Rita Beiswenger, Crescent Avenue Weekday School, Fort Wayne, IN

Ms. Dearman's Pizza Parlor

onion

pepperoni

cheese

green pepper

mushroom

What happened at the beginning of the story?

What was your favorite part of the story?

The Book Bucket

A Pleasing Parlor

Speaking to enter into a play situation

To make a menu of pizza toppings, color a copy of the patterns on page 223. Cut out the patterns and glue them to a sheet of tagboard folded to resemble a menu. Label the items; then laminate the menu for durability. To set up this dramatic-play area, place the menu, pizza pans, plastic utensils, plates, and aprons in your housekeeping area. Also add notepads and crayons for taking orders. Encourage youngsters to visit the area and have conversations to order, make, and then eat bunches of pretend pizzas!

The Book Bucket

Listening to story details

Follow up a read-aloud with questions from this whimsical book bucket! Place a small amount of sparkly confetti in a decorated plastic bucket. Also place question cards, such as those shown, in the bucket. After a read-aloud, reveal the book bucket with great fanfare and a quick toss of sparkly confetti. Have a child remove a card from the bucket. Read the question and then encourage a child to answer it. Continue in the same way with several of the remaining cards.

Sue Fleischmann, Waukesha County Project Head Start
Waukesha, WI

ORDER

Mmm—Pizza Muffins!

Listening to complete a task

To prepare, spray the sections of a muffin tin with nonstick spray. Then obtain a tube of refrigerated biscuit dough and press a circle of dough in a muffin tin section for each child. To begin, explain that it's important to listen carefully so everyone's snack turns out correctly. Then narrate your actions as you place a teaspoon of sauce over the dough and top it with a circle of pepperoni and a spoonful of shredded mozzarella cheese. Have each student show he listened by placing toppings on his own circle of dough in the same order. Congratulate students on their keen listening skills. Then bake the muffins according to the directions on the biscuit tube. When the muffins have cooled, invite students to nibble on their tasty snack!

Ready, Set, Action!

Speaking to describe, developing new vocabulary
Spark some fascinating conversation with this activity! Gather from magazines and newspapers a variety of large photographs that show actions. For example, a girl kicking a ball, a man cooking, or a woman running would all be appropriate pictures. Place the pictures in page protectors and secure them in a three-ring binder. To begin, show students one of the photos and then ask them questions like the ones shown. When students are comfortable with this activity, you may wish to help them make up a story about the photo.

Sharon J. Young, Bright Start (Early Intervention) Agency
Greer, SC

Suggested questions:
What do you see in this photo?
What is the person doing?
Why do you think the person is doing that?
How do you think the person is feeling? Why?
What do you think he/she would do next?
Do you like to cook (dance, run, etc.) like the person?

Special Delivery!

Listening to take a turn
To prepare for this whole-group activity, make a class supply of the pizza pattern on page 224. Cut out the patterns and place them in a clean pizza box. (You may wish to ask your local pizzeria to donate an unused box for classroom use.) Write a class list on a sheet of chart paper and post it in your classroom. After leading students in the provided rhyme, help youngsters identify the first name on the list. When the child hears his name, have him accept the delivery by removing a pizza from the box and saying, "Thanks for the pizza!" Continue in the same way for several rounds, going to the next child on the list for each round.

Pizza delivery—it's piping hot.
That ooey, gooey cheese really hits the spot!
To make sure no one will be missed,
Let's all check our delivery list!

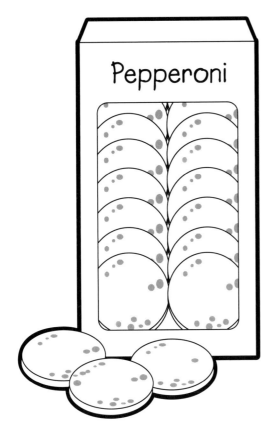

Pepperoni

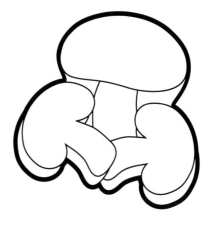

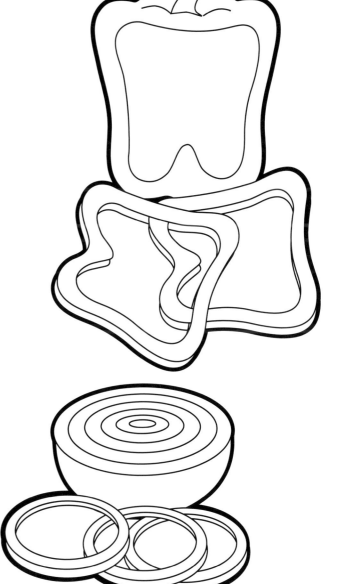

Shredded
Cheese

TEC41026

Pizza Pattern

Use with "Special Delivery!" on page 222.

TEC41026

MATH UNITS

Transport Sort

Boats, planes, and automobiles! These transportation-themed ideas are sure to rev up students' presorting and sorting skills.

ideas contributed by Suzanne Moore, Tucson, AZ

At the Car Wash
Describing objects by one attribute

Make a splash with this unique whole-group activity! Enlarge the car card on page 228 and make three copies; then color and decorate each car differently. Place a transparency over a car. Use a brown permanent marker to color the portion of the transparency over the car to make it appear as if the car were covered with mud. To begin, present one of the cars with the transparency placed on top. Lead students in reciting the rhyme below, removing the transparency during the fifth line. When the rhyme is finished, have a student describe one thing he notices about the car's appearance. Then repeat the process for each remaining car. The wheels are blue!

> One little car is in the car wash line,
> Covered with mud and dirt and grime.
> He went in the car wash—scrub, scrub, scrub,
> Splash, splash, splash, and rub, rub, rub.
> When he came out he was clean and dry.
> The happy little car said, "Thanks! Goodbye!"

What's Missing?
Describing objects by two attributes

To prepare, make copies of the cards on page 228 on three different colors of construction paper. Cut out the cards and lay them on your floor in the formation shown. Have students describe what they see, guiding them to notice the columns of different pictures as well as the rows of colors. Next, have students place their hands over their eyes as you remove one of the pictures. Have the youngsters remove their hands. Then help a child identify which picture is missing, leading him to say both the name of the picture and its color. After students are comfortable with this activity, have them sort the cards into piles by color and then resort them by type of transportation!

Mind Readers

Identifying objects by several attributes

Little ones test their mind-reading capabilities with this giggle-inducing idea! Display five toy automobiles with different attributes. With great drama, tell the students that you are thinking about a car that has four wheels, and they need to read your mind to guess which one it is. Guide youngsters to realize that you gave a very poor clue because *all* of the automobiles have four wheels. Improve your clue by adding a second attribute to your description, such as "The car has four wheels and a green stripe." When youngsters correctly identify the car, play another round of the game!

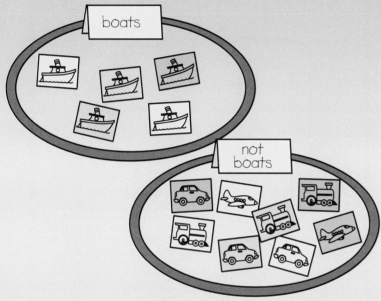

It Is or It Isn't

Sorting

Make several copies of the cards on page 228 in a variety of different colors. Cut out the cards and place them in a gift bag. Place two circles of yarn (or toy hoops) on the floor. Then label the circles as shown. After a child removes a card from the bag and identifies the picture, help him place the card in the appropriate circle. Continue in the same way with each remaining child. Repeat this activity several times, relabeling the circles with different categories, such as red/not red or planes/not planes.

A Spectacular Air Show!

Sorting, regrouping by different attributes

Divide a length of blue bulletin board paper in half and then post the paper on a wall with the labels shown. Make several copies of the plane pattern on page 229, using two different colors of construction paper and reducing the size of some of the patterns. Have each child choose a plane, cut it out, and personalize it (with help, as needed). Next, help each youngster attach his plane to the appropriate half of the paper. Repeat this activity two more times, having students re-sort the planes by different attributes, such as by color or size. These talented pilots can fly in any formation!

Transportation Cards

Use with "At the Car Wash" and "What's Missing?" on page 226 and "It Is or It Isn't" on page 227.

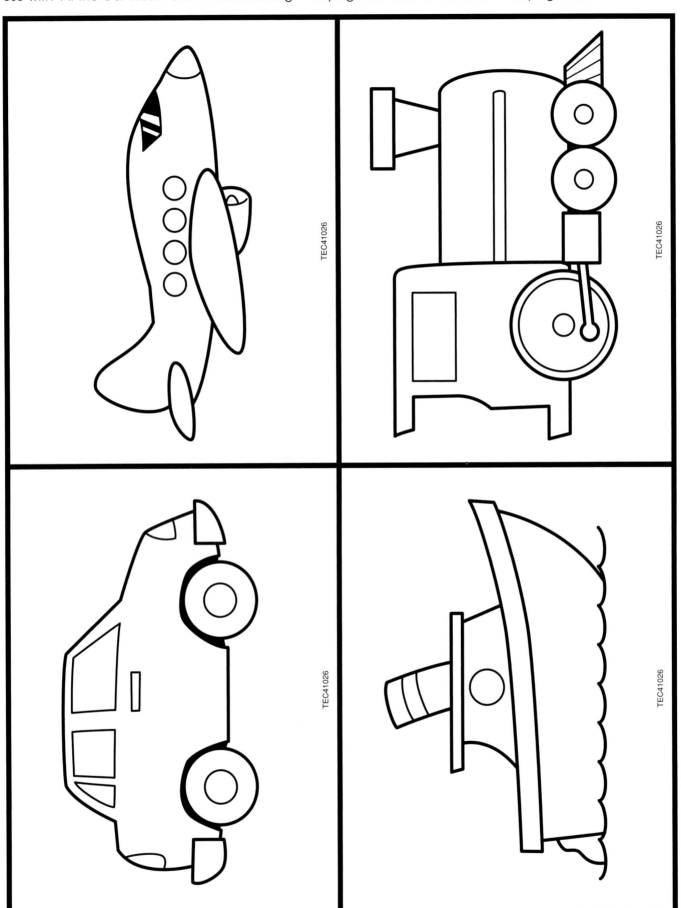

TEC41026

TEC41026

TEC41026

TEC41026

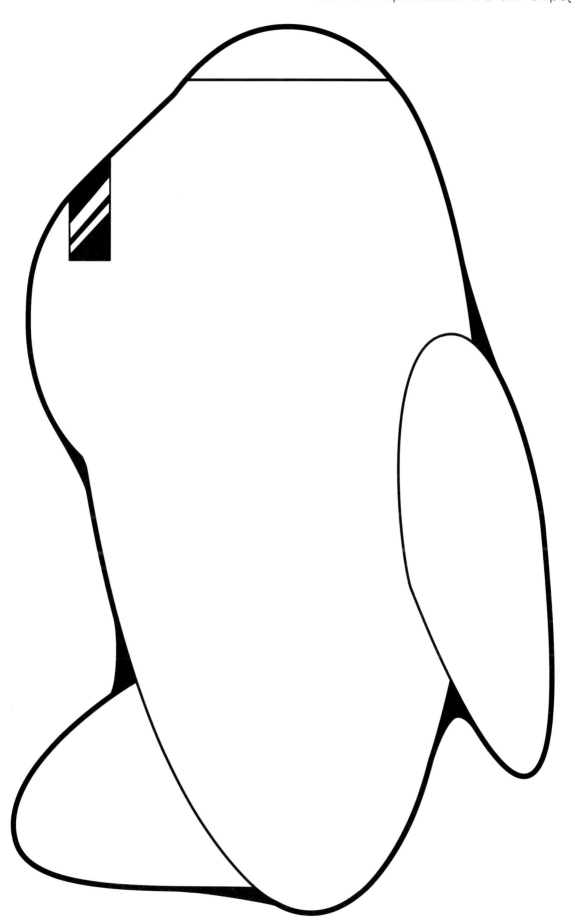

Big, Tall, Long, and Small

Little ones practice comparing and ordering by size with a unit frosted with learning fun. Now that sounds pretty sweet!

ideas contributed by Rebecca Perruquet, Here We Grow Preschool, Danville, PA

Whose House?

Comparing two items: small, large

Here's an idea that will help youngsters compare large and small items! In advance, trim a large and a small house shape from bulletin board paper; then decorate the houses and post them in your room. Place large and small gingerbread man cutouts (patterns on page 232) in separate containers. Then place the containers at a table along with a variety of crayons, colored pencils, and markers. Youngsters visit the table, choose a small and a large gingerbread man, and decorate them as desired. Then she compares the size of her gingerbread men to the houses and attaches them appropriately. If desired, she can choose two new gingerbread men and repeat the process!

long

longer

longest

Candy Cane Factory

Comparing three items: long, longer, longest

Youngsters make candy canes in a variety of sizes at this candy cane factory! In advance, draw three candy canes in different sizes on a sheet of poster board; then label the candy canes as shown. Laminate the poster board for durability and attach it to a table. Place red and white play dough at the center. (If desired, add peppermint oil to the dough for a lovely scent.) To begin, teach youngsters how to roll out white and red play dough and then twist them together to make a candy cane. Point out to students that this factory makes three different sizes of candy canes: long, longer, and longest. Then have students visit the center and make candy canes, placing them on the poster to create the appropriate sizes.

Bunches of Baking Supplies
Stacking objects from largest to smallest

To prepare, gather a variety of nesting kitchen supplies, such as measuring cups, mixing bowls, and measuring spoons. Place all the items in a box, making sure that they are no longer nesting. Challenge youngsters to remove the items from the box and stack them in the correct order with the largest on the bottom and the smallest on the top. As youngsters get proficient at this activity, put a sand timer nearby and challenge them to arrange the items correctly and beat the timer!

A Sweet Surprise
Placing three objects in order by size

This little take-home booklet will delight parents and children alike! Make a simple construction paper pocket booklet for each child; then trim the top to resemble a gingerbread house as shown. Have each child glue a copy of the poem on page 233 to the booklet cover. Have her decorate the cover as well as a set of small, medium, and large gingerbread man cutouts (patterns on page 232). After each child demonstrates how to put the cutouts in order from smallest to largest, have her tuck them in her booklet. Instruct youngsters to take their special projects home to show their families how they can place objects in order.

Home, Sweet Home
Placing four objects in order by size

In advance, make four brown construction paper copies of the gingerbread house on page 233 in different sizes; then cut out the houses. Gather youngsters around the cutouts. Invite a child to find the smallest house, and help him tape the house to your board. Continue in the same way, having students place the houses on the board in a row from smallest to largest. Next, ask students what is missing from the gingerbread houses, leading them to recognize that the houses are not decorated! Have students attach sticky dots, paper squares, and other craft items to the houses to represent candies.

Gingerbread Man Patterns
Use with "Whose House?" on page 230 and "A Sweet Surprise" on page 231.

TEC41028

TEC41028

TEC41028

Poem Card
Use with "A Sweet Surprise" on page 231.

Inside this little booklet

You will find three sweet surprises.

You will see quite clearly

That they come in different sizes.

I will take them out;

Then please watch and I will show

All three placed in order

Laid out nicely in a row.

Gingerbread House Pattern
Use with "Home, Sweet Home" on page 231.

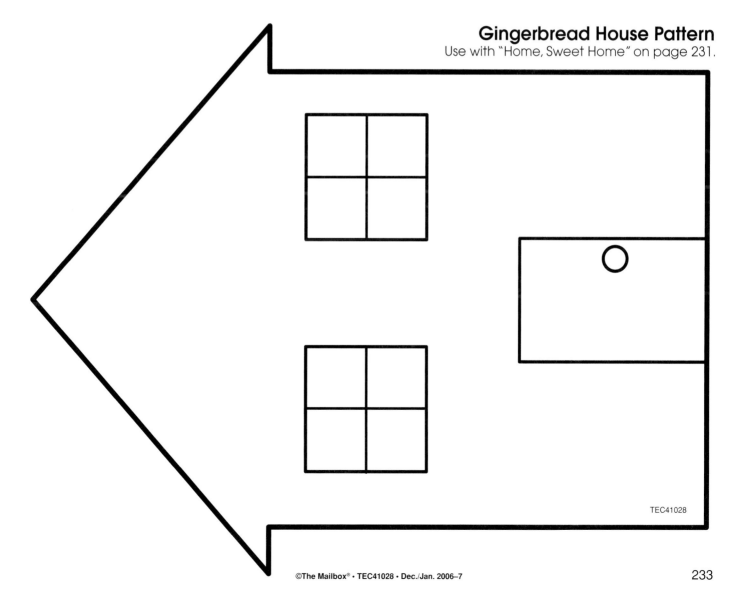

TEC41028

What's for Breakfast? Plenty of Patterning!

Treat your little ones to patterning practice with this buffet of breakfast-themed ideas. What a fun way to recognize the most important meal of the day!

ideas contributed by Lucia Kemp Henry, Fallon, NV

Sounds Like Breakfast!

Making a pattern with sounds

Rattle! Whap! Rattle! Whap! These appetizing sound patterns are sure to remind youngsters of their morning meals! In advance, collect the following items: an empty cereal box, a frying pan, a spatula, a metal bowl, and a whisk. Place a few small manipulatives in the cereal box and then tape the box closed. To begin, give the cereal box to one child and the pan and spatula to another child. Encourage the youngsters to make a simple *AB* pattern by alternately shaking the box and slapping the pan with the spatula. Continue in the same way, having other youngsters use the objects to make *AAB* and *ABB* patterns. When students are comfortable with this activity, add the bowl and whisk. Then students can swirl the whisk in the bowl to make patterns that involve three sounds!

An "Egg-cellent" Booklet!

Making simple and complex patterns

To begin, gather a small group of youngsters at a table and give each child a copy of pages 236 and 237. Guide her through the steps below to complete booklet pages 1–4. Then have her color the cover and final page as desired. Cut out each youngster's cover and booklet pages. (Use a paper cutter to make this a swift and simple job.) Then staple them together to complete the booklet.

Steps:

Page 1: Use a brown crayon to make an *AB* pattern with white and brown eggs.

Page 2: Use a brown crayon to make an *ABB* pattern with white and brown eggs.

Page 3: Use crayons in three different colors to make an *ABC* pattern.

Page 4: Color the eggs and then read the pattern.

234

Big Breakfast Burrito

Extending a pattern

In advance, color several copies of the filling cards on page 238; then cut out the cards. Fold a jumbo tortilla cutout to resemble a burrito as shown. Gather a small group of youngsters and unfold the burrito. Tell students that you need help filling this tasty breakfast burrito; then place only a few cards in the burrito, making a simple pattern. Have youngsters extend the pattern until the burrito is completely filled with tasty toppings. Encourage a child to refold the burrito over the toppings. Then lead students in reciting the chant shown with great enthusiasm, altering the words to reflect the fillings. Continue in the same way, removing the items from the burrito and replacing them with new items to make different patterns.

It's a big, big burrito! It's a breakfast treat Filled with [bacon] and [eggs] for us to eat. Mmmm!

Spilt Milk

Making a pattern with colors

Make an equal number of chocolate and white milk spill cutouts. Attach the cutouts in a row to your floor to make a simple pattern. To begin, ask youngsters whether they have ever accidentally spilled a glass of milk. After they share their experiences, explain that you have "spilled" several glasses of milk on the floor! Invite each child to touch the cutouts as she reads the pattern. Finally, invite students to help you clean up the milk by removing the cutouts from the floor.

Wonderful Waffles

Making a pattern with colors

Have each student place a piece of latch hook canvas over a sheet of newspaper. Instruct each child to dab brown paint on the surface of the canvas with a sponge. Then have her place a light brown construction paper circle over the painted canvas. After she smoothes the surface of the circle with her fingers, have her remove it to reveal her waffle. Next, have her glue a construction paper butter square to her waffle and drizzle her choice of red paint (strawberry syrup) or blue paint (blueberry syrup). When the projects are dry, have little ones help you display them on a wall in a simple pattern. If desired, add to the display a toaster cutout (see page 239) and the title shown.

Patterns Are Popping Up All Over!

Excellent Egg Patterns

by _____

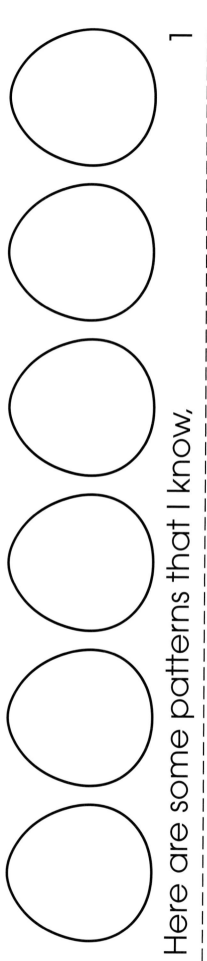

Here are some patterns that I know.

1

With little eggs all in a row.

2

Note to the teacher: Use with "An 'Egg-cellent' Booklet!" on page 234.

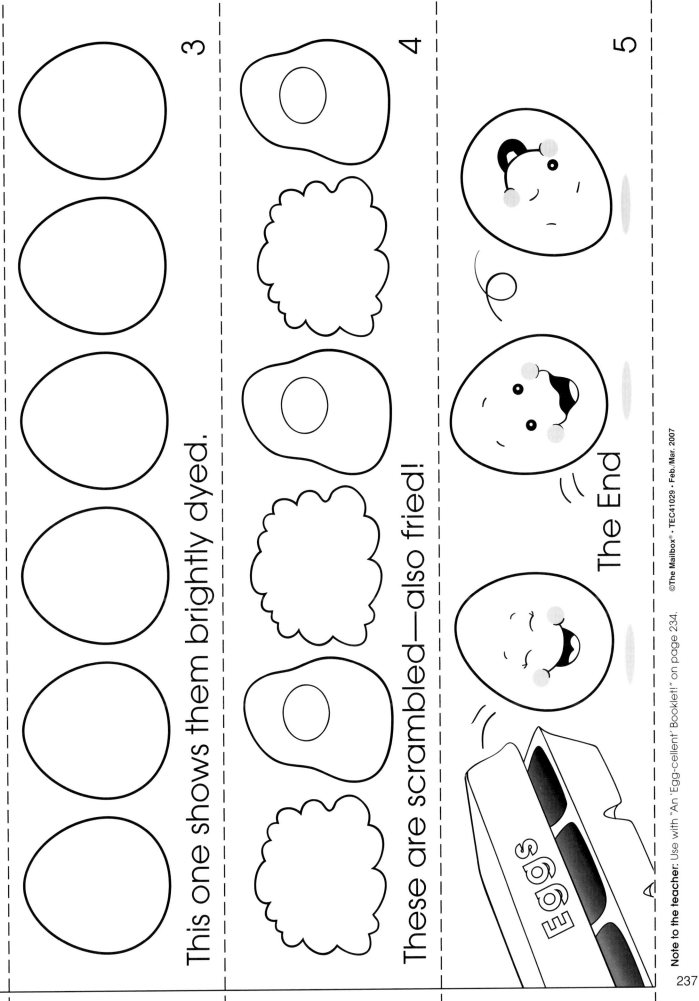

3

This one shows them brightly dyed.

4

These are scrambled—also fried!

5

The End

Eggs

©The Mailbox® • TEC41029 • Feb./Mar. 2007

Note to the teacher: Use with "An 'Egg-cellent' Booklet!" on page 234.

237

bacon

TEC41029

egg

TEC41029

cheese

TEC41029

peppers

TEC41029

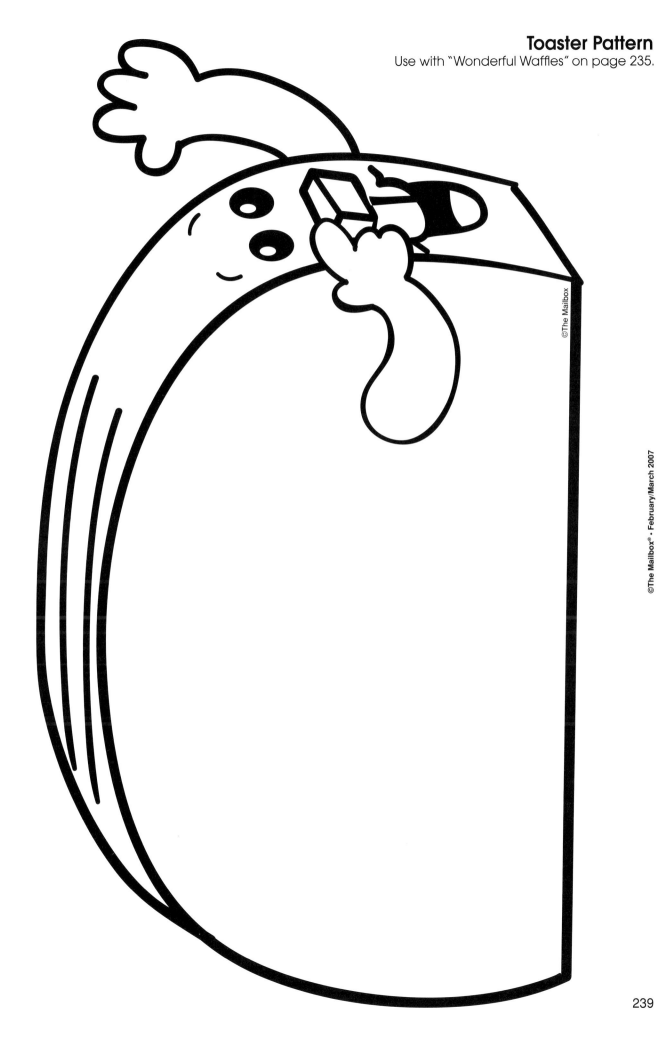

©The Mailbox® • February/March 2007

Counting at the Construction Site

Your little workers build counting skills with this construction–themed selection of learning opportunities!

ideas contributed by Ada Goren, Winston-Salem, NC

Construction Vehicles

Understanding the concept of zero

Little ones add vehicles to a construction site with this engaging activity! Make a copy of a construction vehicle card for each child (cards on page 243), omitting the bulldozer. Draw hills and a counting key on a large sheet of paper as shown. Then display the paper at students' eye level. Introduce the name of each vehicle. Then give each youngster his card and have him tape it to the site. When all the cards are attached, have students help you count each kind of vehicle and then write the corresponding number in each appropriate space in the key. Lead them to understand that there are no bulldozers at this construction site and that the number used to show this is zero. If desired, place vehicle cards and construction paper at a center and encourage youngsters to make their own construction sites.

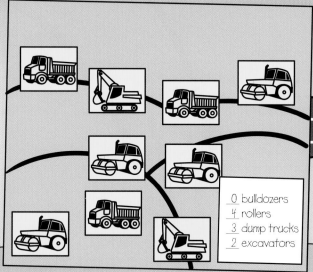

0 bulldozers
4 rollers
3 dump trucks
2 excavators

What a Mess!

Comparing sets

Students help organize this messy toolbox so that all the tools are easy to find! In advance, color and cut out several tagboard copies of the tools on page 244. Place the tools in a real toolbox in a haphazard manner, making sure that each tool is represented a different number of times. Open up the toolbox; then describe with great dramatic flair how messy the toolbox is. Have little ones help you remove the tools from the toolbox and sort them into groups. Then lead students in counting each group and comparing the results, using words such as *more* and *less*. Finally, have students help you place the tools back in the toolbox in a more organized fashion.

Preschoolers at Work

A Hat for Every Worker

One-to-one correspondence

Make a hard hat pattern for each youngster. Have each child draw on a construction paper circle a face that resembles his. Attach the faces to a bulletin board decorated with a construction theme as shown. Then lead students to conclude that construction workers must wear hard hats to be safe at a construction site. Have each child color and cut out his hard hat. Then lead students in counting the number of faces on the board and counting the number of hats. Finally, encourage youngsters to help you attach one hat to each construction worker. Safety first!

Four Big Machines

Developing presubtraction skills

Youngsters are sure to ask for this circle-time chant again and again! Color and cut out a copy of the construction vehicles cards on page 243; then place the cards on the floor. Lead students in reciting the rhyme provided, encouraging a different youngster to remove each vehicle from the group when appropriate.

[Four] big machines at the construction site
Worked, worked, worked with all [their] might!
The foreman called the [dump truck] away.
Then [three] big machines were left that day.

Additional verses: *bulldozer, roller, excavator*

Tool Tray

Naming "how many" concrete objects

Gather several tools (or make tool cutouts from a copy of the patterns on page 244). Have students name the tools. Then have youngsters close their eyes as you place two of the tools on a tray and cover them with a piece of fabric (or paper). Prompt children to open their eyes and join you in reciting the rhyme shown. Then quickly remove the fabric and prompt students to shout out the number of tools on the tray without pausing to count. After youngsters arrive at the correct number, have them name each tool. That's a hammer and a wrench!

Tools are useful, as useful as can be!
Please tell me quickly—how many do you see?

Excavation Station

Counting in proper sequence to five

Youngsters are sure to ask for second helpings of this activity! In advance, cook ground beef with mild taco seasoning. Before the activity, warm the ground beef. Show youngsters a copy of the excavator card on page 243 and explain that the excavator uses its bucket to dig holes in the ground. Give each child a bucket (corn chip scoop) and a bowl. Have him pretend he is an excavator, using his bucket to scoop up five loads of dirt (ground beef) and dumping each one in his bowl. Observe carefully as the child counts to five, making sure he counts in the proper sequence. Then give the little one a few extra buckets to use as he nibbles on his tasty snack.

Happy Hammering

Counting in proper sequence to ten

Place a slab of play dough on a table and put a toy hammer and ten golf tees nearby. Gather youngsters around the table and demonstrate how to line up all the golf tees in the play dough by pushing them in just far enough so that they stay in place. Next, give a child a hammer and encourage him to hammer the golf tees from left to right as you lead the students in counting to ten. Show students how to remove the tees and smooth out the dough. Then allow youngsters to visit the area during center time to repeat the activity independently.

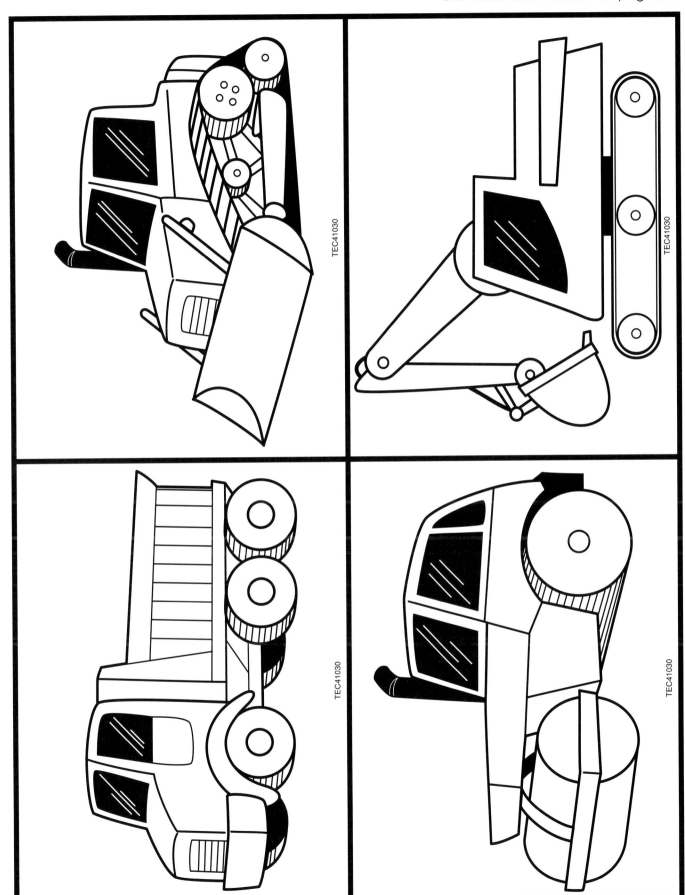

TEC41030

TEC41030

TEC41030

TEC41030

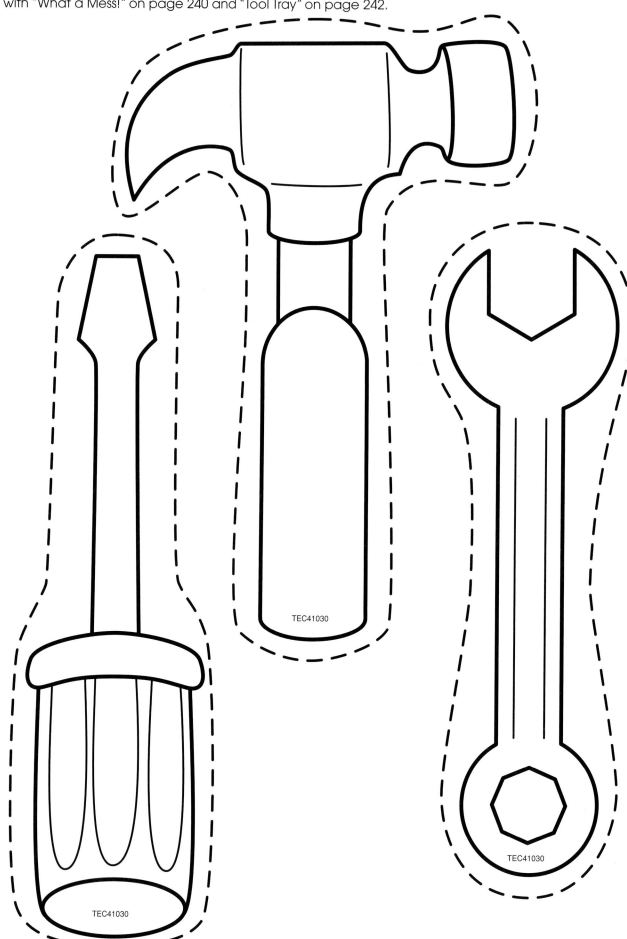

TEC41030

TEC41030

TEC41030

Let's Estimate!

Your little ones will be antsy to begin estimation practice with these picnic-themed activities, which are just perfect for preschoolers!

ideas contributed by Suzanne Moore, Tucson, AZ

Picnic Problems

How many preschoolers can sit on an unusually small picnic blanket? No doubt your little ones will be eager to take a guess! Tell students you are packing items for a picnic but are worried about how many people will fit on the blanket. Spread out a small blanket on the floor, and ask youngsters to estimate how many students can fit on the blanket. (You may wish to explain that an estimate is a good guess and that it's all right not to know the exact number). Write each student's estimate on the board. After each child makes a guess, invite students to sit on the blanket, adding one student at a time. When no more youngsters will fit, enlist students' help in counting the number of children. Then help youngsters compare the number of students on the blanket to their estimates.

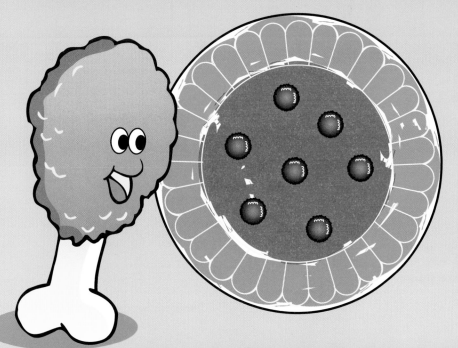

So Many Seeds

Gather a supply of small black pom-poms and place them in a container. Have each student paint or color a paper plate, as shown, so the plate resembles a watermelon. Next, have each student estimate how many pom-poms he can pick up with one hand. After he shares his guess, have him pick up a handful of pom-poms, count them, and then compare them to his estimate. Finally, have him glue his pom-poms to his watermelon craft so they resemble seeds.

Marvelous Macaroni Salad

Youngsters estimate how many pieces of macaroni to put in this picnic-perfect salad! Place a supply of macaroni in a container. Provide access to a spoon and a supply of napkins. Gather a small group of youngsters and give each child a copy of page 247. Have each child scoop a spoonful of macaroni from the bowl and then dump it on a napkin. Have her estimate how many pieces of pasta are on her napkin; then help her write the number on her paper in the appropriate box. Encourage her to spread glue on the bowl on her paper; then help her count the pieces of pasta as she places them on the glue. Finally, have her write in the remaining box on her paper the actual number of pasta pieces. There are 17 pieces of macaroni in my salad!

Marvelous Macaroni Salad!

My guess: 10

I counted: 17

Ants!

To make an oversize picnic basket, place strips of masking tape on a length of brown bulletin board paper so they resemble basket weave. Have youngsters rub unwrapped brown crayons over the masking tape. Then trim the paper to make a picnic basket. Next, make several copies of the ant cards on page 248, cut them out, and place them along with glue near the picnic basket. Encourage each child to glue a few cards to the basket. After displaying the basket on a wall, ask youngsters to estimate how many ants are on the basket. Write students' estimates on sticky notes and attach them near the display. Next, help students count the actual number of ants; then encourage them to compare that number with their estimates. Finally, add student-made food cutouts to enhance the display.

Cooler Estimation

It sure is nice to have ice-cold drinks at a picnic! Place ice in a cooler. Then show students several large bottles of lemonade (or water). After youngsters confirm through touch that the beverages are warm, place the bottles in the cooler. Have students estimate when the drinks will be cold by relating the time to their daily schedule. For example, will the beverages be cold by snacktime, by lunch, or directly after naptime? Record students' predictions on chart paper. Then have students check the bottles throughout the day. When youngsters agree that the beverages are very cold, give each child a cup of refreshing lemonade to drink while you revisit their guesses.

The drinks will be cold

by center time   Josh

before music   Deena

after snack   Samuel

when we play   Emma

after music   D'Quan

Marvelous Macaroni Salad!

My guess

I counted

Note to the teacher: Use with "Marvelous Macaroni Salad" on page 246.

247

Ant Cards

Use with "Ants!" on page 246.

TEC41031

TEC41031

TEC41031

TEC41031

TEC41031

TEC41031

TEC41031

TEC41031

TEC41031

THEMATIC UNITS

Blast Off

to Preschool!

Welcome your newest preschool stars with ideas and activities that are sure to help your year begin smoothly. Now that's out of this world!

A Rocket Ship Welcome
Home-school connection

How will youngsters recognize your smiling face on the first day of school? Why, they'll have received these spiffy welcome cards in the mail, of course! Make a copy of the rocket ship on page 253; then add a message, similar to the one shown, to the ship. Next, trim a photograph of yourself and attach it to the ship. After making a colorful copy of the resulting card for each child, cut out the cards and personalize each message. Then fold each card and tuck it into an envelope labeled with the corresponding address. Before sealing the envelopes, you may wish to sprinkle a small amount of metallic star confetti in each one!

Dear _Hannah_,
It's time to blast off for an exciting year of preschool! My name is Miss Murphy, and I'll be your teacher this year.
Our first day of school is August 28, 2006.

Nate

Mia

For nifty nametags and cubby tags, personalize copies of the star pattern on page 254 or the cow patterns on page 255.

Adorable Astronauts
Room decoration

These self-portraits are appealingly simple! Have each youngster paint a large paper plate gray. Then encourage her to draw her likeness on a skin-toned circle cutout that is slightly smaller than the size of the plate. Next, have her glue her self-portrait to the center of the plate to resemble a child wearing a space helmet. When the project is dry, personalize each astronaut. Then mount these cute crafts on a space-themed board with the title "One Giant Leap Into Preschool!"

Bonnie Martin
Hopewell Country Day School
Pennington, NJ

Who's Here?
Attendance display

To prepare this display, make a colorful class supply of rocket cutouts and flame cutouts (patterns on pages 253 and 254). Label each rocket with a different child's name. Then attach a photograph of each child to his rocket. Laminate the rockets and flames. After mounting the rockets to a wall at student eye level, place the hook end of a piece of Velcro fastener near the bottom of each rocket. Put each corresponding Velcro loop end on the back of a different flame. Then place the flames at a table. When a youngster arrives for the day, he takes a flame and attaches it to his rocket. He's ready to launch into learning!

Jack

Tory

Crunchy Craters
Snack

O-shaped cereal makes perfect moon craters for this easy snack! Give each student a gray circle cutout to represent the moon. If desired, show students a photograph of the moon and point out the craters; then lead students to notice that their moons do not have craters. Next, give each child a cup of O-shaped cereal. Encourage each child to place the cereal on his moon to resemble craters. Then invite him to nibble on the cereal!

J. Lalonde, Gainesville, FL

Rocks in a Box
Storytime

Youngsters make space rocks after a read-aloud of this popular story. Have students settle in for a reading of *Zoom! Zoom! Zoom! I'm Off to the Moon!* by Dan Yaccarino. After the read-aloud, revisit the illustration that shows the astronaut carrying a box of moon rocks. Then invite small groups of youngsters to your art area to make their own moon rocks! Have each child crumple a piece of aluminum foil into a loose ball to resemble a rock. Instruct her to paint her rock with black paint and then roll it in a mixture of silver and gold glitter. When the rocks are dry, place them in a box. Then display them alongside a copy of the book.

Bethany Scully
Shining Star Preschool
Middletown, RI

Dan Yaccarino

Zoom! Zoom! Zoom! I'm Off to the Moon!

High-Flying Cows
Getting acquainted activity

Youngsters are sure to know each other's names in no time with this unique idea! Make a class supply of the cow patterns on page 255. Then transform each cow into a personalized stick puppet as shown. Mount a large moon cutout at student eye level and place the cows nearby. After you gather youngsters around the moon, give one child her cow puppet. Encourage the child to move her cow as if it's jumping over the moon as you lead students in reciting the rhyme shown above. Finally, help students identify the name of the cow's owner. Play several rounds of this fun activity.

Hey diddle dee, whose cow do we see
Jumping up over the moon?

Alexis

Stardust Dough
Center

Mix fine glitter with a supply of white or yellow play dough. Then place the dough at a table covered with laminated black bulletin board paper. Provide access to a variety of star-shaped cookie cutters. Then encourage youngsters to visit the center and decorate the night sky. Look at all the sparkling stars!

Shooting Star Helpers
Classroom job display

Make a class supply of star cutouts (see the pattern on page 254) and personalize each one. Then staple several lengths of colorful curling ribbon to each star. Label a length of black bulletin board paper with several decorated job title cards. Display the bulletin board paper and place the stars nearby. To assign jobs, mount a different star under each title. Then lead youngsters in singing the song shown.

(sung to the tune of "Twinkle, Twinkle, Little Star")

Twinkle, twinkle, little stars,
Look at who our helpers are.
We work hard throughout our day,
Helping others—that's our way.
When our day is at an end,
We know we have helped our friends.

Marlene Koontz, S.C.A.P. Head Start, Schenectady, NY

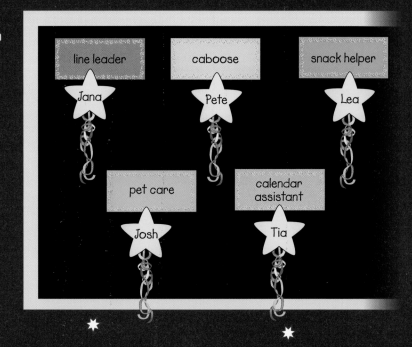

line leader
Jana

caboose
Pete

snack helper
Lea

pet care
Josh

calendar assistant
Tia

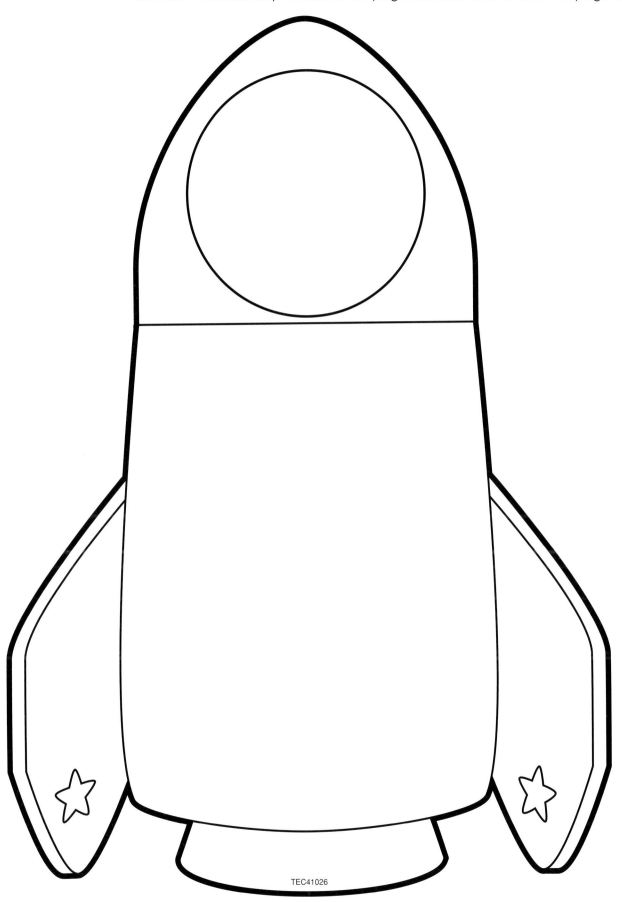

TEC41026

Flame Pattern
Use with "Who's Here?" on page 251.

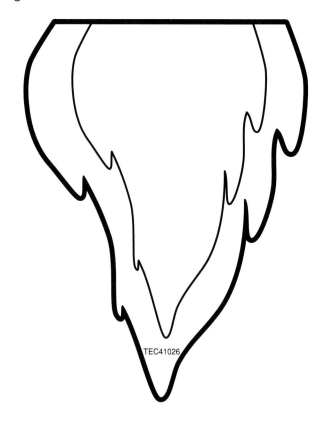

TEC41026

Star Pattern
Use with "Shooting Star Helpers" on page 252.

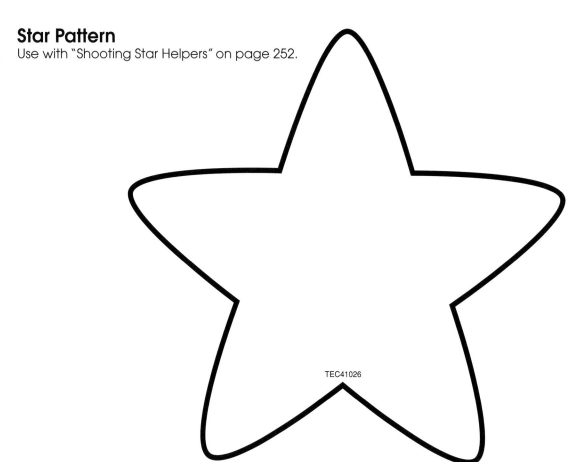

TEC41026

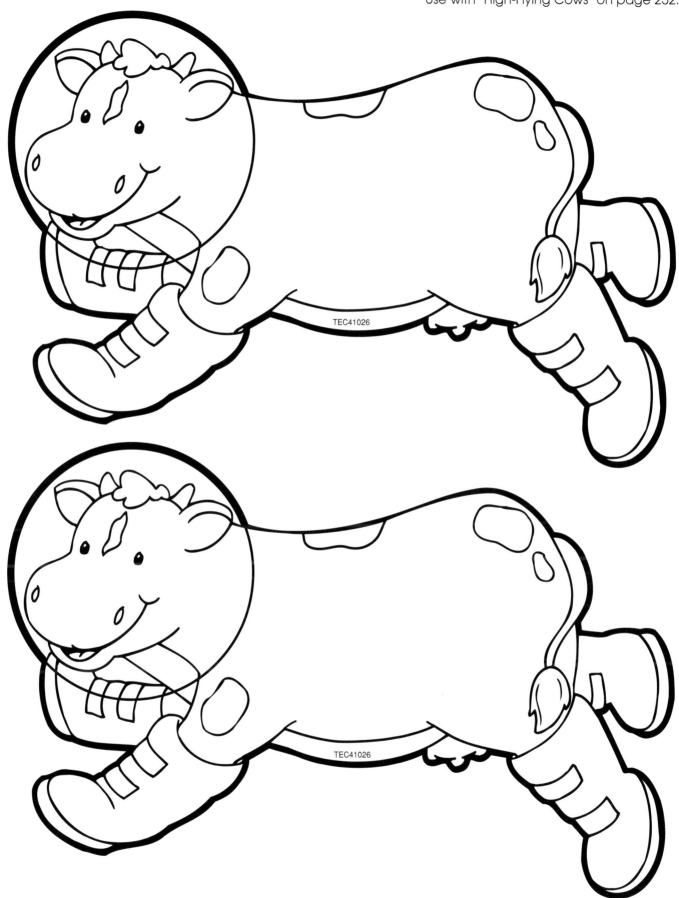

TEC41026

TEC41026

Signs of Fall

How will your youngsters know that fall is coming? Why, nature will show them, of course! Help little ones recognize signs of fall with a collection of colorful activities.

ideas contributed by Barb Stefaniuk, Kerrobert Tiny Tots Playschool
Kerrobert, Saskatchewan, Canada

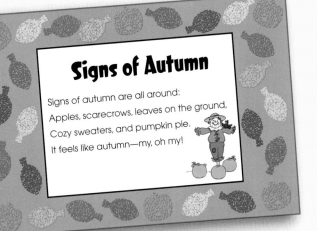

Signs of Autumn

Signs of autumn are all around:
Apples, scarecrows, leaves on the ground,
Cozy sweaters, and pumpkin pie.
It feels like autumn—my, oh my!

Feels Like Autumn!
Reciting a rhyme

Little ones decorate their very own fall poem to take home and share with their families. For each child, make a copy of the poem on the back of the centerfold. Lead students in reciting the poem several times; then have each youngster color his poem page as desired. Instruct him to glue his poem to a sheet of 12" x 18" construction paper. Then have him make prints around the poem with pumpkin- and leaf-shaped sponges. Lovely!

Sara Andrew
Clark Elementary School
Charlottesville, VA

Gather 'em Up!
Identifying characteristics of animals

Here's a circle-time activity that will have your little squirrels scurrying about. In advance, gather enough brown pom-poms (nuts) so that each child has four. Explain that squirrels can remember where nuts are hidden long after they've placed them there. Then have each student hide four nuts throughout the classroom. Later in the day, remind youngsters of the fact mentioned above; then have them search for the nuts. Could each child find all four? If so, your youngsters have something in common with this bushy-tailed critter!

Fall Brings...
Recognizing seasonal changes

To prepare, make a copy of the cover and booklet pages on pages 259–261. Read the text aloud; then invite the child to color pages 1–3. Next, guide each youngster through the directions below to complete each page. When the glue is dry, help each student cut out the pages and staple them behind the cover.

Booklet directions:

Page 1: Tape pieces of curling ribbon to the pumpkins to resemble vines.

Page 2: Spread glue over the grass and then sprinkle silver glitter over the glue to resemble frost.

Page 3: Press your finger on a red ink pad; then make prints on and below the tree to make foliage. Repeat the process with other fall colors.

Page 4: Use a crayon to trace the child's long-sleeved shirt. Draw hair on the youngster to resemble your own hair; then color the page as desired.

Cooperative Fall Colors
Mixing the color orange

Little ones will rake in the compliments on these colorful fall trees! Gather shallow pans of red and yellow tempera paint and place a separate bath puff in each one. Draw an outline of a tree trunk on a large sheet of newsprint for every two youngsters. Then place the papers and pans at your art center along with a supply of brown crayons. Have two students visit the center and work together to color the trunk brown. Then instruct each youngster to take a bath puff in hand and press it repeatedly on the paper to make foliage, overlapping prints to see the yellow and red paint make the color orange. Now that's teamwork!

...pumpkins round,

frost on the ground,

falling leaves,

and longer sleeves.

Fall Brings...
by Mathew

Bear Goes to Bed
Developing phonological awareness

To begin, explain that during the fall bears go to bed and then nap off and on throughout the long winter. Give each youngster a copy of page 262. Then tell them this bear has met some friends on the way to his bed, which is tucked in a cozy cave. Have the child say the words *bear* and *bed,* emphasizing the /b/ sound in both of the words. Next, give each child a bingo dauber and have him press it on each friend the bear meets on the way to its bed, saying each name as he goes along. Hey, those names begin with the /b/ sound as well!

The Fruits of Fall
Identifying characteristics of fall

Here's a quick snack to emphasize a favorite fall fruit. In advance, make a fruit dip by using a mixer to combine one 16 oz. package of cream cheese and one jar of marshmallow crème. Give each child several thin slices of apple and a small plate with a dollop of the fruit dip. Explain that apples are a fruit usually harvested in early fall. Then invite the youngster to tint her dollop of dip with yellow, red, or orange food coloring to give it some fall flair! Finally, invite her to nibble on her snack!

Happy Holidays!
Sorting

The holidays Halloween and Thanksgiving are sure clues that it's fall! Cut out copies of clip art pictures relating to a variety of different holidays, including several Halloween and Thanksgiving-themed pictures. Place two yarn circles on the floor and label one circle "Fall" and the second circle "Not Fall." Then gather youngsters around the circles and have them sort the pictures appropriately into the hoops. Try this activity for winter and spring as well!

Not Fall

Fall

Fall Brings...

by _____

Fall Brings...

by _____

Booklet Pages 1 and 2

Use with "Fall Brings..." on page 257.

...pumpkins round,

©The Mailbox® • TEC41027 • Oct./Nov. 2006

1

frost on the ground,

2

falling leaves,

3

and longer sleeves.

4

Note to the teacher: Use with "Bear Goes to Bed" on page 258.

Signs of Autumn

Signs of autumn are all around:

Apples, scarecrows, leaves on the ground,

Cozy sweaters, and pumpkin pie.

It feels like autumn—my, oh my!

Bunches of

Your little ones will go batty for activities featuring this fascinating and gentle nighttime creature!

A Cozy Cave
Building on prior knowledge

No doubt youngsters will be delighted with this crafty cave scene! In advance, cut out several tan construction paper copies of the bat pattern on page 267 and set them aside. Have each youngster press a piece of sponge into brown paint and then make prints on a 12" x 18" sheet of tan paper. If desired, have her sprinkle sand over the wet paint. When the paint is dry, trim the sheets to resemble stalactites and stalagmites; then attach them to a wall (or a length of bulletin board paper) to make a cave. Next, have students tell you what they know about bats as you write each child's words on a prepared bat cutout. Attach the cutouts to the cave. As students learn more about bats throughout your study, add more bats to the scene.

Bats can fly.
Joshua

Bats have wings.
Juan

Bats come out at night.
Jenniece

I saw a bat one time.
Kayla

Bats can live in caves.
Darion

Brown-Bat Basics
Investigating living things, following directions

To prepare, place white glue and small squares of brown felt (fur) at a table. Also provide access to a supply of crayons, including several black crayons without wrappers. Gather a small group of youngsters at the table and give each child a copy of page 268. Guide students through the directions below; then allow them to add any other desired details to the picture.

Directions:
1. This bat is a little brown bat. Color the bat brown.
2. The little brown bat is awake at nighttime. Color the moon and stars yellow. Use the edge of a black crayon to make a dark sky.
3. The little brown bat has a furry body. Glue a piece of fur (felt) to its body.
4. The little brown bat eats bugs. Draw flying bugs for it to eat.

Bat Ideas!

Chow Time!
Sorting

Youngsters may be surprised to find out that some bats eat bugs and others eat fruit! Cut out enough copies of the bug and fruit cards on page 269 so there is one for each child. Label a container "Bug-Eating Bats" and a second container "Fruit-Eating Bats." Then attach a corresponding card to each container. Scatter the remaining cards around the room. Gather youngsters around the containers and explain that some bats like to eat bugs and other bats like to eat fruit.

Next, dim the lights and have your little bats "fly" around the room hunting for food. When each child finds a card, have him bring it to the circle area and then sit down. When all your bats have landed, turn the lights back on and have the children sort the bugs and fruit into the corresponding containers.

adapted from an idea by Juli Engel
Santa Teresa, NM

Fruit-Eating Bats

Bug-Eating Bats

Mamas and Babies
Matching symbols

Make several brown construction paper copies of the mother and baby bat patterns on page 270. Label each mother and her baby with matching symbols. Place an extra large cardboard box in a center to resemble a cave; then glue the baby bats inside the cave. Place the hook side of a piece of Velcro fastener next to each baby bat. Attach the loop sides of the Velcro fasteners to the mother bats. Before youngsters visit the center, explain that each mother bat leaves the cave to hunt for food every night and then flies back and finds her baby. To complete the center, a youngster chooses a mother bat. Then he "flies" her into the cave and places her next to her baby by matching the symbols. He continues in the same way with each remaining mother bat.

Lisa Addington
Chadwicks, NY

Bat Mobile

Developing fine-motor skills

This adorable craft is sure to be a hit with your youngsters and classroom visitors! For each child, use a white crayon to trace a pair of simple bat shapes, as shown, on a sheet of black construction paper. Help each child cut out the bats. Have her put glue on only the center portions of the bats and then attach them to opposite sides of a yellow construction paper moon. After she adds hole-reinforcer eyes to each bat, have her bend both sets of wings forward to give the appearance of flying. Finally, suspend the finished projects in your classroom.

Janet Boyce
King's Kids
Hutchinson, MN

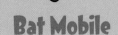

Five Little Bats

Reciting a song

Cut out five brown construction paper copies of the bat pattern on page 267. Ready each bat for flannelboard use; then place the bats on your flannelboard. Lead youngsters in performing the first verse of the song five times, removing a bat each time and substituting the appropriate numbers in each repetition. As you lead little ones in performing the final verse, place all of the bats back on the flannelboard when indicated.

(sung to the tune of "Five Little Ducks")

[Five] little bats went out for a flight	*Link thumbs and flap fingers.*
On a crisp and clear fall night.	*Hold arms in a circle (moon).*
Mother Bat called, "Please come right back!"	*Cup hands around mouth.*
But only [four] little bats flew back.*	*Link thumbs and flap fingers.*

*For the fifth repetition, alter the final line to "But none of the little bats flew right back."

Final verse:

Mother bat went out for a flight	*Link thumbs and flap fingers.*
To look for her five little bats that night.	*Hold edge of hand to forehead.*
When Mother Bat saw them, she said, "Boo!"	*Cup both hands around mouth.*
And right back home all five bats flew!	*Link thumbs and flap fingers.*

Janet Boyce

TEC41027

268

©The Mailbox® • TEC41027 • Oct./Nov. 2006

Note to the teacher: Use with "Brown-Bat Basics" on page 264.

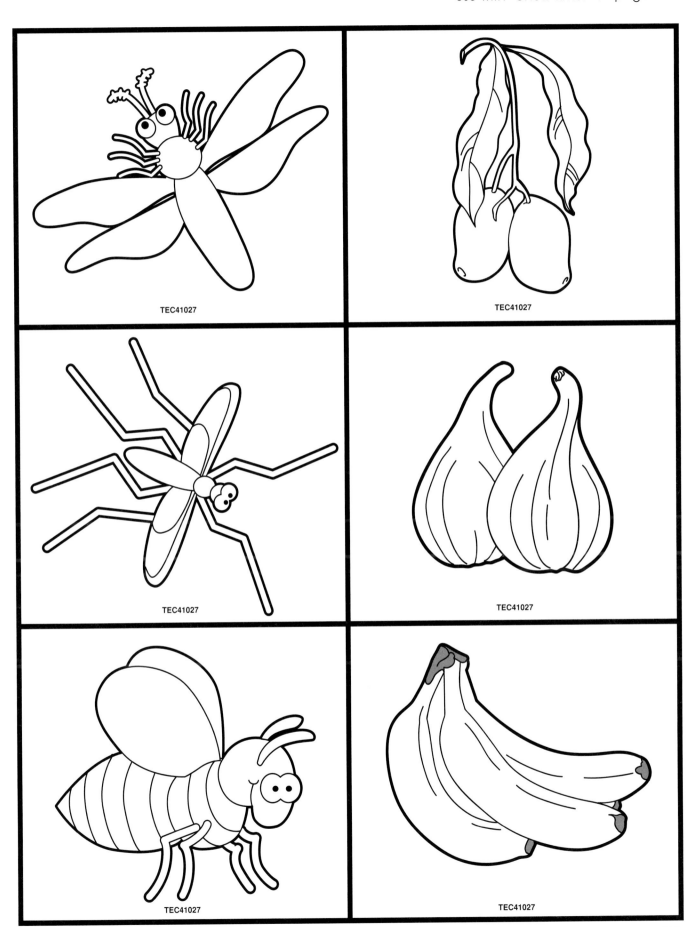

TEC41027

TEC41027

TEC41027

TEC41027

TEC41027

TEC41027

Mother and Baby Bat Patterns
Use with "Mamas and Babies" on page 265.

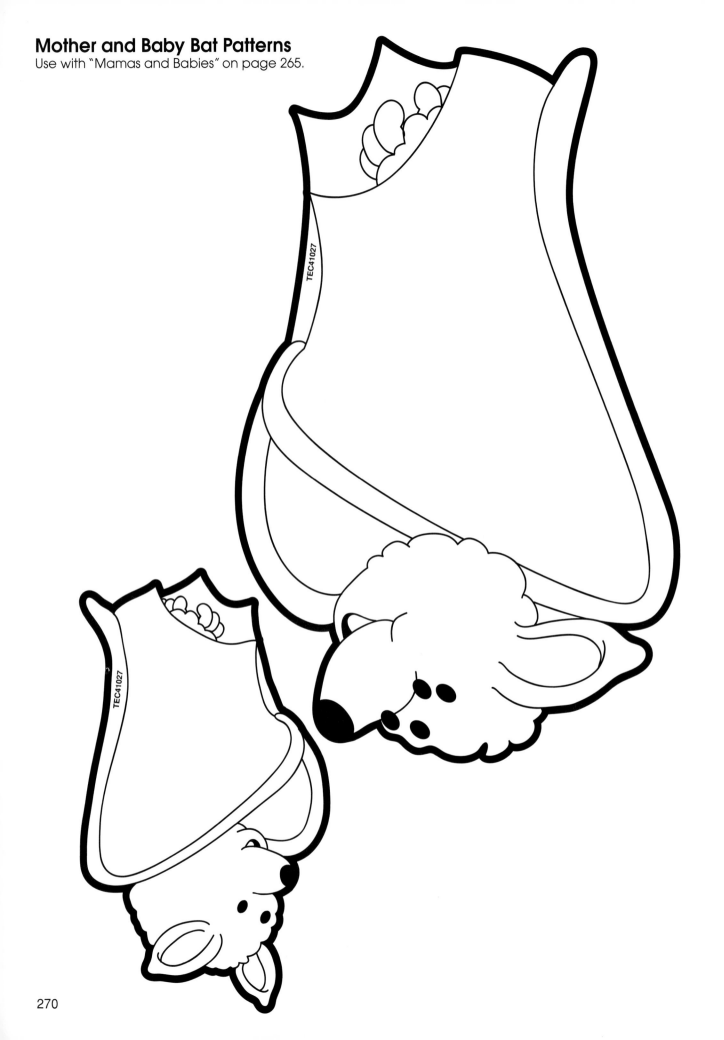

TEC41027

TEC41027

All About ME

Delight little ones with ideas that help them express information about themselves. No doubt you'll be delighted as well as you learn all about your students!

Mirror, Mirror

Developing awareness of similarities and differences
Youngsters focus on faces with this pleasing chant! Give students opportunities to view themselves in a mirror. Then lead them in saying the chant below. After several repetitions of the chant, guide students to notice that faces have the same number of features, yet the features look different. For example, you might say, "Both Ava and Lee have two eyes, but Ava's two eyes are blue and Lee's two eyes are brown."

When I look in a mirror I see my face,
And all of my parts are in their place.
I have one mouth, two ears, two eyes,
And one nose in the middle—just the perfect size!

Home, Sweet Home

Identifying one's address
Little ones practice identifying their addresses with the help of these three-dimensional projects. Have each child color a paper bag. Invite him to add details to paper door and window cutouts and then glue them to the bag. When the glue is dry, encourage him to stuff his bag with newspaper strips and fold down the top. Next, staple to the project a construction paper roof labeled with the child's name and address. Then display the resulting homes. Whenever you have a few minutes, help a child locate his home and say his address.

Matt
230A North Drive
Midland, MI

271

Bigger Each Day!
Sequencing

Spotlight students' growth with this sequencing activity! In advance, color and cut out a copy of the sequencing cards on page 274. Lead youngsters in performing the action chant shown. Then help them sequence the cards to show how they really have gotten bigger throughout their lives!

I can look at a book and put on my socks.	*Pantomime actions.*
I'm getting bigger each day!	*Stay seated on floor.*
I can brush my teeth and pick up my toys.	*Pantomime actions.*
I'm getting bigger each day!	*Move to a kneeling position.*
I can brush my hair and wash my face.	*Pantomime actions.*
I'm getting bigger each day!	*Jump to a standing position.*

My Favorites!
Please help your child place the following items in this special bucket; then send the bucket back to school with your youngster.
1. Two favorite photographs, one of which shows your family
2. A favorite snack to share with the class (We currently have 16 students.)
3. A favorite book

The photos and book will be returned to you after our sharing time.
Thank you!

My Favorites
Speaking to describe

Use clear Con-Tact covering to attach a note similar to the one shown to a large, clean ice-cream bucket (or other container). Then send the bucket home with a youngster. When the child returns the bucket with the requested items, set aside a special time for the student to explain the photographs and share her snack. Then read aloud the youngsters' favorite book. What a delightful sharing time!

Happy and Sad
Speaking to discuss emotions

To prepare for this whole-group activity, use a permanent marker to draw eyes and a nose on a large felt circle. Place the resulting face on your flannelboard. Put a length of red yarn near the board. To begin, invite a child to tell about a time when she was happy. When the youngster finishes sharing, invite her to place the yarn on the face to show how her mouth looks when she's happy. Next, ask a different child to share a time when she was sad and then invite her to manipulate the yarn appropriately. Continue in the same way for several rounds.

Stand Up Song

Expressing knowledge about self

This active song helps youngsters develop listening skills! Gather students in your large-group area. Then sing the song shown, encouraging youngsters who have sisters to stand up. When the song is finished, enlist students' help in counting the number of youngsters who have sisters. Then have the students sit down. Sing several rounds of the song, substituting the underlined portions of the song with one of the suggestions provided.

(sung to the tune of "Skip to My Lou")

If you [have a sister], please stand up.
If you [have a sister], please stand up.
If you [have a sister], please stand up.
We want to know all about you!

Song suggestions: *have a brother, like spaghetti, have a pet, like play dough, eat bananas, are in preschool*

Pocket Booklet

Following directions

To make a booklet for each child, fold up the bottom two inches on each of two 9" x 12" sheets of construction paper; then staple each resulting flap to make a pocket. Fold each prepared paper in half and glue the resulting pages together to make a four-page booklet. Next, help each child cut out the strips on a copy of page 275. Encourage her to glue the strips, in order, to the pockets. Title the book as shown. Then guide students through the directions below to fill pages 1–3. Finally, tuck a photograph of the child in the final pocket.

Page 1: Use paint to make a handprint on construction paper. When the paint is dry, cut out the print.
Page 2: Draw a picture of your family.
Page 3: Color a cake cutout (pattern on page 275). Glue paper strips (candles) to the cake to represent your age. *Write the child's birthdate on the cake.*

Ideas contributed by Janet Boyce, King's Kids, Hutchinson, MN; Jo Ellen Brown, Hawthorne Child Development Center, Albuquerque, NM; Cynthia Holcomb, ESC Region XV, San Angelo, TX; Angela Lenker, Montgomery Early Learning Center/Head Start, Pottstown, PA; Barb Stefaniuk, Kerrobert Tiny Tots Playschool, Kerrobert, Saskatchewan, Canada; Kara Taylor, William Paca Old Post Road Elementary, Abingdon, MD; Jan Trautman, Samaritan's Purse, Lira, Uganda

Sequencing Cards

Use with "Bigger Each Day!" on page 272.

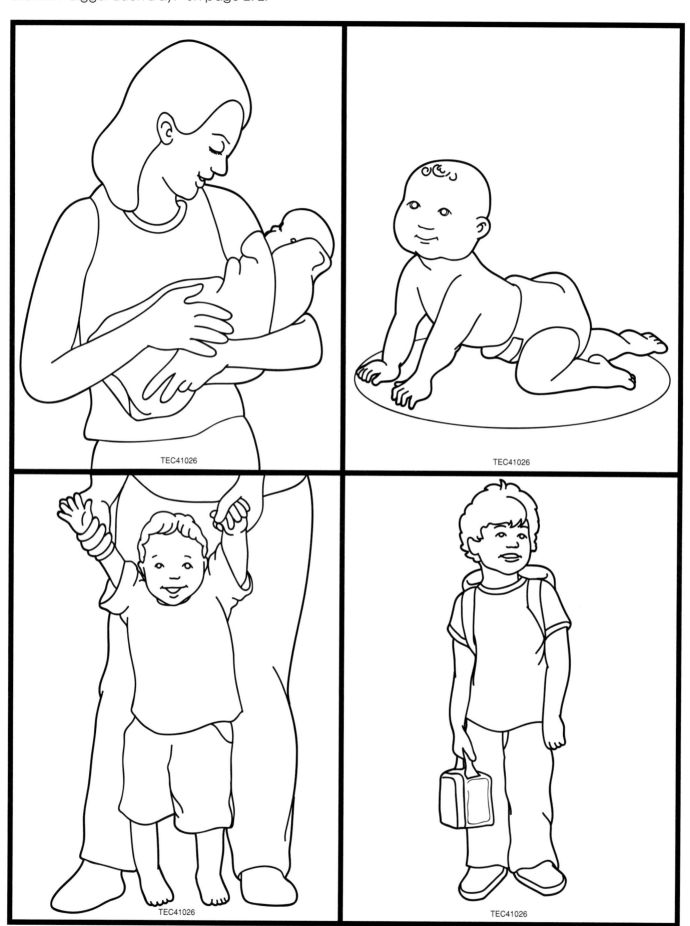

TEC41026

TEC41026

TEC41026

TEC41026

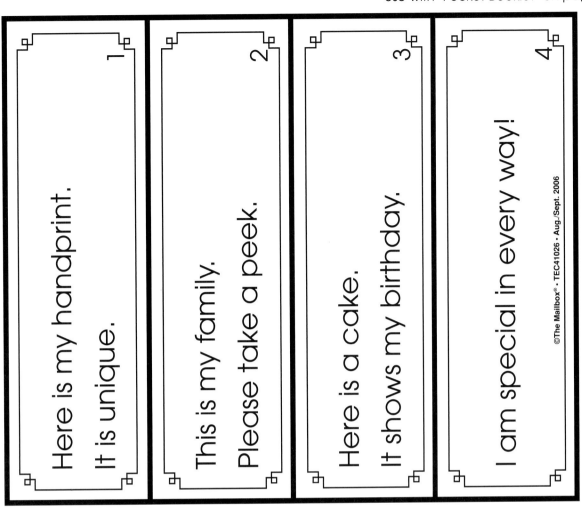

1

Here is my handprint.
It is unique.

2

This is my family.
Please take a peek.

3

Here is a cake.
It shows my birthday.

4

I am special in every way!

©The Mailbox® • TEC41026 • Aug./Sept. 2006

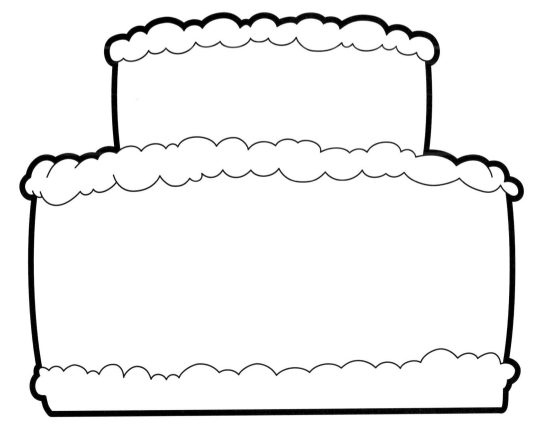

Friends Are

Focus on friends with this adorable selection of learning opportunities just perfect for your little ones!

ideas contributed by Suzanne Moore, Tucson, AZ

What Is a Friend?
Reciting a rhyme
Youngsters name characteristics of school friends with this adorable rhyme! Lead students in reciting the rhyme, encouraging them to pat their legs to the beat.

Friends at school can play and share.
Friends at school are kind and fair.
Friends at school will talk to you
When you're feeling sad and blue.
Friends at school are big and small.
Friends at school are best of all!

Cynthia Holcomb
Education Service Center XV
San Angelo, TX

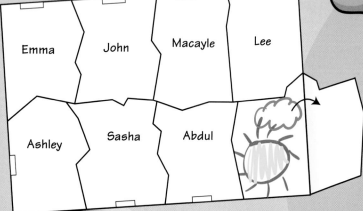

Puzzle Pictures
Working cooperatively to create artwork
Friends work together to make this splendid masterpiece! In advance, puzzle-cut a large sheet of white poster board to make a puzzle piece for each child. Tape the pieces to an identical sheet of poster board so that the pieces can be lifted like flaps as shown. Then label each piece with a different child's name. Place the poster board at a table along with crayons. Invite two youngsters to the table and encourage each child to find her name and then lift up the puzzle piece. Have her color the area under her puzzle piece as desired and then replace the flap. Continue in the same way until each child has had the opportunity to add to the artwork. Finally, gather youngsters around the project and gently remove each flap to reveal the finished artwork, pointing out that working with friends to finish a project is fun!

Fabulous

A Friendship Booklet
Developing an awareness of friendly behavior

Give each child copies of pages 279 and 280. Encourage him to color the pages as desired. Then help him cut out the pages and place glue on the tab. Assist the youngster in attaching the pages to make a booklet. Accordion-fold his booklet. Then instruct him to glue a preprogrammed front cover and a back cover to the booklet as shown. After reading the text to the child, invite him to color the booklet. Then guide him through the directions below to complete each page. Encourage each student to take his friendship booklet home to share with his family.

Directions:
Page 1: Glue a length of string from the cat's paw to the kite.

Page 2: Frost each cookie with glitter glue.

Page 3: Glue a pom-pom to the scene to resemble a ball.

Page 4: Make a fingerprint at the top of each string to resemble a balloon.

Beautiful Bracelets
Developing vocabulary

Friends use kind words. Help youngsters discuss a variety of kind words with this cute little activity. Cut out enough construction paper copies of page 281 to have at least one strip for each child. Then staple each strip to make a bracelet. To begin, explain that friends use kind, polite words when they talk to each other. Have youngsters suggest several kind words as you write their words on a sheet of chart paper. Next, tell youngsters that they are all invited to wear a special bracelet today to help them remember kind words. Read the words written on a bracelet; then give the bracelet to a youngster to wear. Continue in the same way until each child has donned a bracelet. Throughout the day, take special notice of youngsters who use kind words with their friends.

Preschool Pals
Speaking to play a game

Youngsters identify all their classmates as potential friends with this fun chant and game. Take a photograph of each child and then laminate each photo for durability. Place the photos in a pocket chart with the backs facing front. Invite a youngster to choose two photos from the pocket chart and then reveal them to her classmates. Lead all of the students in the chant shown, substituting the appropriate youngster's names. Have her replace the photos. Then repeat the process several times, inviting a different child to the pocket chart each time. When youngsters are comfortable with this game, you may wish to place the photos in a center for independent exploration.

I'm looking for friends, and who do I see? [Sarah] and [Liam] looking back at me!

adapted from an idea by Wendy Williams
YMCA Children's Center
New Fairfield, CT

Here's a quick tip to reinforce friendly behavior every day! In addition to the typical jobs on your classroom job chart, include a job titled "Kindness Cop." Have your kindness cop keep an eye out for youngsters being friendly toward others. Then invite him to give a kindness report at the end of each day, mentioning the nice things he has seen.

Tamara Scholl, Logan Head Start, Logan, OH

A Mix of Friends
Measuring

Each youngster contributes to this sweet friendship snack! Send a note, similar to the one shown, home with students. When the day arrives to complete the snack, have each child pour his carefully measured cereal into a large mixing bowl. Encourage students to help you mix the cereal. Finally, encourage youngsters to help serve this snack mix to each other. That's what friends are for!

Laura Johnson
South Decatur Elementary
Greensburg, IN

Nancy M. Lotzer
The Hillcrest Academy
Dallas, TX

Dear Family,
We're making a friendship snack! Please help your youngster measure one cup of a favorite cereal into a resealable plastic bag. Have your child bring the bag to school on **Thursday, February 22.** We'll be adding the cereals together to make a snack mix.

Thanks so much!
Ms. Johnson and Ms. Lotzer

Friends laugh.

1

Friends share.

2

Glue.

Friends play.

3

Friends care.

4

Thank you.

We're friends.

Let's play!

You're nice!

TEC41029

TEC41029

TEC41029

TEC41029

Lovely

Brighten youngsters' winter days with these luminous activities that are just perfect for the season!

ideas contributed by Ada Goren, Winston-Salem, NC

Let It Shine!
Singing a song

Watch students' faces light up when they sing this twist on a familiar song! In advance, give each child a small cardboard tube. If desired, invite her to decorate the tube. Then have her glue yellow and orange tissue paper inside the tube to resemble a candle. Invite youngsters to hold their candles. Then lead students in singing the provided song, encouraging them to sway to the music. Repeat the song two more times, substituting the underlined word with different holiday names, such as Christmas and Hanukkah.

(sung to the tune of "This Little Light of Mine")

This little light of mine—I'm going to let it shine.
This little light of mine—I'm going to let it shine.
This little light of mine—I'm going to let it shine,
Let it shine at this fine [Kwanzaa] time!

Fabulous Farolitos!
Appreciating cultural differences

These lovely luminaries will add a soft glow to your classroom! Explain to youngsters that Las Posadas is a Mexican celebration that occurs just before Christmas. *Farolitos* are paper bag lanterns frequently displayed during Las Posadas. Each lantern contains sand and a small candle. Invite each youngster to make a lighted bag similar to a farolito. Begin by having each child decorate a lunch-size paper bag as desired. Encourage him to place a scoop of sand in his bag to stabilize it. Have students place their farolitos around the perimeter of the room. If desired, place a glow stick in each one. (Glow sticks are available at many toy stores and novelty companies, such as Oriental Trading Company, Inc.) Then dim the lights and have students enjoy these lovely decorations!

Lights

Brilliant Holidays
Recognizing familiar holidays

Spotlight the importance of lights in many different holiday celebrations with this snappy rhyme. Make a copy of page 287 for each child and encourage her to color the pictures. Then have her press her finger in yellow tempera paint to make flames above the candles in the menorah and the kinara and to make lights on the tree. When the paint is dry, lead students in reciting the rhyme shown, encouraging them to point to the appropriate picture during each verse.

Sparkling lights on an evergreen tree
Give off a pretty glow.
That's a sign of Christmas
That many people know.

Candles in a menorah
For eight days burn bright.
That's a sign of Hanukkah.
Yes, that's right!

A kinara with seven candles
Put out on display—
That's a sign it's time
For the Kwanzaa holiday.

It's Rudolph's Nose!
Contributing to a class book

Rudolph's luminous nose is the subject of this whimsical class book! Take a photograph of each child gesturing as shown. Make a class supply of the left text card on page 285. Help each student write her name in the spaces provided and cut out the text card. Then have her glue the text to the bottom of a 9" x 12" sheet of black construction paper. Have her glue her photo to the paper as shown. Then help her squeeze a dot of glue on the paper and sprinkle red glitter over the glue to resemble Rudolph's nose. Next, use the right text card on page 285 and the Rudolph pattern on page 286 to make a final page for the book. When the glue is dry, add a cover and bind the pages together to make a book titled "What Do You See?" Youngsters are sure to enjoy a read-aloud of this special book!

What does Rudolph see on this dark, dark night?
Rudolph sees children smiling with delight!

What does Emma see on this dark, dark night?
Emma sees Rudolph's nose shining bright!

Counting Candles
Counting

Little ones count candles in a menorah with this sweet little rhyme! Cut out a simple menorah shape, as shown, and decorate it as desired. Also cut out nine construction paper strip candles and flames. Lead students in reciting the poem shown. Then have them revisit the information in the poem, reviewing that there are nine candles, with four on each side and the *shammash,* or leader candle in the middle. Have students help you count the candles and flames and then attach them correctly to the displayed menorah. Next, have students verify that there are nine candles in all. Leave the display out so youngsters can count and place the candles on their own.

See the menorah all silver and blue
With nine little candles for us to view.
There are four on the left
And four on the right
And the *shammash* in the middle lights
them up at night.

A Sparkly Snack
Following directions

This simple snack will remind little ones of a lighted holiday tree! In advance, make a batch of marshmallow cereal treats, molding each treat while warm to resemble a tree. Fill a resealable plastic bag with green-tinted frosting; then snip a corner off the bag and encourage each youngster to squeeze some frosting onto his tree. Finally, encourage him to shake sprinkles over the treat. The sprinkles will stick to the snack to resemble sparkly holiday lights! Finally, have little ones nibble on these festive treats!

Susan Isner
North Elementary
Elkins, WV

Light Up the Night
Developing fine-motor skills

To prepare, make a large house cutout from black bulletin board paper and attach it to a wall in the classroom. Make a supply of lightbulb cutouts. Drape green yarn on the house as shown. Place the cutouts at a table along with scissors, glue sticks, and small pieces of cellophane, aluminum foil, and sequins. Encourage students to visit the table and glue desired items to bulb cutouts to make them sparkle and shine. When the glue is dry, have them tape the lightbulbs near the green yarn to resemble strings of lights.

What does _____ see
on this dark, dark night?
_____ sees Rudolph's
nose shining bright!

What does Rudolph see on this dark,
dark night?
Rudolph sees children smiling with
delight!

TEC41028

Rudolph Pattern

Use with "It's Rudolph's Nose!" on page 283.

TEC41028

©The Mailbox® • TEC41028 • Dec./Jan. 2006–7

Note to the teacher: Use with "Brilliant Holidays" on page 283.

Critter COVERINGS

Fur, feathers, scales, and hair–these are some things that critters wear! Little ones are sure to enjoy investigating the coverings of some of their favorite critters!

ideas contributed by Lucia Kemp Henry, Fallon, NV

How Does It Feel?
Comparing textures

Youngsters explore texture as they place each covering on the appropriate critter! Use clip art to make a sheet similar to the one shown and then copy a class supply. Place the papers at a table along with white glue, felt squares, craft feathers, and small sequins. Invite a small group of youngsters to the table and give each child a paper. Have her color the animals. Next, help her glue sequins (scales) to the fish, feathers to the bird, and felt (fur) to the mouse. Then have your sense-savvy scientists touch the coverings, name them, and describe how they feel!

Jessica

Playing Pretend
Reciting a rhyme

Youngsters pretend to be scaly, feathery, and furry with this little action rhyme. If desired, repeat this rhyme several times, replacing the animals' names with other scaly, feathery, and furry critters!

Let's be fish with flashy scales.
Let's be birds with feathery tails.
Let's be bears with furry feet,
The scariest bears you'll ever meet!
Let's change back to kids again.
It's so much fun to play pretend!

Wiggle your scaly fins.
Shake your feathery tail.
Stomp your furry feet.
Show claws and look scary.
Point to self.
Clap.

Furry Feet

Creating a story innovation

Read aloud the book *Four Fur Feet* by Margaret Wise Brown, encouraging little ones to chant along with this simple story and stomp their feet whenever they hear the words *four fur feet.* Next, make several copies of the robin card on page 291. Enlist youngsters' help in using Sticky-Tac to attach a robin card over the furry animal on each page of the book. Next, reread the story, replacing the words *walked* and *four fur feet* with *flew* and *feathery wings,* respectively. As you read, encourage youngsters to recite with you as before and flap their arms whenever they hear the words *feathery wings.* If desired, repeat the process with snake cards, saying the words *slithered* and *dry, rough scales* while students wiggle an arm to resemble a snake.

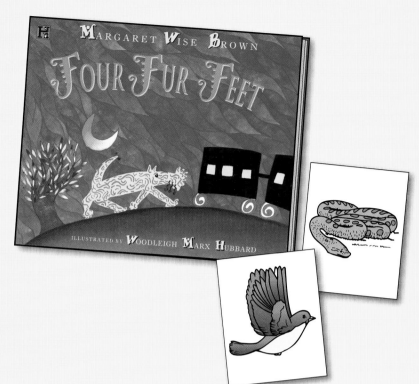

Got It Covered!

Singing a song

Review different animal coverings with this song and activity. In advance, enlarge and copy the robin, fish, and bear cards on page 291. Then color and cut out the cards. Hold up the bird card and have little ones identify the picture. Then lead students in singing the first verse of the song below. Continue in the same way with the fish and bear cards, completing the appropriate verse after showing each card. (You may wish to take a moment during the mammal verse to explain that some mammal coverings are called hair rather than fur.)

(sung to the tune of "Camptown Races")

Oh, what are birdies covered in?
Feathers, feathers.
Feathers cover birdies' skin so they are not bare.
Feathers cover here! Feathers cover there!
Birds have special coverings. Feathers are what they wear.

Oh, what are fishies covered in?
Scales, scales.
Scales cover fishies' skin so they are not bare.
Scales cover here! Scales cover there!
Fish have special coverings. Scales are what they wear.

Oh, what are mammals covered in?
Fur, fur.
Fur covers mammals' skin so they are not bare.
Fur covers here! Fur covers there!
Mammals have special coverings. Fur is what they wear.

Lift the Flaps
Making a booklet

Give each child a copy of pages 292 and 293. Have each student color the cover, booklet pages, and patterns as desired. Have her draw a face and hair to resemble her own on the final page; then help her cut out the patterns. Next, instruct her to use a glue stick to attach the patterns to the appropriate booklet pages to show the feathers, scales, and fur. After the child cuts out the cover and pages, stack them in order and staple them together; then fold each page on the line to make a flap. Help each child read her booklet, lifting each flap accordingly to answer each question. No doubt youngsters will be eager to show these adorable booklets to their families!

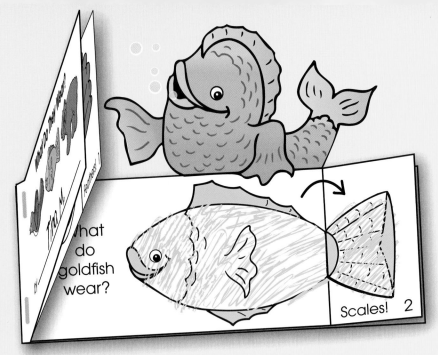

Thinking Maps
Organizing data

These thinking maps are a simple way for preschoolers to organize information. Draw an oval on each of three different sheets of construction paper and then label each oval with a different animal covering. Display the papers in your circle-time area. Cut out a copy of the cards on page 291; then place the cards facedown near the thinking maps. To begin, have a child choose a card and identify whether the critter pictured has feathers, scales, or fur/hair. Encourage him to tape it to the appropriate thinking map. Invite youngsters to identify the animal; then write its name under the card. Continue in the same way with each remaining card. What an easy way to organize information!

Furry, Scaly, and Feathery
Developing fine-motor skills

Invite students to use their imaginations to invent an animal that might have fur, scales, *and* feathers! Post a length of bulletin board paper on a wall and have students suggest what such an animal might look like. As youngsters suggest characteristics, draw their suggestions to create the animal. Then have students help you name the animal. Next, attach the drawing to a tabletop and provide access to torn pieces of paper (scales), faux fur (or yarn), and craft feathers. Place a container of glue and paintbrushes at the table. Encourage youngsters, in turn, to visit the area, spread some glue on the creature, and then place fur, feathers, and scales on the glue. What a delightful animal!

TEC41028

TEC41028

TEC41028

TEC41028

TEC41028

TEC41028

TEC41028

TEC41028

TEC41028

What Do They Wear?

by _____

What
do
robins
wear?

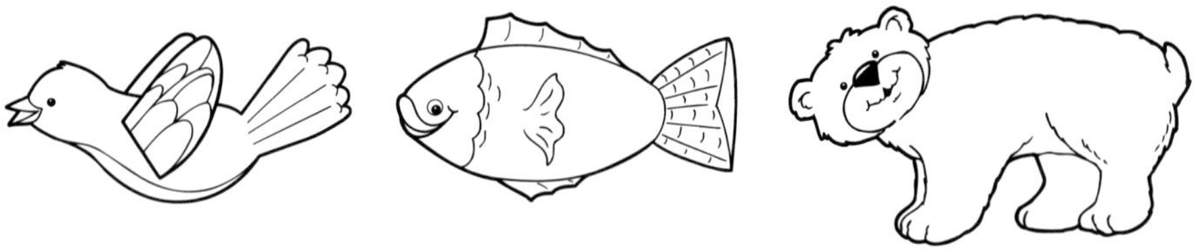

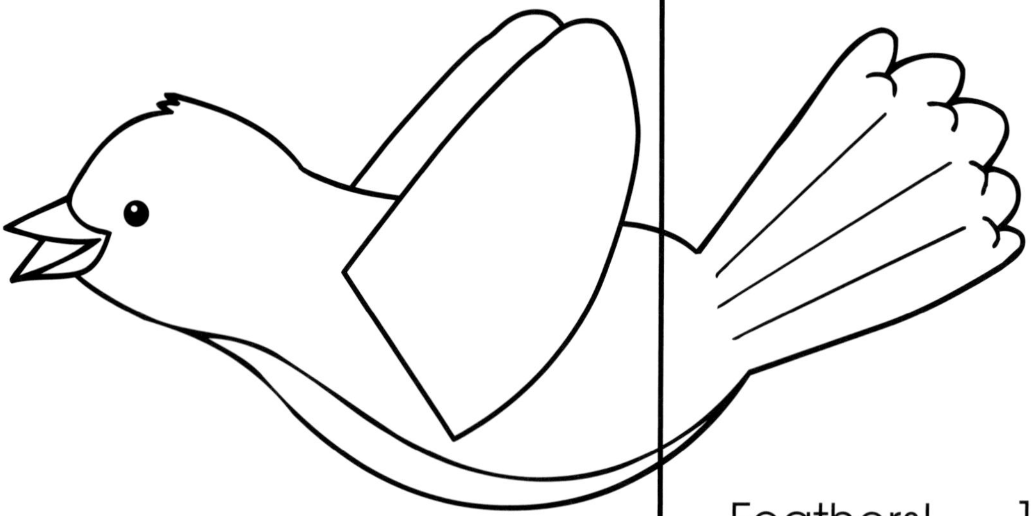

Feathers!   1

What
do
goldfish
wear?

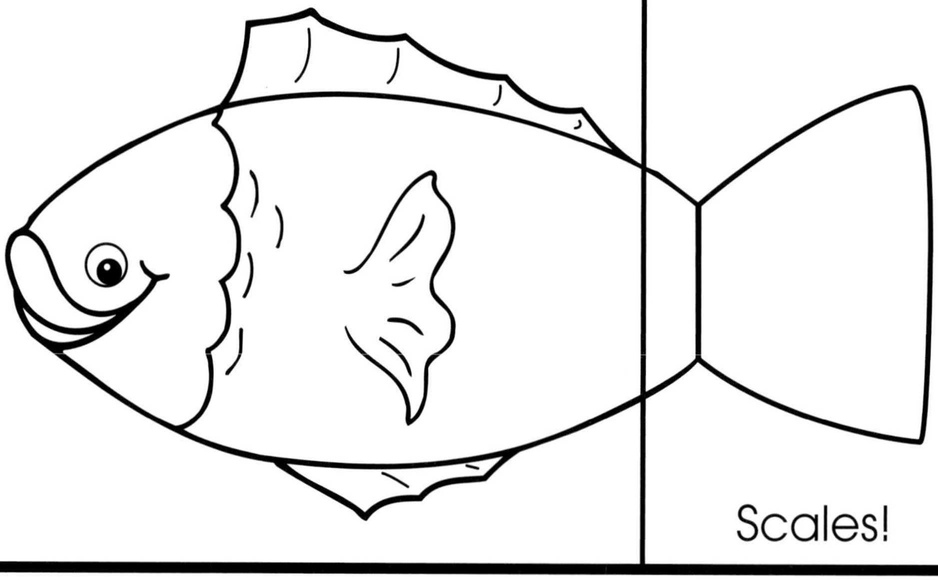

Scales!   2

What
do
bears
wear?

Fur!   3

What
do
you
wear?

Clothes!   4

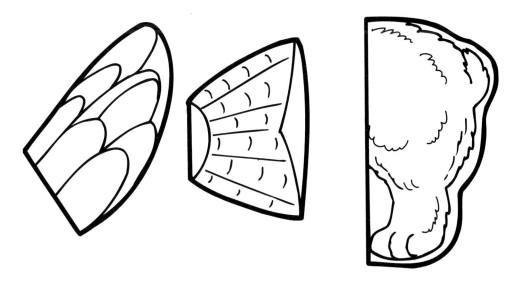

Signs of Spring

The snow is melting, the birds are singing, and there's plenty of mud. Spring must be on its way! March into this lovely season with this selection of adorable learning opportunities.

Blooming Trees
Expressing oneself through art

This simple and unique art technique results in a lovely spring tree! Make a brown tree cutout, minus foliage, for each child. Have her glue her tree to a large sheet of paper. Then instruct her to use an eyedropper to place drops of green and pink tempera paint on the tree's branches. Next, encourage the child to place a piece of waxed paper over the drops and smooth her hand over the paper. Then have her remove the paper. What a lovely blossoming tree!

Belinda Durham
Kamelot Kids Preschool
Mansfield, MA

It Must Be Spring!
Counting

To make this flip booklet, fold a 12" x 18" sheet of light-colored construction paper in half lengthwise for each child. Cut five flaps in the booklet; then label each flap as shown. Place the booklets at a table along with colorful ink pads. To begin, invite a child to the table. Have him stamp fingerprints under each flap to make the items indicated. Use a fine-tip permanent marker to add details to each print. Help each youngster read his booklet and count the pictures.

Mirielle Strasser, Da Vinci Academy, Elgin, IL

Windy Weather

Performing an action rhyme

Youngsters are sure to be delighted by this action rhyme about a well-known sign of spring. Lead students in performing the rhyme with enthusiastic motions!

I see the wind when the clouds glide by.	*Move hands gently overhead.*
I see the wind when the kites fly high.	*Point upward.*
I see the wind when my clothes flip-flap.	*Wiggle legs and arms.*
I see the wind when it blows my cap.	*Pat head.*
I see the wind when the flowers bend low.	*Bend over and touch floor.*
I see the wind when the flags all blow.	*Flap arms to resemble flags.*
I see the wind when it moves my hair.	*Smooth hair.*
I see the wind almost everywhere!	*Throw arms outward.*

Elizabeth Brandel
Milwaukie, OR

Mud Surprise!

Exploring the life cycle of a plant

This mud investigation has a surprise ending! In advance, place soil in a plastic tub (or sand table). To begin, read aloud *Mud* by Mary Lyn Ray, guiding youngsters to note the illustrations of green grass poking up through the mud. Have students watch as you add water to the soil to make mud. Encourage children to explore the mud with small plastic gardening tools during your center time. (You may need to periodically add more water to the tub.) While youngsters are out of the room, mix grass seed with the mud. After a few days your little ones will notice the green grass beginning to poke through the mud just like the grass in the book's illustrations! If desired, have each child take some sprouting grass home in a paper cup to share with her family.

adapted from an idea by Cindy Lazaroe
United Methodist Children's Learning Center
Houma, LA

Nest, Sweet Nest
Developing independent interest in books

This lovely nest is a fun holder for a selection of spring-related books! In advance, place a supply of natural raffia in your sensory table. Send a note home with youngsters explaining that the class is making a big bird nest to celebrate spring. Encourage children to bring items from home that a bird might find to put in her nest, such as pieces of ribbon, yarn, cotton batting, or strips of fabric. Have each youngster add his items to the raffia to make a large cozy nest. Arrange spring-related books in the nest along with plastic eggs and stuffed-animal birds. Encourage youngsters to visit the nest during center time to look at the books.

adapted from an idea by Dawn Unger
Lotus School
Spring Grove, IL

Spring Song
Reciting a song

This bouncy little ditty is terrific fun when it's accompanied by flower tambourines! For each child, place a handful of dried beans between two paper plates. Then securely tape the edges to make a tambourine. Have each child glue petal cutouts around the edge of his tambourine. Then, when the glue is dry, invite youngsters to tap on their tambourines as they sing the song! After several repetitions of the song, gather the tambourines for safekeeping.

(sung to the tune of "Sing a Song of Sixpence")

Pink and yellow flowers
Are nodding pretty heads.
Bees are buzzing nicely
Around the garden beds.
Trees are filled with blossoms.
The robins start to sing.
And this will surely let us know
The season must be spring!

Deborah Garmon
Groton, CT

Springtime Babies
Developing hand-eye coordination

Spring means it's time for baby animals! Make two construction paper copies of the adult duck pattern and several copies of the duckling patterns on page 297. Cut out the copies and securely attach each cutout to a different block in your block center. Invite youngsters to the center and encourage them to line up the ducklings behind their parents.

inspired by an idea by Angela Brody
Indiana County Head Start
Indiana, PA

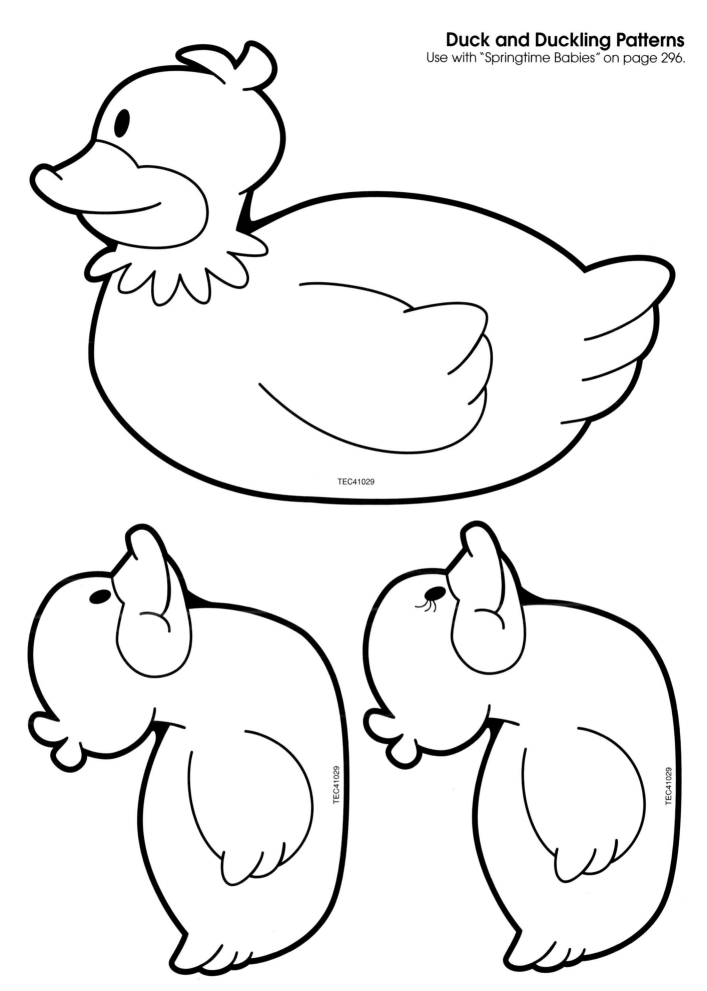

TEC41029

TEC41029

TEC41029

Hooray for Rabbits!

Little ones are sure to be all ears for these adorable rabbit–themed activities!

Funny Bunny

Reciting a rhyming chant
Youngsters will jump at the chance to perform this engaging action chant!

Here is a bunny with ears so funny!
And this is her hole in the ground.
When a noise she hears,
She perks up her ears

And hops in her hole with a bound!

Hold up two fingers, slightly bent.
Point to floor.
Cup hand around ear.
Bend two fingers as before; then straighten them.
Pretend to jump in the hole.

Janet Boyce
Cokato, MN

A Bunny Booklet

Following directions
   Give each child a copy of pages 301 and 302. Read aloud the text. Then invite him to color the pages as desired. Next, guide each youngster through the steps below to help him complete the pages. When the glue is dry, cut out the pages and stack them under a construction paper cover titled as shown.

Steps:
Page 1: Glue pink felt inside the rabbit's long ears.
Page 2: Glue construction paper rectangles to the rabbit to make long front teeth.
Page 3: Glue crumpled green tissue paper to the page so that it resembles plants.
Page 4: Stretch out cotton balls and then glue them to the rabbit to make soft fur.

Anissa Collins, Ivydale Elementary, Ivydale, WV

All About Bunnies! by Joshua

A rabbit has long ears.   1

A rabbit has long front teeth.   2

A rabbit eats plants.   3

A rabbit is soft.   4

298

Collecting Colors
Identifying colors

No doubt this whole-group game would get the Easter Bunny's stamp of approval! Gather several egg cutouts, each in a different color. To begin, have youngsters sit in a circle. Then invite a child to pretend to be the Easter Bunny. Give the child a basket and prompt him to hop around the circle as you lead the remaining students in the chant shown. When the chant is finished, encourage the Easter Bunny to stop in front of a child and give her the basket. Hold up one of the eggs and have the youngster with the basket identify the color. Then instruct her to walk around the room, find something that is the same color as the egg, and then place it in the basket. This youngster then becomes the Easter Bunny for the next round of play!

Little bunny, little bunny, hop, hop, hop!
Little bunny, little bunny, won't you stop?

Michelle Freed
Papillon, NE

Rabbits and Rain

Making connections between spoken and written words

Youngsters reflect on this serene story with a bunny craft! To begin, read aloud the story *Rabbits & Raindrops* by Jim Arnosky. Point out that Jim Arnosky painted the raindrops perfectly round because this is how raindrops are shaped when they fall. Have each youngster attach hole reinforcers to a 12" x 18" sheet of blue construction paper to resemble the raindrops in the story. If desired, invite her to use a white gel pen to make a line leading down to each raindrop. Next, have her glue torn pieces of green tissue paper to her project to make the rabbit's leafy shelter. Finally, encourage the student to tell you what she liked about the story as you write her words on a bunny cutout (pattern on page 303). Have the child glue the bunny to her scene.

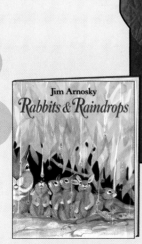

I liked the bunny that got splashed by a raindrop. That was funny!

Kaitlyn

So Soft!
Exploring texture

Gather a variety of soft items, such as cotton balls, cotton batting, tissues, fabric, and pom-poms. Cut the items into smaller pieces, if necessary. Then place the items in a container and place the container at a table. Make a supersize bunny cutout. (If desired, use the pattern on page 303 as a guide.) Place the bunny at the table along with a shallow container of glue and a paintbrush. Explain to youngsters that bunnies have very soft fur. Then invite students to the table during center time and encourage them to explore the items with their sense of touch. Encourage children to brush glue on the bunny and then place items on the glue. Have youngsters continue to visit the center until the bunny is covered with soft items.

Fun and Fluffy
Following directions

These easy-to-prepare treats look just like fluffy little bunny tails! Have students assist you in mixing up a batch of instant white chocolate pudding mix. When the pudding has set, encourage each child to place a dollop of pudding on a plate and then top it with a dollop of whipped cream. Invite little ones to nibble on their treats. Hey, that looks just like a bunny's tail!

Voilà! A Rabbit!
Developing gross-motor skills

Youngsters will delight in pulling these rabbits out of a hat! In advance, reduce the size of the rabbit pattern on page 303; then make several copies. Cut out the rabbits and write a different movement or action on each one. Place the rabbits in a hat. Whenever you have a few extra minutes in your daily schedule, invite a child to pull a rabbit from the hat. Read the instruction on the bunny; then lead students in completing the movement. For oodles of giggles, tuck an additional labeled animal in the hat, such as an alligator. Now how did that alligator get in there?

Hop like a rabbit ten times!

Joan Glaubitz-Morrison
Amboy, MN

2

A rabbit has long front teeth.

1

A rabbit has long ears.

4

A rabbit is soft.

3

A rabbit eats plants.

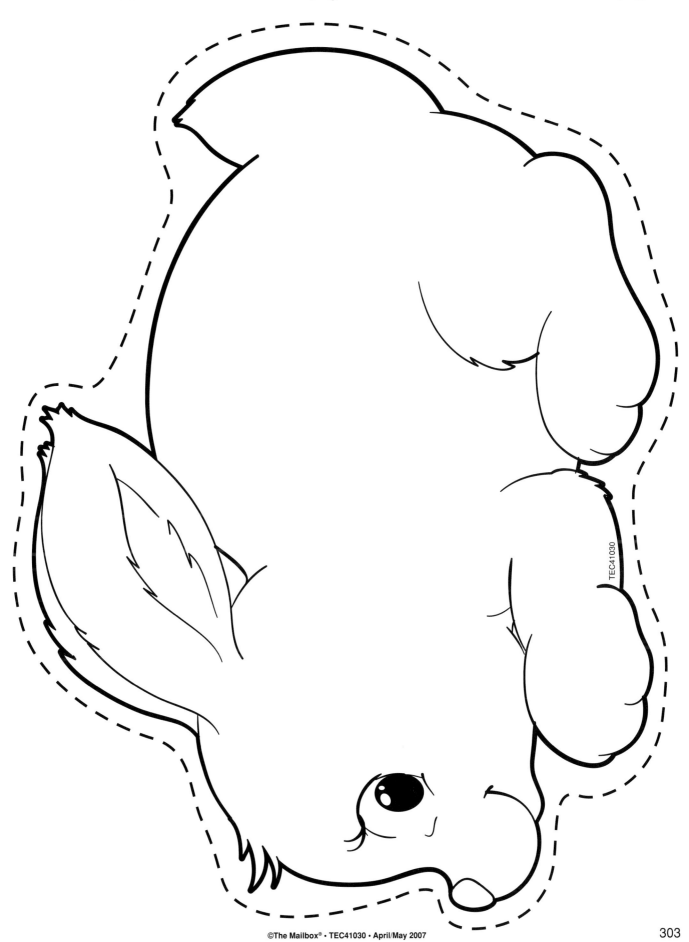

TEC41030

Who Lives in the Forest?

Deer, opossums, bears, and mice—forest critters sure are nice! Introduce youngsters to the creatures of the forest with this cuddly collection of learning opportunities.

Many Critters
Investigating living things

Youngsters identify forest inhabitants when they contribute to this simple scene! Color and cut out two copies of the animal cards on page 306. Cut a length of blue crepe paper to create a stream. Then attach a large piece of paper to a wall at children's eye level. To begin, have each youngster draw and cut out a tree. Encourage each child to attach his tree to the paper to make a forest. Next, explain that animals live in this forest. Have students identify and then attach the animal cards to the forest scene. Finally, explain that the animals need water to drink. Have a student help you attach the crepe paper stream to the display. What a lovely forest!

Lucia Kemp Henry
Fallon, NV

Awesome Opossum
Following directions

Make a pink construction paper opossum cutout (see page 307) for each child. Have each student dip a comb into gray tempera paint and then drag the comb over the opossum. Encourage her to repeat the process until a desired effect is achieved. When the paint is dry, help her cut out her opossum. Next, explain that an opossum is a marsupial and that most marsupials have pouches on their stomachs. Baby opossums stay nice and safe in the pouch. Help each child glue a pink felt pouch to her opossum. Then encourage the child to draw eyes on her opossum and attach a pom-pom nose, ear cutouts, and a pipe cleaner tail. Finally, invite her to tuck pink pom-pom babies into the pouch.

Karen Sheheane
Centenary United Methodist Preschool
Quincy, FL

The Moose Are Missing!

Developing presubtraction skills

This sweet little moose rhyme is great fun! Color and cut out five copies of the moose pattern below and ready them for flannelboard use by attaching a piece of felt to the back of each one. Place the moose on your flannelboard. Then recite the first verse of the chant below with your youngsters, having a youngster remove a moose when appropriate and hide it nearby. Continue in the same way, reciting four more verses, subtracting the number by one for each verse and hiding a different moose each time. As you lead students in reciting the final verse, encourage a youngster to be the mother (or father) moose, retrieve each hidden moose, and then place them back on the flannelboard.

[Five] little moose went out to play,
Out to the lake that's far away.
One little moose, he went astray.
So how many moose were left to play?

Final verse:
Big Mother Moose had quite a fright,
So she went to the lake that night.
She found her moose that went astray.
No more going to the lake to play!

Debra Liermann
Small Wonders Preschool
Lakeville, MN

Moose Pattern

Use with "The Moose Are Missing!" on this page.

TEC41030

Forest Cards

Use with "Many Critters" on page 304.

Green Tree
National
Forest

TEC41030

Sand and Soil Explorations

Little ones are sure to dig this collection of learning opportunities about sand and soil!

ideas contributed by Carole Watkins
Holy Family Child Care Center, Crown Point, IN

Let's Compare!

Making comparisons

No doubt your little scientists will enjoy this hands-on exploration! Place a shallow tub of sand and a shallow tub of soil on a protected surface. Then gather a small group of young-sters around the containers. Invite children to explore the sand and soil and then to share their impressions. Next, give each child a copy of the recording sheet on page 311. Encourage her to use crayons to draw the sand in the top container on the sheet; then have the youngster describe the sand as you write her words in the space provided. Repeat the process for the soil. If desired, after each youngster has had the opportunity to complete this activity, place the containers at a center along with magnifying glasses and plastic tweezers for further investigation.

Sand and Soil

Sand is lighter than soil, and it feels soft.

Soil is brown, and there are some sticks in it.

Sand

Soil

Sand and Soil Snack

Following directions

Invite youngsters to mix pretend sand and soil to make a tasty yogurt topper! Have each child mix a tablespoon of graham cracker crumbles (sand) and a tablespoon of crushed chocolate sandwich cookies (soil) in a reseal-able plastic bag. Encourage each child to sprinkle his sand and soil mixture over a cup of vanilla yogurt. What a tasty snack!

Cameron

Grow a Letter
Investigating living things
Not only can youngsters use this idea to investigate how plants grow in soil, but they also can practice letter-writing skills! To begin, help each child place a layer of soil (or potting soil) in a disposable pie tin. Have each child use a craft stick to write the first letter of his name in the soil. Help him sprinkle grass seed over his letter. Then encourage him to lightly water the grass seed. After several days, the seeds will sprout in the shape of the letter. If desired, have youngsters use scissors to trim the grass if it grows too tall.

Which Is Heavier?
Exploring weight
Gather a small group of youngsters around a balance scale and separate containers of sand and soil. Have them touch and explore the sand and soil. Then ask students whether they think a cup of sand or a cup of soil is heavier. Write each child's name on a sticky note and attach the notes to the appropriate containers to record students' predictions. Next, have students help you place a cup of soil on one side of the balance and a cup of sand on the remaining side. Have students discuss the results and then compare the results to their predictions.

David Ana Chris   Jesse Leo

Soggy Sand
Exploring volume
Let youngsters experience the unique texture and uses of wet sand! Combine water and sand in your sand table or tub until the mixture reaches a pleasing packing consistency. Then provide access to a variety of cups, containers, and utensils. Encourage students to pack sand in the containers and then remove the molded sand.

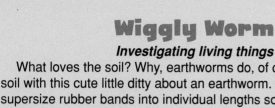

Wiggly Worm

Investigating living things

What loves the soil? Why, earthworms do, of course! Celebrate soil with this cute little ditty about an earthworm. In advance, cut supersize rubber bands into individual lengths so they resemble worms. Give each child a worm. Then lead students in singing the song shown as they wiggle their worms to the beat!

(sung to the tune of "I'm a Little Teapot")

I'm a little earthworm
In the ground.
I love the soil,
And that's where I'm found.
I can wiggle waggle;
Watch me go
Deeper, deeper down below.

Randi Austin, Lebanon, MO

Seth

Dear Family,
Have a terrific time at the beach! If you have an opportunity, please help your preschooler place a sample of beach sand in this resealable plastic bag. Then, when you return from your vacation, have your child bring the sample to school.

Thanks so much!
Ms. Maurer

A Selection of Sand

Making comparisons

Invite students to collect sand while on vacation! Before a child in your class leaves for a vacation at a beach, give him a personalized resealable plastic bag that contains a note similar to the one shown. Whenever a sand sample is brought to school, display it in a plastic container with the youngster's name and the location of the beach where it was collected. It's fascinating to compare the different types of sand!

Tracie Maurer
Boys and Girls Club of Northern Westchester Preschool
Mt. Kisco, NY

Sand and Soil Shakers

Exploring sand and soil

Remove the labels from two two-liter soda bottles. Place sand in one bottle and soil in the remaining bottle so that each bottle is about one-fourth full. Then pour water in the bottles until they're about half to three-fourths full. Use hot glue to secure each lid on its bottle and then label each bottle as shown. Place these finished shakers at a center. A child shakes the bottles and then watches as the sand and soil settle to the bottom.

Keely Peasner, Liberty Ridge Head Start, Bonney Lake, WA

Sand

Soil

Sand and Soil

Sand is _____

_____

Soil is _____

_____

Note to the teacher: Use with "Let's Compare!" on page 308.

What's in the Soil?

Note to the teacher: Have youngsters color the page. Then explain that soil has small rocks, sticks, and leaves in it. Have each child make gray fingerprints on the page to make rocks. Then have her glue pieces of sticks and leaves to the page. Finally, have her glue small pieces of brown yarn to the page so the yarn resembles earthworms.

INDEX